TO SARA
who has choreographed the
perfect marriage

Contents

Acknowledgements

This is not an authorised biography of Fred Astaire, although many people who know and admire him co-operated in its preparation, sharing memories that bring instant smiles, occasional sadness and, rarely, irritation. I am particularly indebted to: Larry Adler, Pandro S. Berman, George Burns, Sammy Cahn, Joan Caulfield, Barrie Chase, Louis F. Edelman, Nanette Fabray, Eddie Foy Junior, Leonard Gershe, John Green, Rita Hayworth, Michael Kidd, Jack Lemmon, Ann Miller, Richard Quine, Cesar Romero, David Rose, Olga San Juan, Walter Scharf, Ted Shapiro, Sidney Sheldon, Morris Stoloff, John Scott Trotter, Charles Walters and Trudy Wellman. Particular thanks are due to David Niven for granting permission to quote correspondence between himself and Fred Astaire. I should like to thank, too, the librarians of the British Library, London, the Lincoln Center Library of the Performing Arts, New York, and the British Film Institute for their help. Tribute should also be paid to those newspapermen who through the last seventy years have recorded the phenomenon known as Fred Astaire.

MICHAEL FREEDLAND

A*

Shoes With Wings On

There were still nearly thirty years to go when an American national magazine decided to tot up the credit and loss account of the twentieth century. When they came to choosing their 'Entertainer of the Century', they picked Fred Astaire.

If they had selected anyone else, the letters would have poured in and the complaints would have multiplied. How can you choose anything of the century with a quarter of it still to go? How can the Man of the Year be selected in September or the movie of the year be chosen in February? Yet such things do constantly happen and every time they do someone scoffs.

But no one did complain about the choice of Astaire. His was genuinely a household name, as vivid to the older generation as the memory of the Charleston and a stolen kiss in the jump seat of an open car. More important, their grandchildren knew it, too – some of them as well as that of the latest pop group who would consider themselves lucky to survive the season.

What was Fred Astaire's secret? Partly that he could put into a pair of feet the energy required to fly a jet plane yet make it all look like a glider swimming in a cool breeze. Partly because he could sing songs in a voice that of itself would never win any vocal prizes, but in a way that would make him the idol of the songwriters. Cole Porter, George

Gershwin, Jerome Kern and Irving Berlin all said they would rather have him sing their songs than anyone else – because he not only had a sense of rhythm as instinctive as the desire to breathe but because he had a deep respect for the meaning of lyrics.

It was Kern who said of him: 'Astaire can't do anything bad.' And possibly the reason was the work he put into achieving that seemingly effortless pose. When he danced down a street, it was the result of weeks of planning every foot motion, almost every flex of his muscles – but it wouldn't have worked had he not made it seem as though he were doing it all on the spur of the moment, as naturally and easily as a small boy would kick a ball. It produced an incredible limiting factor to the vocabulary of the people who knew him. Invariably they would all choose the same word to describe him: perfectionist. Astaire's legacy has been to make the tap dance respectable.

Before Astaire there was ballet and 'the other sort', which usually amounted to the kind of thing chorus girls did. In vaudeville, there was the old soft shoe routine. From New Orleans, through the blackface minstrel shows and on to Broadway, performers like Zip Coon and Jim Crow – who themselves had something of an effect on the English language – added the 'buck and wing'. But it took Astaire to refine that quaint jazz shuffle into tap dancing and in turn to be regarded himself as a latter day Nijinsky.

To an actress, the chance to dance with Astaire was both the culmination of a dream and a demand for a work schedule so tough that it could bring her to tears. Yet in most cases he was that rare breed: a generous showman. Ann Miller said of him, 'It's as though I've always danced with him. He has that way with women. He tried to do the steps that made her look good. I appreciate that. It's very unusual in a man dancer.'

There's probably only one person who will not accept that there was anything at all unusual about Astaire and that's himself.

He once said: 'I'm not one of those people who can say, "I was born in the world without a shirt to my back and when I was old enough to pour my own cup of coffee . . ." I can't go into that whole deal.'

In fact, he steadfastly refuses to live in the past or even reflect on what the rest of us would like to call his glories. Ask him why, and he'll reply that it simply isn't his 'racket'. The most important thing is that he's glad he 'made a buck'. He wouldn't add that he's also glad that he made a lot of other people happy. But he did.

I Wanna Be A Dancin' Man

It was a combination of the discipline in the Austro-Hungarian Army and Prohibition in Nebraska that produced the Entertainer of the Century. If it hadn't have been for the first of those two factors, Fred Astaire would never have been born; had it not been for the second, he quite possibly might never have been a great star.

His father, Frederic Austerlitz, was one of three brothers, all of them officers serving Franz Josef in the Austro-Hungarian Army; Frederic, a mere subaltern, Otto and Ernest rather more senior. They came from a family of brewers, but had decided to make the Army their career instead. Their mother's maiden name was Astaire.

Frederic was a handsome chap with a curly moustache. Out of uniform he wore a homburg with a crease in the front which made it resemble a Boy Scout's hat. But somehow, when that was combined with a bow tie and a tweed coat, it gave him the look of a suave opera singer.

His brother Ernest had a similar moustache – in fact it was much the same as Kaiser Wilhelm affected – and was tall and slim. He was also very conscious of his importance as an officer in the Imperial Army, for when he saw Frederic approach him and then fail to salute, he had his younger brother arrested and incarcerated in the divisional guardhouse. It was the final straw for Frederic, he decided he had had enough, and as quickly as he could decently manage it, he left the Army, his homeland and family and set sail for America.

He settled in Omaha, Nebraska, got a job in a leather firm and there he met and fell in love with a local beauty named Ann Geilus. She was a schoolteacher and still a teenager when she married Frederic, who was about ten years older. The year of the wedding was 1896. A year later, Mrs Austerlitz gave birth to a baby girl. They called her Adele. Eighteen months afterwards, the family increased still further. Their second child was a boy. They named him Frederick – the final 'k' to the name making it look more American than the way the child's father spelt his.

He immediately became known simply as Fred – or Freddie. The day he was born, 10 May 1899. Adele, meanwhile had become 'Delly'.

Mr Austerlitz was now back in the family trade. After deciding he didn't like the leather business in Omaha, he had gone to work for a local brewery, the Storz Brewing Co., and was doing very well there. But he was not one of those brewers who thought of nothing but beer. On the contrary, whenever the opportunity presented itself, he would go to the theatre. Years later, his daughter would say that Mr Auster-litz was stage-struck – he even subscribed to a theatrical paper – although Fred maintained that he simply enjoyed the entertainment the theatre offered and had no ambitions to 'tread the boards' himself. Certainly, his wife found no overpowering appeal in the smell of greasepaint. But whether their father did or did not have any theatrical aspirations, the Austerlitz children knew very early on that any move they would make in that direction would not be discouraged.

At the age when most other children are considered due for nursery education, Adele was enrolled at Chambers' Dancing Academy and was soon regarded as the star attraction when the school put on its shows. Contrary to legend, Fred merely went along there for a ride in the family horse and buggy, when his mother took Adele to her lessons, and then collected her. There is a story, however, that on Adele's second day at the school her brother was copying her steps.

Freddie's involvement was soon to become more definite; he was no more than four years old when a big adventure beckoned. He heard he was going for a two-day train ride – to New York. The destination was less exciting to young Master Austerlitz than the method of getting there; all he could think about was the train and the things he would see from its windows. Once on that train, he had formulated his final idea of how he intended to spend his future. He was going to be a breakman – or what in Britain would be called the guard.

Frederic Austerlitz, Senior, stayed behind at Omaha to earn the family's keep while the others stared wide-eyed at all they surveyed. New York with its tall buildings and bustling streets was not at all like Nebraska. They had come without any introduction to the city other than their father's theatrical newspaper, although this was to prove useful. From it, they cut out an advertisement for a dancing school run by a Mr Claude Alvienne.

Mrs Austerlitz carted her young brood to Mr Alvienne's premises above the Grand Opera House on Eighth Avenue and introduced them. He agreed to give the youngsters a trial. Very soon after they joined the school, Adele was selected to take part in a benefit performance at the Metropolitan Opera and Freddie was taken along to sit in the audience and clap his sister.

Both of the children took to dancing immediately. Fred says in his own autobiography *Steps In Time* that he 'didn't mind' the lessons. Indeed, Mr Alvienne and his wife – who was quite famous at one time as the dancer La Neva – thought they had considerable talent. Enough talent to be given the featured roles in the school's production of *Cyrano de Bergerac*. What foresight! What powerful intuition of the kind of future his two young charges were going to have! Not quite. He decided that Adele should play Cyrano and Fred, Roxanne – he was shorter than his sister and it seemed to look better that way.

Fred was conscious of the opportunity he now had. 'Mr Alvienne is going to make me a star,' he told Adele, who replied 'Don't be silly!' Well, Fred was learning to dance. He was also beginning to sing – in fact, he was singing more than he was dancing at this stage, and he wasn't yet five years old.

He and Adele were told that they had to watch the established performers at work. Their model was the Danish ballerina, Adeline Genee and they saw her perform in *The Soul Kiss* twenty-eight times.

It was while at Mr Alvienne's establishment that Fred decided on the sort of dancer he was going to be – or rather Mr Alvienne decided for him. At the back of the school's stage, he set up two wedding cakes, each with a collection of electric light bulbs glowing from it, and in front of them a bride and bridegroom. Adele, all in white, was the bride, Fred was the bridegroom. He wore tails, white tie – and a top hat. In the annals of the theatre, an historic moment, that. The fact that his ensemble was complemented by a pair of black silk knickerbockers should not be allowed to diminish the importance of that moment.

The two danced on the cakes and on the stage around them. Mr and Mrs Alvienne told them how good they were.

It was at Keyport, New Jersey, that an even more historic moment dawned. In the small theatre at the end of the pier, with the waves of the Atlantic Ocean lapping the supports below, Adele and Fred Austerlitz did their wedding cake dance and people paid to see them do it. Or at least they paid to see Adele and Fred Astaire. At five years old, the Austerlitz children had changed their names. Austerlitz, their mother was advised, wouldn't look good on theatre bills; so she searched for alternatives and decided on her mother-in-law's maiden name. It not only looked better, it looked French. Their professional debut had to come in style. And they got fifty dollars for their efforts – the very first money Fred and Adele earned.

The Keyport theatre critic liked them, and spurred on by this encouraging response, the Astaires – already that was how the children were known – went looking for work in other vaudeville theatres. They found it more easily than a lot of older, more seasoned performers and with the same act went from the Atlantic Coast to the Pacific, only stopping briefly for an attack of scarlet fever.

In December 1905, a critic wrote: 'Two little ones, Adele and Fred, give an electrical dancing novelty in vaudeville.' It was one of the first of thousands of such reviews.

It was also one of a crop of reviews that took these impressive youngsters to what was known in the vaudeville business as the Big Time. Whenever he had the opportunity, Frederic Austerlitz Senior, used to leave Omaha and drop into New York as much to see the Broadway shows and get to know the important show people as to visit his family. An attractive character, Mr Austerlitz had the gift of being able to make friends easily. One of these friends was Frank Vincent, who booked acts for the famed Orpheum Circuit – one of the huge chains of theatres that managed to slice the world of American vaudeville between them. The man from the circuit saw the Astaires and said he liked what he saw. As a result, Fred and Adele were in the Big Time and looked all set to stay there, until a batch of do-gooders called the Gerry Society stepped into the picture.

The Gerry Society had been active in America for a number of years. Their aim was to kill off what they considered to be a traffic almost as dangerous as the white slave trade, the employment of children in the theatre. In State after State they managed to persuade the authorities to ban young performers.

The Astaires had two things in their favour that other child enter-tainers did not always have – for most of them appeared to have run away from home – a mother to watch every move they made and even more important to give them private tuition in more than just the art of tapping their toes. As they went from place to place on trains, to hotel rooms and backstage in the theatres, their mother took her bundle of school books and gave them lessons. Meanwhile, she changed her name, too – to Astaire.

When she heard that the Gerry Society were about to pounce, she dressed Fred in long trousers and told the two children to lie about their ages. The Society were still not impressed and called their mother to a conference. When Mrs Austerlitz left the meeting, she told her children she had done the impossible – the Gerry Society were not going to stop them performing.

But what the Gerry Society could not do, the theatre managers did. They decided they didn't like the Astaires any more – or, rather, they liked Adele but wondered just what Fred had to offer. They were get-ting taller and their routine didn't suit the effects of their advancing years – after all, Fred was about nine, and a veteran of what seemed like a thousand campaigns. As he claimed nearly seventy years later, his singing got worse and worse.

Mr Austerlitz and his wife were intelligent parents and decided not to fight what appeared to be the writing on the wall. They agreed that their children would leave the stage and go to school – a proper school this time.

They had also found a new home. It was at Highwood Park; the residential part of Weekhawken in New Jersey. To the children's parents, one of the most important features of this new environment was that it offered a good state school. So for the first time, Adele and Fred sat in a classroom and at the same sort of desks as any other chil-dren of their age; and Mrs Astaire's training was paying off. The

7

lessons she had given Fred meant that he was able to compete on more than merely equal terms with boys and girls of his age. Within days he went up a class so that he was with children a year older than he was.

In later years, the people of Weekhawken were proud to remember the Astaires, and even if their views were clouded by pride, they came to the same conclusion: they were nice kids to know. Edward Spengeman, the town's postman, said they were always hanging around when he came to the house, because they hoped he would be bringing a letter from their father, who was still living in Omaha. 'They were the liveliest kids I ever saw. They were always jigging or practising some new step.' Miss Brundage, his teacher and Mrs Fiske, the school principal, used to watch the progress of the Astaires with pride and made sure that their names were on the school's list of honours.

Fred himself says he hates looking back on those days. 'It's boring for an old-timer,' he insists. But, as long as they have been able to find an audience, the people who remembered the Astaires have been talking about the kids they knew at school. They recalled that Fred used to hate being asked to give an impromptu performance, either at school or at some social function. He'd shrug his shoulders or mop his curly brown hair, but he wouldn't dance. If they insisted that he do something for them, he would compromise with a rendition of 'Asleep In The Deep', which his mother had taught him.

One of his contemporaries insisted that Fred would have preferred to play baseball and usually managed to get a game after a performance – with an apple or a slice of cake as a bonus.

One of his proudest possessions was a bag of marbles that his father sent him from Omaha. When one of his friends admired the collection, he split the lot with him. 'The best-natured kid on the block,' said the pal some thirty years later. But he wouldn't discuss dancing with any of his friends. They were convinced that he considered it sissyish – something that Fred has never admitted himself. He has been rather more willing to recall the time that one of his friends punched him on the nose.

For two years the Astaires were like two ordinary children at an ordinary school. And then their mother decided they should try to think about the theatre again. With her they went to see the latest shows, all the big acts at both the neighbourhood and the New York theatres. Among the acts they saw again and again were a husband and

8

wife team of ballroom dancers who for a time dominated the exhibition dancing scene, Vernon and Irene Castle.

Mrs Astaire also changed their school, and while continuing to coach them, enrolled the pair at Ned Wayburn's dancing school, which she rightly considered to be a training ground for stars. If all his pupils didn't end up with a Number One dressing room, it was unlikely to be Mr Wayburn's fault. As a director of shows, he was unsurpassed and Flo Ziegfeld bore testimony to that fact by frequently employing him. He did more than teach Adele and Fred new dance steps. He wrote them a vaudeville routine – and charged their mother $1,000 for it, which she paid in quarterly instalments.

The act Wayburn wrote put Fred in what he liked to consider his favourite stance, with a baseball bat in his hand and a ballplayer's outfit on his back. The act even had a name – 'A Rainy Saturday'.

They worked hard, Fred much harder than Adele, for he was beginning to take the job of being an entertainer seriously. He gave up playing in the streets and concentrated on working, meticulously pacing out the details of the toe dance and the soft shoe routine. Adele, meanwhile, thought it was a lot of fun and enjoyed playing the clown. Yet when she danced it was as natural and perfect as anything ever seen in a ballet.

But it was difficult to get anyone to appreciate just how perfect either she or her brother was. Not until Wayburn got them a booking at a benefit show at the Broadway Theatre did anyone see their act. And when they did, it all seemed well worth the effort. A critic reported they were a 'clever singing and dancing team' and as a result they were given their big chance at one of the smartest vaudeville theatres in New York, Proctor's on Fifth Avenue. Topping the bill was a Mr Douglas Fairbanks.

If they thought they had reached perfection, the result of the engagement at Proctor's soon put their careers into perspective. Not only were they opening the show – a killing spot in those days when vaudeville was as much a part of everyday life as a television screen is today – but they were not very good. Fred sang 'When Uncle Joe Plays A Rag On His Old Banjo' and the only accompaniment to the sound of his simultaneous singing, dancing and even at one point, piano playing, was the noise of marching feet. An empty theatre was beginning to fill up for the matinée, while the Astaires were on. It was as if they were

9

being used as interval music and the audience were more interested in finding their places than looking up at the stage and at the young performers. Adele and Fred found it all too distracting.

They returned to the theatre that night despondent. When they saw the running order of acts for the evening performance, they were even more distraught. Their name wasn't among them. When they asked why, the answer was all too clear – they had been fired. Fred agrees that the reason he and Adele were fired was that their act was 'lousy'. But they were hurt just the same.

Show business has a phrase for what the Astaires were doing now. They were 'picking up time' – whatever work they could get, sandwiched in between the daily lessons their mother still gave them. Not only were they picking up time, but they were picking up small time, the sort of vaudeville that never saw a real headliner. It seemed that the Big Time was slipping firmly away from their grasp and for seasoned vaudeville entertainers like themselves that was a sad situation.

They hoisted bags into trains and carried them off again, staying at one seedy lodging house after the other. The houses were usually full of vaudevillians – some of them hard-working decent people patiently waiting for a break. There were also thieves and perverts sharing the same dining table, living in rooms next to theirs.

Things seemed to get better when they were earning $150 a week and had the second from last position on the bill. But more than once they were second to a dog act and the dogs had the best dressing room. Another time, they had to climb a ladder to get to their own dressing room because a troupe of trained seals had to have the only one downstairs.

Today Adele remembers their rehearsals as boring occasions that she tried to get over as quickly as possible, if Fred would let her. He, meanwhile, tried not to. If he felt she was slacking he would make her do the steps over and over again. The little brother, who was at least a foot shorter than she and whose voice was now beginning to break, was proving even tougher than the stage directors and orchestra leaders – some of whom were themselves so bored with what was happening that they let them perform just as badly as they wanted to. More often than not, they would get to the theatre on a Monday morning, hand their music to the conductor and then hear him play everything in the wrong tempo. When he repeated this at the first actual performance, it would be little Fred who fought the Astaires' battles. Hopefully, it would get better for him and there would be opportunities for improvement. Vaudeville was officially known as the 'two-a-day' – two performances a day. But often, it was one continuous performance from early afternoon till late at night. As one wag suggested, two-a-day would mean that the theatre had burned down in the middle of the afternoon.

With Fred's voice broken, the dancing part of the act became more important than ever, so he took it upon himself to make sure that the stage was just right and that he and Adele wouldn't slip when they did their routine. Before every performance, he would go on to the stage and sprinkle it with rosin.

Even though the kids and their mother were frequently in one part of the US, or maybe in Canada, while their father was in another, they were a close family. Mr Austerlitz would come to visit the travelling players whenever he could, and would help supplement their income. When they failed to pick up enough time, they had to live on almost non-existent savings. When they were working, their salary cheque had to cover the cost of those train trips from one tank town – the showbiz term that summed up all the love and frustration of vaudeville circuitry – to another, as well as their costumes and the money they had to pay to the keepers of theatrical lodging houses.

Sometimes, things were so desperate that Mrs Astaire had to pawn a small diamond to see them through the week. On another celebrated occasion, she cut an egg in half and divided it among the children.

They would dance anywhere they could get work. During this time a friend spotted Fred and asked him what had happened to the toe dances he used to do when he was six or seven. Years later, he recalled Fred's answer: 'Aw, I'm grown up. And it's too sissy of a fellow to toe-dance.'

Matters were complicated still further by that problem of Prohibition in the State of Nebraska. In 1916, the state went dry and Mr Austerlitz had to start thinking about getting a new job. That was a lot more easily said than done, but he changed his name to Astaire, and kept trying. If his children had ever contemplated a premature retirement, this new turn of events had to put the idea completely out of their minds. So they stayed in small-time vaudeville and continued to make tours of the theatres.

When things were going well, the Astaires could pull in up to $175 a week – with enough saved to give them holidays on the East Coast. They were more forced holidays than eagerly awaited vacations because there was little or no work in the summer months. Fred learned to play golf – another seed sown for the future – and perfected the game he had learned from the older vaudeville pros, pool. Even his mother approved of this. If there ever were any doubts in her mind about the wisdom of show business careers for her children, they were based on the company that they – and Fred in particular – kept. She wanted him to mix more with people his own age and not become too sophisticated before his time, which is an interesting thought.

They went back to work at the end of each summer – or, rather, they chased the work where it lay. They would play anywhere that there was a vaudeville theatre ready to have them. If the theatre manager didn't like an act, he would write a report to the circuit head office. If the report was really bad, there was a fair chance the act would lose its next booking. One such comment sent into the office might have read: 'The girl sticks out her tongue at the audience' which is precisely what Adele had done. She thought the people out front were too slow in their applause – so gave them what she considered to be an effective reward. She did it only, however, when she was sure no one was looking. But the manager was standing in the opposite wing and did notice. What he didn't know was that, when he turned his back, Adele stuck her tongue out at him, too.

Life was never at a lower ebb for the two Astaires than when the pair hit Detroit. Fred was no more than fifteen, but he and Adele were old enough to be right in the middle of a vaudeville artists' strike. They were not members of the 'union', the White Rats, but just the same they were laid off and were short of money, too.

Mrs Astaire pawned her jewellery again and a fur coat, too. They had, meanwhile, changed their act.

For six months they had been training with Aurelia Coccia, who had a vaudeville dance routine with his wife Minnie Amato. Coccia taught them the tango and, says Astaire in *Steps In Time*, had more influence on his own dancing than any other man in his career. Above all, he taught Fred and Adele showmanship.

Another dance act they watched avidly was that of Bert Kalmar and Jessie Brown. The Astaires stood in the wings, staring at the couple with what, years later, Fred called 'thrilled envy – wondering if we could ever equal their finesse and reach their headline billing'.

More than thirty years later, Fred had not only more than equalled that finesse, he played Kalmar in the film *Three Little Words*.

When they did get the odd spot on a vaudeville bill, they were still being talked of as a pair of kids, Adele and her little brother. But things were changing and when finally, they got back on to the Orpheum Circuit, between them the Astaires were now earning the fabulous sum of $225 a week. What was more, they were working with big stars now.

One of the headliners they worked with was a man called Wellington Cross, who years later would give up show business to become right-hand man to Elizabeth Arden. Cross had a young piano player called Ted Shapiro. He was about six months younger than Fred and when they were on the same bills together, Fred and Ted were close friends. They also had a useful arrangement between them. Mrs Ann Astaire didn't like the idea of her children smoking – so Shapiro held the packets of cigarettes that Fred secretly bought. When he smoked, the young piano player kept an eye out for the approach of the 'enemy'. If Mrs Astaire did come in their direction, Ted would be the one to take the cigarette and smoke it – much to the lady's distaste, but she never did find out that Fred had been smoking all the time. 'Fred kept me in cigarettes for months', Shapiro now laughs. Not long after this episode, Ted began an act with Sophie Tucker that was to last for forty-five years and achieved a status never given before or since to an accompanist.

Mrs Astaire did not know about another of Fred's tastes either. Just occasionally, he wasn't about when he was expected to be. He had discovered the magic of the racetrack. He felt something like a truant, but when his mother wasn't looking, Fred would disappear on an afternoon in New York and secretly worm his way into the Aquaduct or Belmont Park tracks. It was a taste not shared by anyone else in his family.

Anyone concerned with the effect it could have on his work had little to worry about, he watched the other acts as closely as the horses. One of these was a couple called Eduardo and Elisa Cansino. Like the Astaires they, too, were brother and sister, but unlike them at the time, they topped every bill they were on. They were the leading team of Spanish dancers in the business and both Fred and Adele were captivated by their poise and style. Adele, in fact, confesses to this day that

13

she fell madly in love with Eduardo. A generation later, Fred was still influenced by the pair. As a result of that influence, he helped give the first big chance to Eduardo's daughter. By then she was known as Rita Hayworth. The Astaires had not had anything like a normal childhood, but they took to it much better than many juvenile performers who were 'born in a trunk'. As Fred has said: 'People talk about when they were hard up. Most of us don't remember that. I've just had a great time.' Adele has said that as far as she was concerned, showbiz was 'an acquired taste – like olives'. They enjoyed the life because the pressures were those they forced upon themselves – or, to be fair, the pressures Fred forced upon them. He was convinced Adele was the better dancer, so he worked to keep up with her. But he also wanted to make sure she would keep up with herself, or maintain what he believed to be her own high standard. 'Oh, I can slide through without practising,' she would say. To which Fred would reply, 'You can slide through maybe, but you're not going to. You're going to get it right.' Adele coined a name for him at moments like this – 'Moaning Minnie'.

The Orpheum office obviously thought they were getting it right often enough to offer them as much as $350 for a single week's work, which was incredible money for a pair of teenagers in those days Their first dance routine with Fred as a detective arresting Adele, a gangster's moll, brought the house down at the Palace Theatre in Chicago and brought them a string of further bookings, too. As before, they were opening the show. But that did not matter so much any more. It was a big-time show and now there was a newsreel preceding them. If people walked in while the film was showing, no one on the screen was either going to complain or be fired for not concentrating. But the Astaires made such an impression that they were moved up to third place. Eddie Cantor was on the same bill – as part of the Cantor and Lee act.

The success of the Astaires meant that he had to wait to get on. There was too much applause to let the curtain fall on schedule, straight after the youngsters had gone through their prepared act. Encore followed encore.

So while Fred and Adele were on stage lapping up the applause, Cantor was running backwards and forwards in the wings, mumbling to the stage manager as he did so: 'What's this? The Gans–Nelson fight? How do you expect me to follow this?'

Reviewers were noticing the Astaires, too. Most of them deciding without a shadow of doubt that the real star in the family was Adele. The Philadelphia *North American* declared: 'The bill began with a pair of excellent dancers, Fred and Adele Astaire. The girl who was also the possesser of remarkably good looks, being especially graceful of movement.'

The New York *Star* reported: 'We have never seen the Castles and we might also say we never wish to after the superb exhibition of modern dances by Fred and Adele Astaire. Their grace and charm completely won over the audience and called for repeated applause.'

That sort of reaction made the Astaires think about their future even more seriously than they had before. Their act had to have a title, a phrase that would always be linked with the name Astaire on a vaudeville bill. They didn't exactly find inspiration when they decided on calling themselves 'Fred and Adele Astaire, The Youthful Brother and Sister', but it didn't hold them back either.

They not only sought out and obtained new bookings but new material, too. They would go round the music publishers' offices, pop into the booths where the pluggers were demonstrating songs and would then dance to the melodies banged out by the pianists. At Remicks, in New York, a young plugger was so impressed by the way they performed that he said he would like nothing more than to write a brand new show for this unusual pair of kid dancers. They told him they would like nothing better themselves and made a note of his name – George Gershwin. At Waterson, Berlin and Snyder's offices, the Astaires occasionally spotted one of the three principals – a curly-haired, Russian-born songwriter whose material was so good that Messrs Waterson and Snyder decided that the only way to keep him out of any other publishing firm's clutches was to give him a partnership. His name was Irving Berlin. In those days he was already too important to deal personally with artists like the teenage Adele and Fred.

Nevertheless, the Astaires knew enough about their business to pick material that was peculiarly right for them. The New York audiences were showing them so much appreciation that there would hardly have been time to move out of the city, even if they had wanted to. One thing they did want was a chance to play the Palace, the Broadway theatre about which Judy Garland fifty years later was to say, 'If you haven't played the Palace, you haven't lived.' To that extent, the

Astaires never did live. They never played the Palace, apart from the one in Chicago and that in itself was an achievement. Nor after 1916 did they ever again play in vaudeville.

A scout from the Shubert Brothers, the toughest, most ruthless impresarios of the age, saw to that. The Astaires were in New York on Fred's seventeenth birthday. The scout went back stage, knocked on their dressing room doors and invited the pair to take part in the next Shubert show. They accepted. Had they turned down the offer, they would be turning down Broadway.

Clap Yo' Hands

Broadway in 1917 was more than just a place name. It had already become a word in the English language, even if you couldn't find it in a dictionary. But you didn't have to look it up; to anyone who had ever spent a couple of cents for a seat in the gallery it meant Big Time show business – and the capital letters were part of the definition. When America entered World War One, Broadway had also somehow come to symbolise patriotism. Every theatre seemed to be filled with people who had come into the auditorium not merely to escape the misery of war news, but to revel in the exhilaration of finally being given the chance to beat the Hun.

There were parades through the street; flags in almost every show. Those productions that were not so blatantly banner-waving were helping the cause Woodrow Wilson had ordained for America – simply by being escapist. And *Over The Top* was that kind of show, its billing was littered with names that are now part of Broadway and Tin Pan Alley folklore. The score was by Sigmund Romberg, Harold Atteridge wrote some of the sketches and Justine Johnstone and Mary Eaton were the leads. It also featured Fred and Adele Astaire. Before long, they were joined by Ed Wynn, a tall slightly overweight comedian who wore spectacles without lenses in them. Fred and the older Wynn became firm friends and cemented their friendship on the golf course.

But the friendship of Wynn and Astaire was stronger than the show. It had started off at New Haven, Connecticut by being called the *Nine O'Clock Revue* and was very popular with the students at Yale. Possibly this approval from an institution of learning was the reason the artists were quaintly introduced with this note in the show programme: 'To make the lucidity of the libretto conspicuous, the following musical interruptions take place . . .' The show lasted a mere seventy-eight performances, but these were enough for the Astaires to be noticed.

The Shubert Brothers – Lee and Jake, who six years earlier had made the biggest Broadway discovery of all time, Al Jolson – were among those who did notice. They signed the Astaires for *The Passing Show of 1918*, the next production at the 'flagship' of their empire, the Winter Garden. It was probably Broadway's most attractive theatre and the one which Jolson had been making his own.

Heywood Broun laid it firmly on the line in the *New York Tribune* that he felt Fred was about to make something of an impact there, too. 'Fred Astaire stood out,' he wrote. 'He and his partner, Adele Astaire, made the show pause early in the evening with a beautiful loose-limbed dance . . . it almost seemed as if the two young people had been poured into the dance.'

They were poured in fact into the sort of show business for which the Shuberts had become famous. Not only were they working six nights a week at the Winter Garden – and matinées, too – but on Sunday evenings as well. This was another Jolson institution – started because he wanted the show people who were themselves working during the week to have a chance of seeing how good he was. The Sunday entertainment laws did not allow the usual kind of theatrical show, there couldn't be costumes or sets, for instance, so they called these shows concerts. Jolson frequently headed the bill himself and other entertainers – usually the ones under contract to the Shuberts – were the supporting acts, as much as they would be on a vaudeville bill. The Astaires filled one of these spots week after week.

Today, both remember Jolson as one of the most dynamic performers they ever came across – if not always the most polite man on their side of the footlights. Another with whom they worked was W. C. Fields, also something of an egoist.

In *The Passing Show*, both Fred and Adele were adorned with chicken feathers for a number called 'Twit, Twit, Twit, Twit' and

18

Adele sang 'I Can't Make My Feet Behave' – although, in fact, she made them behave exceedingly well. They were billed as 'Fred and Adele Astaire, New Songs and Smart Dances'.

Fred, however, didn't think their dancing was smart enough. And he didn't think Adele did nearly enough rehearsing. He would constantly tell her to get it right and not just hope everything would be OK for the next performance. More than once, he stayed up all night just to get the movements perfect. He would notice when she was slacking, almost before she would herself. If she missed the odd step or two and at the end of the show would slope off, feeling – as she put it – 'very cute', Fred had other ideas.

'Babe, you missed a step tonight,' he'd tell her. 'Think we'd better stay on after the show and rehearse.' And rehearse they would, no matter what other plans they had for the evening. Nineteen-year-old Fred was boss although if there were troubles with orchestra conductors or musical directors, Adele was now better able to fight them than before, and didn't leave it all for Fred as she once had.

He, by then, was getting ready to fight a different sort of battle. Fred was told he would be drafted any day and probably sent over to France. But it was late 1918 and before the draft board could get round to calling him, the war was over. After 125 performances, *The Passing Show* passed into 1919 and went on tour. In Detroit, Astaire the perfectionist came unstuck. He fell asleep in the afternoon and woke up to realise that he only had five minutes to go before curtain-up time. He was also eighteen storeys above street level and the hotel was six blocks away from the theatre – but he got on the stage in time, without make-up and in his street clothes.

The Passing Show was followed by a production with music by Fritz Kreisler called *Apple Blossoms* – the most notable feature of which was not the world-famous violinist's score, but the fact that it was produced by Charles Dillingham, a rival of the Shubert Brothers and also one of the main competitors to Florenz Ziegfeld. In the years since those early post-First World War days, the near viciousness of the Shuberts has become a legend on Broadway, the extravagance and subsequent debts of Ziegfeld are equally part of theatrical history. But Dillingham remains a gentleman. The Astaires, in particular, loved him. As well they might. Dillingham must today be given credit for really seeing the potential that these two young dancers offered. He had been told that Fred worked at every number as though his life depended upon it. And he realised that Adele was a clown who could also join in a contest with the lead dancers of the New York Ballet and probably win. He wanted them for *Apple Blossoms*.

The day the Astaires met him for the first time, Dillingham was sitting in his office quite obviously overcome from the effects of a long hot New York summer. He was mopping his balding head with a piece of blotting paper. 'Well, kids, what do you expect to get?' he asked. Fred, up till then thought of as too shy to ask the directions to the theatre, replied: 'Five hundred and fifty dollars!'

Dillingham appreciated the significance of the way in which the figure was put, as well as the embarrassment of the young man. 'What's the 500 dollars for?' he asked. But he didn't argue the point. The Astaires got their $500. The other $50 went to their agent. And all they had to do was dance two numbers in the operetta, the story of which was loosely based on a tale by Alexandre Dumas. The star of the show was a man who was then one of the leading figures in American musical comedy, John Charles Thomas.

While the show was having a trial run at Atlantic City, Dillingham took the Astaires out to dinner at the resort's best hotel. Then, after the opening in New York, he wined and dined them in the manner to which he, as a scion of one of the city's Society families, had become accustomed. In some ways, this was also the introduction of the Astaires into Society. They had never regarded 'doing the town' as an important part of getting ahead. Ironically, the two dancers hated doing the sort of steps other people of their age enjoyed on ballroom floors. They rarely went to night clubs. Fred certainly had few friends and was quite content to save his contacts with other people for the time when he was on the stage.

In *Apple Blossoms*, the contact came from the almost thunderous applause of the audience – an audience who had been informed of the Astaire's presence at the Globe Theatre on Broadway and 46th Street through a programme which listed the cast in their section of the show like this:

Julie	Miss Lena Parker
Polly	Miss Juanita Fletcher
Molly	Adele Astaire
Johnny	F. Astaire

20

Neither of them merited a title to their name and poor Fred didn't get more than an initial. But the impact was made. And more than that, it was an opportunity both to introduce the Astaires to a much wider public than before – and to clear up any misunderstandings.

On 16 November 1919, the *New York Times* reported:

'Fred and Adele Astaire who romp off with a very considerable portion of the honours in *Apple Blossoms* are actually brother and sister.

' "When a pair of dancers calling themselves the Astaires come out of vaudeville, it is customary to discover that one of them is named McGurn and the other Lieblich and that it was by cleverly combining these two that they arrived at Astaire." (A double or treble reading of that sentence should make the author's intentions fairly clear.) The piece went on: "The Astaires, furthermore, are as young as they look – another cause for surprise. Adele is twenty-one and Fred is twenty. . . ." The writer did, however, have one criticism: "In addition to her skill as a dancer, the girl of the team possesses vocal ambitions, which she is unable to further in *Apple Blossoms*." '

Kreisler's music, which was very definitely Kreisler on a rather bad day, would not have helped her even if she had had that opportunity to practise her art. But Kreisler liked the Astaires as much as the critics did, and he had even acted as their rehearsal pianist in the early days of the show. Another composer also helped out in this role, George Gershwin, who was still working as a song plugger. He came along to see how things were going for his friends and ended up working – because the regular pianist had gone off for the day.

The friendship between Gershwin and the Astaires was blooming like the *Apple Blossoms* of the title. Together, they would go to night clubs and spot the talent whom each would predict would one day 'make it'. They would play 'in' games on the piano together, with Fred playing a chord that struck Gershwin as fascinating; 'What was that?' he would ask. 'What was that?' Occasionally, the roles would change, with George demonstrating a dance or two that Fred had to promise to think about.

Looking back now it is certain that the Astaires contributed more to *Apple Blossoms* than anyone else. It is also certain that without them, it

21

would never have run as long as it did; the Broadway histories now record that the show ran for a total of 256 performances. When Charles Dillingham looked for a follow up, he believed he had found it with *The Love Letter*. It opened in October 1921 at the same theatre as *Apple Blossoms* and again with John Charles Thomas in the lead. The credits also included William Le Baron writing the book and lyrics (as he had done for *Apple Blossoms*) and Victor Jacobi, who had shared the music score of the previous show with Kreisler, and was now providing all the music himself. The show also had the Astaires.

The Love Letter was no great masterpiece, in fact, there appeared to be no love lost at all between the show and the patrons. After thirty-one wilting performances, it died. But despite the disappointments of such a microscopic run, there was one compensating factor, one that was to have an important effect on the Astaires' theatrical career. It was called the run-around.

The Astaires opened the show with a number called 'Upside Down'. Edward Royce, a British-born choreographer, dreamed up the idea of having them run round and around the stage like a team of circus horses who had plumes rising from their heads. The Astaires' main decoration was a massive dose of energy, but the audience went wild as the circles they described got wider and wider until they had left the stage altogether. It sounds simple, almost childish. But, it established an Astaire trademark.

Most of the kind words that critics could find for *The Love Letter* were reserved, as before, for the Astaires. One man – who obviously had not read what the *New York Times* said when reviewing *Apple Blossoms* – wrote admiringly of their 'Parisian chic'.

The show did not close, however, before it could be seen by a man selling ties in a Fifth Avenue store. Fred was buying a tie and the man selling it to him was called Alex Aarons. His father owned the shop as well as being a top man in one of the biggest American theatrical production firms. Aarons junior, had no desire to sell ties indefinitely. In fact, the sooner he could get out from behind the counter and go into show business himself, the better he'd like it. He'd like it even more, he said, if the Astaires would join him. This was not an invitation that could be turned down lightly, providing that Charles Dillingham would 'lend' them for the run of the show. With Aarons' father's connections, it seemed as if it couldn't go wrong. He also had another ace up his sleeve. Almost by the way, he added that there was a young man ready to do the score. His name, George Gershwin.

With the memory of George's wish that day in the Remick's song plugger's booth still quite fresh, it represented the clinch to a deal being carried off. Fred and Adele talked it over with their agent and they agreed it was a show they wanted to do just as soon as *The Love Letter* closed. And Dillingham raised no objection either. The only problem was that Gershwin was not available to do the entire score. The young man had just had a fantastic success with his hit 'Swanee' which was to prove, in fact, the most profitable number in his entire career – and was contracted to the showman George White to provide the music for his latest 'Scandals' production. But he did promise to produce a few numbers for the Aarons' show, which was going to be called *For Goodness Sake*.

When it finally opened, it was clear the Astaires had made a very good move. The piece was a tale about a marital upset – a husband thinks his wife is playing around with someone else, and decides that the only way to get her sympathy is by pretending to commit suicide. Fred and Adele played friends of the warring spouses.

They were number six in the list of artists appearing, but signing the contract for the show was the most sensible thing they had yet done in their careers. Robert Benchley, writing in the New York magazine *Life*, summed up the reaction of most people who saw it:

'There isn't much to say about *For Goodness Sake* that you couldn't say about most musicals except that the Astaires are in it. When they dance, everything seems brighter and their comedy alone would be good enough to carry them through, even if they were to stop dancing (which God forbid).'

They didn't stop dancing. And when they danced, it was like the turning of an ignition key on a car's dashboard. A rather indifferent audience was suddenly galvanised into near mass hysteria. And as in *The Love Letter*, it was the run-around that made the people out front stand up and cheer. One minute it seemed that Fred and Adele were the circus horses again; the next they were a team of trick cyclists. The number had the ridiculous title of 'The Whichness of the Whatness and the Whereness of the Who.' It was as crazy as the run-around itself. But what everyone connected with *For Goodness Sake* knew as the 'nutty dance' had established a new show business convention. It was what people had come to see. When Adele appeared to fall flat on her face at the end of the dance, the cheering was almost deafening.

All this pleased the young brother and sister more than anything they had done so far. It also thrilled their parents. Mr Astaire senior had tried a whole variety of business ventures, but none of them too successfully – and he was finally coming around to the idea of retiring on his children's laurels. To a man with his sort of adoration of the theatre it was a marvellous moment. For his wife, who had jumped on and off trains with her kids and had put up with the discomforts of the theatrical boarding houses, it was all she had ever been waiting for. It seemed that nothing could stop *For Goodness Sake*. But those who thought that, hadn't bargained with New York in the summer. With no air-conditioning in the Lyric Theatre, the show offered no competition at all to the notion of sitting at home with your feet in a bowl of cold water or in a speakeasy with fans whirring overhead. The show closed after 103 performances. All that remained of *For Goodness Sake* now was the tour.

The Broadway season is the one stars, impresarios and audiences tend to remember. In contrast, the tour was an extra that found its way into the contract, with an additional fee written into the legal agreement. That way, there was consolation for the boredom of re-doing in the sticks what had been so exciting on Broadway, and a contribution towards the fares and hotel expenses that sometimes had to be paid by the stars themselves.

In Bridgeport, Connecticut during 1922 something happened which even Fred considered to reflect well on his talent. He and Adele were so sensational, that they took one curtain call after the other. There was a magnetism about the way the audience picked up the message they were transmitting across the footlights and they could do nothing wrong.

Earlier that day, Fred had walked around the town and picked up some shopping. Among his purchases was a red and green plaid bathrobe. As he put it on after the show that night, it struck him that perhaps that bathrobe had something to do with the success of his performance. Show people can sometimes be very irrational and there was nothing less rational than to think that a bathrobe could be more responsible for success than mere talent. But it came to be a lucky charm that symbolised a lucky night. For years afterwards, no opening night, no first day of the screening of an Astaire film, would be allowed to pass without the bathrobe going on first. It was an indulgence he could now afford to allow himself. After *For Goodness Sake*, there could be no doubt that both he and Adele were stars.

'S Wonderful

An extraordinary amount of hard work had got the Astaires to the point where Charles Dillingham decided to keep them for himself. He wasn't going to be persuaded by Aarons or anyone else to release them from his contract this time, and he was about to pay them for the privilege – to the tune of $1,000 a week.

Now, he was going to build a show entirely around the brother and sister who, to use the Broadway cliché, had taken the town by storm. He was doing so at a time when people wanted to know all they could about Adele and Fred. When 'Delly' could be heard screaming from her dressing room that 'Fred's got a girl out front – a blonde', the news raced round New York. Whether he had a girl out front or not, it certainly wasn't a serious affair. Fred was still as shy as ever and he wasn't going to do anything that would break his habit of working until the muscles in his legs seemed locked into one position – unless it was a game of pool or a hand at gin rummy. As for Adele, she was beginning to appear at the smart places and nearly always with an escort who had his name in the Social Register. She was important enough in her own right for newspapermen to want to know her views on the latest fashions or on the fads of what was considered to be beauty.

It took more than a snide comment from a columnist to get her champing on the bit, but she was gaining a reputation for the speedy riposte. It was the age when girls flattened their chests but showed their legs. When a certain French actress was hailed as having the shapeliest legs in the world, Adele was quick to add her comment on this momentous announcement. 'Who was the judge?' she asked. 'Did he confine his observations just to those in France?' Miss Astaire made no claims on her own behalf, but it didn't take too close an observation to note that when men looked at her legs, they weren't only concerned with her dancing.

Dillingham's new show was called *The Bunch and Judy*. Most of the critics liked it, although one writer described the performance as 'an artless piece', which didn't seem to bode well for the stars. But the audience loved the run-around – this time to a piece called 'How Do You Do, Katinka?', and Heywood Broun wrote in the *New York World*, 'Fred and Adele are the most gracious young dancers available in the world of musical comedy. Indeed, the Astaires are distinctly attractive even when they are not in motion, and once they begin to dance they are among the immortals.' Faced with *The Bunch and Judy* as it stood, those were brave words, if uncannily intuitive.

There was one scene in the show involving the Astaires playing bagpipes. It was this one that their father said he liked best which they took to be the most generous comment he felt able to make. The music was by Jerome Kern and Kern himself came along for rehearsals. But far from that encouraging the stars and the other performers, including another brother and sister team, Johnny and Ray Dooley, there were moments of foreboding right from the workouts on tour. At the dress rehearsal they were ceremoniously dropped on to the floor from a large table being carried across the stage by the male chorus. After only one performance, scenes were rewritten, numbers were changed. Fred didn't like the scene where he was supposed to fall overboard from a ship. He also objected to wearing a powdered wig. In *Steps In Time*, he says the whole number in which he wore it 'bothered' him.

But if the critics were basically sympathetic, the audiences were plainly much less warm about the show than they had been for the previous Astaire appearances. It showed, too, in the box office takings.

There were, however, the bright moments. On 9 December 1922 Adele celebrated what the show's publicists liked to call her twenty-first birthday. She was, in fact, now twenty-four but twenty-one seemed more appropriate for a pretty girl who was always making people laugh. Dillingham gave her a big party on the stage of the Globe Theatre. Her parents were there and so was everyone from the show. Eighty-one presents were hauled on to the stage, including a ton of coal. It had been brought in a truck which drove up to the door of the theatre on 46th Street. The driver said he had been sent by a coal merchant from Pittsburg. With the gift, was a card that said: 'In hard times, black diamonds are more useful than white ones.'

Dillingham offered to buy the coal and use it to heat the theatre. At the supper party after the show that night, the impresario paid her the price of the 'black diamonds' – a bouquet of orchids.

He and the other 'angels' of *The Bunch and Judy*, needed the coal more than the young dancer. Times were indeed hard for them. After just over three weeks, *The Bunch and Judy* closed, and from that moment on, the Astaires called it 'The Bust and Judy'. It was the first time they had starred in their own show and it was the biggest flop they had experienced since their names were removed from the bill at Proctor's Fifth Avenue. As far as they were concerned, they weren't really the stars they had genuinely believed themselves to be. And they wondered if Dillingham thought they were, either. He decided not to take up the option he had on them for $1,250 a week and didn't even give them a Christmas present. Alex Aarons, however, backed his hunch. If *The Bunch and Judy* failed, it was because it wasn't much of a show, not that the Astaires weren't good performers. He wanted to extend his operations and he thought that Fred and Adele deserved to have a wider audience than they had experienced so far – even with a whole string of country-wide vaudeville tours behind them.

He had been having talks in London with Sir Alfred Butt, an MP, who was also a theatre producer. The Astaires, he told Butt, were made to measure for London and he had just the vehicle for them. As for the dancers, he simply asked: 'How would you like to do *For Goodness Sake* in London?'

He was playing it safe – and choosing their most successful show – the one to which he had beaten Dillingham. He was also giving Fred and Adele a much bigger slice of the action than they had had on Broadway.

It didn't take much to convince Adele and Fred that this was an opportunity they just could not afford to miss. They were going to London and were going there as stars. For the crossing they were sailing on the *Aquitania* – first class, of course. When they arrived in London, they would be accommodated at the Savoy, which really was the pinnacle of success. But they made one condition which the British management found difficult at first to accept: if they go, their mother must go, too. Their father had not been well and wasn't up to making the journey, but he told them he was feeling fine and it was right that Adele should have a chaperon. Sir Alfred wasn't completely impressed by the argument, but he accepted what appeared to be the inevitable.

The first performance on the tour took place on the *Aquitania* itself, at a concert organised by the captain for the crew's benevolent fund. It was not an evening for people prone to sea sickness. The passengers in long dresses and dinner suits were jostled from one end of the ballroom to the other. The phrase used for the way the pair had to dance that night was given an altogether different meaning a generation or two later – it was pure rock and roll.

When they got to London, they were shown the sights, smelled the sooty London air and announced they loved every inch of the place. They wondered about the theatres, though. The stages looked different and sitting in the stalls for the first night of a revue that floundered before their eyes was an experience that sent shivers up and down their spines. The Gallery First Nighters, a London institution, were treating the cast in much the same way they would candidates at an election meeting.

The man who excited them most was Jack Buchanan, who with his top hat and tails routines would inevitably before long be called the British Fred Astaire. It would be a little while, however, before they themselves were presenting Mr Buchanan with any direct competition. For the moment, they were about to experience British audiences in the provinces. They need not have worried.

There were changes in the routines, changes in the dialogue and changes in the other players. One of the New York numbers 'Tra La La' was withdrawn and in its place was a new Gershwin song, 'Stairway to Paradise', which before long was to rank as one of the composer's greatest standards. But the biggest change of all – apart from the rise in status of the Astaires – was the title. *For Goodness Sake* became, without any reasonable explanation, *Stop Flirting*. It was a pointless change; the original title was hardly an Americanism – although much of the dialogue was – but the people who came to see

29

the show in provincial England and later in Scotland were not in the least bit perturbed. All they knew was they had found a show to love and a pair of performers to take to their hearts. After the Second World War, American musicals were to dominate completely the English stage. *Stop Flirting* provided a useful dress rehearsal for what was within twenty-five years to become a theatrical phenomenon.

The show opened at the Royal Court Theatre, Liverpool, early in 1923. With what the young Astaires must have thought was fairly typical British phlegm, the *Liverpool Dispatch* gave them a warm welcome to a city which would itself one day have an important place in the British pop scene. It said: 'The hit of the evening was a comedy dance by an exceedingly clever American couple, Miss Adele and Mr Fred Astaire, whose dancing throughout is a feature of the programme.'

The comedy dance was the run-around, or as it had now become, 'The Oompah Trot'. The famous Colonel Bogey chords had been incorporated into the final bars of the routine and everyone seemed to be oompahing their way out of the theatre.

The Astaires had proved themselves to be infectious. As the *Glasgow Citizen* reported when their man went round to the Kings Theatre dressing room to talk to the stars soon after the opening: 'When I danced round to the stage door – what's that? Danced? Yes, I danced. I couldn't walk after watching the Astaires all evening – I found them coming off the stage where they had just had their photograph taken. The photographer must have had his quickest lens working, for if ever feet twinkled, the Astaires have 'em.'

No one had known quite what to expect of Fred and Adele. In these pre-radio, pre-talking pictures days, the American accent came as something of a shock to the provincial Briton. The Astaires were either fawned over or patronised as country bumpkins who had finally found a big city.

Both had certainly found Scotland. Before they arrived in the country, they did their homework, learnt all they could about Edinburgh and Glasgow, swatted up on the Highlands and Lowlands and read everything they found about Mary Queen of Scots. When there was a Scots ear to listen, they were ready with their potted Scottish history course. And so was Mother. Every time anyone was shown into Adele's dressing room, the first person to be introduced was Mrs Astaire, who was plainly having a great time with Delly and the boy whom she persisted in calling 'Sonny'. She was moved by the plaudits of critics and audiences alike.

The *Glasgow Evening Times* said: 'I can't think of any stage production, musical comedy or any other, that makes so many genuinely laughable situations out of a thin story as *Stop Flirting* does.'

Every time they changed their steps, the couple announced to the audience what they were doing. One critic commented,

The terms were double-Dutch to me, but their dancing was parexcellence. This new American pair were in great demand. But their supply seemed to exceed the demand, for they always had some new trick to set out no matter how often they were recalled. Their parts were minor but they tied over so many 'blind spots' with some excellent fooling. They have an alluring American drawl and Miss Astaire's 'golly' eyes are a wealth of comedy, in themselves great partners.

Another writer in the *Evening Times* said,

Everyone concerned with the production of *Stop Flirting*, which is being played at the Kings this week prior to going to London, must have rejoiced at the enthusiasm with which it was received. But indeed the music was so bright and the players so exuberant that the audience had to be the same . . .

In some ways, *Stop Flirting* recalls the *Belle of New York*. The American trail is over it all, the music is tuneful and lovely and the stage is continually crowded with bright young men and pretty girls dancing in harmony with jazz airs and merrily singing in chorus. . . . The brightest attraction is, however, Adele Astaire and her partner Fred Astaire [which gave some indication of who was regarded as boss at the time]. These clever Americans introduced us to a new art. Grotesque and eccentric dancing is familiar, but humour combined with vivacity and art and nimble daintiness is a novelty which was last night rewarded by enthusiastic recalls.

It was the same story in Edinburgh and again when they finally opened in London. It was at the Shaftesbury Theatre on 20 May 1923, an evening represented in the Astaire memory by a sea of women in evening dresses and men in stiff white shirt fronts – all of them calling out 'core', 'core' after every twirl on stage. The gallery was ecstatic and, far away in a haze, there were the equally emotional shouts from that unique institution of the British theatre, the 'pit'. Adele and 'her partner Fred' had all the encouragement they needed. At the end of the show, Adele went down to the footlights and told the still cheering audience: 'My brother and I thank you from the bottom of our hearts and – and we want you all to come and have tea with us tomorrow.' Fred was less forthcoming: 'She said it,' he added.

The *New York Times* thought the reaction important enough to print a telegram received from London. 'Adele and Fred Astaire by their dancing carried away the audience and the number of encores they received actually impeded the action of the piece.' The headline said it all, 'Or as one says in the cruder western hemisphere, they stopped the show.'

It was encores all the way – except that they didn't content themselves with mere encores. As the man in Glasgow almost said, the supply met the demand and there was a complete new routine every time they came on, with dance numbers and songs interpolated where no one expected them to be. There had never been an audience like it. The reserved Englishman, as far as they were concerned, was for the story books. Champagne was popping after the show and the newspapers told the tale the company thought they would. 'Adele Astaire,' said *The Star*, the London evening paper, 'could dance the depression out of an undertaker.'

The following Sunday, *The People* reported 'Adele is a genius; not only does she dance with perfect grace, but she imparts a sense of fun into all she does. She is also a clever comic actress and her quaint little voice is very attractive. Her partner is also a clever dancer.'

It was the beginning of a love affair with London. Fifty years later Fred was still saying: 'I may even live there one day.' As much as anything it was a love affair with a way of life. Britain had emerged from the war shaken, but determined to have a good time. The twenties were gay and exciting for people who had money and a desire to enjoy themselves and there was no Prohibition or its effects to make chasing that good time the sordid experience it was in the States. The white ties in the audience summed it all up – if a black bow was spotted the Astaires felt that the show was running down. But more than anything the well-dressed audience symbolised London.

Fred fancied himself as a snappy dresser. Now he haunted Savile Row in the way he used to visit the Tin Pan Alley music publishers, he would buy a tie that he had seen someone he admired wearing. If he played golf, it would be in just the right sort of plus-fours, and he always sported the kind of hat that he fancied the smart man-about-town would wear.

Meanwhile, both he and Adele were being courted for parties. Fred was still bashful, still 'Moaning Minnie' if he felt his sister wasn't putting enough work into one of her routines, but he had to admit that he was now having more of a good time than he had ever had before. If going to select parties was the way to meet people, he went. But the big thing that happened during the run of *Stop Flirting* was a visit to the theatre by the Prince of Wales. The show had just moved from the Shaftesbury to the Queens and the Prince was sitting in the eighth row with a party of friends, a lady to his left. He obviously enjoyed the experience, for later in the week he came back again and this time went round to the Astaires' dressing rooms after the performance. With him was his friend 'Fruity' Metcalfe, who suggested that the dancers join the royal party at the Riviera Club afterwards. Adele, who had been dancing her heart out – and every other part of her body, too – on stage, danced with the Prince and the news was not long getting out. The New York social set were suitably impressed.

There were altogether ten visits by the Prince of Wales and other members of his family to *Stop Flirting*, during which time the heir to the British throne had become the idol of the kid from Omaha. Fred was never actually seen tugging at his tie as the Prince would, but almost every other clothes idea he practised was copied religiously. Fred even found out where the Wales dress suits and waistcoats which had an unusual cut were made and tried to order an exact replica of the waistcoat. The man at Hawes & Curtis made it known, ever so politely, that they could not possibly do that – so Fred found another tailor who could and did.

The Astaires had become part of London society themselves, and the centre of a host of advertising campaigns. They lent their names to toothbrushes and pick-me-ups and succeeded in convincing a somewhat gullible public that their lives would never be the same without these products. In an effort to keep the public interested in *Stop Flirting* a rash of ten-shilling notes could be seen sprouting out of wallets casually 'lost' on the pavements of London. It was an irresistible temptation and only when they were picked up, could the unlucky finder see the 'wallets' were made of paper and the ten bob was an advertisement for *Stop Flirting*, hiding behind a photograph of a section of a banknote. What the Bank of England thought about these is not on record.

Stop Flirting moved from the Queens to the Strand Theatre and back to the provinces when this latest London venue was needed for a pantomime. While the show was on tour in Birmingham, another royal relationship was cemented. Prince George – for ever afterwards, simply 'PG' to Astaire – came along to see the show with a friend and called at Fred's dressing room afterwards. This youngest of the royal brothers, who, in 1942 as Duke of Kent was to be killed in a plane crash, would before long become a close friend. But as Fred now recalls, 'I always called him "Sir" .'

Back in London after the pantomime season, it seemed that the Astaires would never *Stop Flirting*. *The Times* was glad that they were so firmly entrenched.

Mr Fred and Miss Adele Astaire are examples of the comparative small body of American comedians who have come to this country and have instantly conquered [said the paper].

Less than a year ago, they were unknown over here. Then they appeared at the Shaftesbury Theatre in the musical comedy *Stop Flirting* to which they have been attached ever since. The piece ended a successful run in London and then went on tour. Now it has ended a successful tour and come back to London.

On Saturday night at the Strand Theatre it was received again with the utmost enthusiasm. The applause was a great tribute to the two Astaires, for without them, the piece would not be very exhilarating. They both dance as well as ever and act as easily and with a distinct sense of comedy. Whenever the action begins to languish, they come to the rescue with a song or dance. . . . There seems no reason why *Stop Flirting* should stop running until the Astaires stop dancing.

When one gallery first-nighter told Fred he had seen the show 114 times, anything a critic could write was superfluous – particularly bearing in mind the love affair that was growing between the Astaires and Britain. If nothing else, London had introduced Fred to serious horse racing – and there was every sign that this attachment was developing into a passion. Fred got to know the Leach family, the two brothers, Jack the jockey and Felix the trainer. When he saw how keen the young Astaire was on the Turf, Jack told him, 'You are now a member of the racing swine.' With accounts at the leading London bookmakers, he was taking it all very seriously indeed. He was now able to go to the races without feeling he was playing truant.

He also considered it was a suitable time to start thinking about music more seriously, too. With his recently-found friend, Noël Coward, he took a course in composition at London's Guildhall School of Music. He says that he didn't benefit all that much. Certainly Coward got more dividends from the course than he did, but at the back of the mind of the twenty-four-year-old performer was an idea that he would one day like to write an important tune himself.

What was always being brought home to the Astaires was how very much more vociferous the British audiences were compared with those in America. They had never heard people out front yell the way the people in London and the provinces were doing, long after the first nights. Sometimes, they would join in the action, too. In one scene, Jack Melford, another of the principal players in *Stop Flirting*, sang a comedy song about being drunk.

A man stood up in the stalls and cried out: 'I don't see there is anything funny about drunkenness; that is nothing to laugh at.' At that, the unhappy theatregoer called to his wife and shouted, 'We're leaving.' The rest of the audience were astonished and just sat wondering whether the man was really upset or was a 'plant'. They did not wait long to react, however. The very next scene Fred appeared on stage and joked about Prohibition. The audience roared – while the man was still marching out of the theatre, clutching his wife's arm.

If London was the scene of the Astaires' greatest triumphs to date, it was also the place where they first experienced a family bereavement. During the run of the show, their mother had gone home to the States. Her husband still was ill and not responding to medical treatment and she thought she ought to be near him. They were together when he died. Sir Alfred Butt gave Fred and Adele the news, but the legend was that the show must go on – and that night it did.

Frederic Astaire or Austerlitz, had been the one to set his children on a dancing career. So, by proceeding with the show, Fred and Adele were really thanking him. Soon their mother returned to London, but was so ill herself on arrival that she was sent to a nursing home. Both Fred and Adele frequently visited her there and became favourites of the other patients, one of whom was Sir James Barrie, creator of Peter Pan. Wouldn't it be a good idea, he suggested, if Adele would one day star in the traditional Christmas play, in the title role of the boy who never grew up? A marvellous idea, but it never happened.

The impact of the Astaires in London extended way beyond the sort of social strata in which they were now moving. A woman approached Mrs Astaire with a story about her son being unable to get any work – because he didn't have any decent clothes to wear. Fred made up a large parcel from his own wardrobe and had them sent round to the woman's address in a poor part of London. Almost by return came a note: 'Thanks for the parcel you sent me, but I'm sorry to say there weren't any shoes in it.'

Occasionally, there were moments when Fred wondered whether he had been deceiving himself about the success of *Stop Flirting*. Despite all the raves in the press, all the flattery of the people who went back stage, there was usually at least someone who remained unimpressed. In 1924, Fred talked about the young lady who told him what she thought of *Stop Flirting*, 'The star is simply too awful for words,' she said, 'and it's surprising managers can be found to produce such drivel – and with such a terrible cast.' Only later was she told she had been talking to Mr Astaire himself.

There had been six hundred performances of *Stop Flirting* and Fred and Adele didn't miss one of them. But in August 1924, they announced that they were packing up and going home. They weren't bored with the show, even less were they growing tired of London. But the strain of dancing what they worked out to be a total of 10,000 miles in the one show was telling – particularly on Adele. She had been to see her doctor and he ordered her to stop immediately and take a complete rest.

In her rose and white dressing room at the Strand, she poured her heart out. 'We have lost our hearts to England – your lovely country.

We want to come back again soon.' They had never expected to be in Britain for anything like the eighteen months that *Stop Flirting* had run.

> Everyone wants us to stay [said Adele]. We hate to disappoint our friends in front. Even when we're feeling off colour, we try to give our very best to our performance. When we get home, we shall have a long rest and then come out in a new show, which we trust will be sufficiently successful to warrant our bringing it to London. So we are not really saying good-bye, as we expect to be back quite soon.

And then Fred said something which took eighteen months to have its full repercussions. He thought British people were so polite. But the Americans?

> In America, everyone is so rude. They say they have no time to say 'Please' and 'Thank you'. But here, although London is so big and bustling, everyone is always saying 'thank you' in the shops and the buses; the taxi drivers and the policemen, in the restaurants and the hotels. We feel that we shall not be able to stand rudeness when we get back home and I am sure we shall tell Americans they must come to London to learn to be polite. [And there was this sign of the times] Your servants here are wonderful, too, and our servants might take a lesson from them.

What had really impressed them was being in a lift and hearing an attendant say 'Thank you' as they got out. As Fred said: 'I was tickled to death and didn't know what to say.'

On the final night at the Strand Theatre, the audience didn't know what to say either. But they reacted much more directly, they threw flowers on to the stage as well as anything else that was accessible and safe. It was the most incredible experience either of the Astaires had yet had on any stage. But there were to be more – and soon. For the moment, Adele admitted she was homesick. Fred said it was a matter of commitments in New York. Guy Bolton had written a new show and Alex Aarons was going to produce it again. They had to go now because the New Yorkers had such short memories and they were frightened they would be forgotten. 'But we can always come back,' said Fred. It was a promise to be kept. In the meantime, Fred was going to Scotland for a short holiday and Adele, worn out but with her usual impish impatience of anything that looked like stultifying her activity, was going to Devon. The holidays did them both good. On the long voyage home on the *Homeric*, no one even pressed them too hard to perform, although Fred did agree to lead the passenger's favourite guessing game – how many miles the ship would cover in a day.

They were saving their energies for the new show.

Lady Be Good

They were all set for what even then looked like being their biggest opportunity so far. Fred and Adele were going to get $1,750 a week, with a promise of $250 more when they went on tour. Most important of all, they were finally going to do a complete show with George Gershwin.

The package handed to the Astaires by Aarons was for a production called *Black Eyed Susan*, a species that seemed constantly to crop up in song titles of the period but which they both agreed was a fairly uninspired name for a show. Yet it was going to be Broadway again and it would be the first opportunity since the disaster of *Bunch and Judy* to show New York what London had already discovered, that they now were really big stars.

It was an almost identically enticing prospect for George Gershwin. For the first time, he was contracted to do an entire score for a show, with his brother Ira writing the lyrics. George was still barely twenty-six-years-old, but he had already stormed his way to the top of the American musical scene, both with a rash of hit standards and his much more serious 'Rhapsody in Blue'. To date, there had been no formal partnership agreement with any lyricist although many of his early songs were with Irving Caesar and more recently with Buddy De Sylva. Just occasionally, he and Ira would work together as they had done in *For Goodness Sake* and in the show *Primrose*. But in this, his elder brother shared the lyric credits with a man called Desmond Carter and, as in his whole life, had been very much in George's shadow. In *For Goodness Sake* Ira didn't even have the self-confidence to write under his own name. Instead, he adopted the pseudonym of Arthur Francis.

Like the Astaires, George had recently returned from England where he, too, had become the darling of the Prince of Wales set. He had never been more serious than he was that day in the booth at Remicks when he told Fred how much he wanted to write a show for him and Adele. Now he felt he could at last prove it.

The combination of the Astaires and the Gershwins seemed too good to go wrong. Certainly, that was the view of Alex Aarons. This time, he wasn't producing the show alone, but was sharing the role with Vinton Freedley, who had also been connected with *For Goodness Sake* – but in a totally different capacity from the one he adopted now; in those days he had been the romantic lead.

The contract for *Black Eyed Susan* was signed the moment Fred and Adele had stepped down the gangplank of the *Homeric* in New York, and before they were finally cleared through customs. Fred rested the important document on one of his cabin trunks and scribbled his name at the foot of the page, before handing it over to Adele.

Black Eyed Susan didn't stay so named for very long. Before the Gershwins had completed the score, Aarons and Freedley had decided on a title they thought would be much more appealing. It would be called, they announced, *Lady Be Good*.

The Astaires, Aarons told them, would sing and dance for as long and as well as their talents would allow. As far as he was concerned, this meant that they would never leave the stage. But they were to be allowed the occasional breathing space. Walter Catlett, one of the most original and best-loved comedians on Broadway – and before long in Hollywood, too – would be on hand to make people laugh while the Astaires had their feet up. And to him, and not Fred, must go the credit of first singing 'Oh, Lady Be Good' in public. Note the 'Oh' at the beginning, which distinguished the song title from the name of the show. Catlett made everyone realise how good a singer Fred could be.

It was not the only musical misjudgement in the saga of the show. After the try-out in Philadelphia, the management decided one song had to come out of the production entirely, because they thought it slowed up the action. As a result, it remains a classic example of how even the most experienced people in show business don't always know that business. The tune had been written specially for Adele by the Gershwins. Aarons and Freedley had borrowed $10,000 for *Lady Be Good* on the strength of that number alone – from a backer who had previously been determined not to lend them a cent. But the song was removed in Philadelphia just the same. Fortunately it was to be more adequately appreciated later on. Its title: 'The Man I Love'.

Having said all that, there was much more that was right with *Lady Be Good* than was wrong. The story was as flimsy as ever, but the Astaires – playing a real-life brother and sister dancing team who fall on to bad times – were dancing better than even they had done before and were singing better, too.

The run-around was exquisite and more nutty than ever before, to the accompaniment of the Gershwins' 'Swiss Miss'. But if *Lady Be Good* must inevitably be remembered for what was all but the title song – and for the one that got away 'The Man I Love' – one other number stands out as classic Gershwin – 'Fascinating Rhythm'. Adele and Fred did a routine for this with Cliff Edwards, a top artist of the time, better known as Ukelele Ike. The audiences had no doubts about cheering this in Philadelphia and again when the show finally opened at the Liberty Theatre on Broadway.

For weeks Adele had been trying to slip away from rehearsals to go on to nightclubs, unashamedly assisted in this by George Gershwin, while all Fred had wanted to do was spread more rosin on the stage and practise. He would have sandwiches sent up to him night after night while he paced the floor with just a rehearsal light to keep him company. As opening night neared, Adele would get caught up in the momentum and work just as hard as her brother. But while he thought of nothing more than just getting a perfect production out of it all, Adele desperately wanted to get back to 'café society'.

It was worth all the hard work; even Adele could appreciate that. After the first night, the enthusiasm of all concerned was bubbling over as wildly as the champagne.

The *New York Times* spared no compliments to describe their dancing on the Liberty stage that night in December 1924, if it did get a little pen-tied:

It is agile, clever, tricky, whatever you like to say about it. What really comes along is more elusive and vital than these. The art of words

41

cannot say it. Just as Sullivan wrote the comedy of music, this art of the Astaires is the comedy of the dance. It alone can express itself.

The brother and sister, [the paper declared], are easy and familiar. They are like two puppies in a frolic on the stage. They are like a good-natured brother and sister at some fraternity dance at a Western college. . . .

Miss Astaire is an amusing actress. She and her brother are charming, lovable together. They are clever dancers. The Astaires are pleasant to see together. They contrast happily with the rose-hued professional chorus around them. They have a jolly domestic twitter to all their antics.

The show as such shows go is a good one. Above all there was the unique Astaire style. The dancing itself remains inexplicable. It is abstract as music is, scarcely imitative at all, quite free and completely itself.

The New York *Herald Tribune* was much more straightforward:

Fred and Adele we salute you! Last night at the Liberty Theatre, this young couple appeared about 8.30 o'clock and from an audience sophisticated and over-theatred received a cordial greeting.

At 8.45, they were applauded enthusiastically and when, at 9.15 they sang and danced 'Fascinating Rhythm', the callous Broadwayites cheered them as if their favourite halfback had planted the ball behind the goal posts after an 80-yard run. Seldom has it been our pleasure to witness so heartfelt, spontaneous and so deserved a tribute.

It was plainly also the reaction of the audiences – and the people who wished they could be part of those audiences. The show was booked up for months. Brokers had seen the way it was moving in Philadelphia and had snatched up all the New York tickets that they could get hold of.

Not only was it considered the 'thing' to see *Lady Be Good*, an even greater sign of success was to be seen seeing the show. If you could also get into the Astaires' dressing room after a performance, you felt one step closer to an inclusion in the Social Register.

Middle-aged ladies dressed in furs and positively dripping in diamonds would call on Fred, sometimes to be shocked to the roots of their dyed blonde hair by a choice remark or a risque story from Walter Catlett, who shared Fred's dressing room. As Fred says in *Steps In Time*, this proximity to Catlett was not only very amusing it also provided the comedian with a good opportunity to borrow money – which he always returned.

As the show progressed, Fred continued to rehearse, to practise a new step or perfect another that appeared to go wrong. Adele occasionally let the odd thing slip, not that anyone but Fred ever noticed. But Fred, of course, always did.

About this time, Adele went to the gala opening of a rather smart dancing school. An observer of the occasion thought that her appearance that day summed up completely the difference in approaches to the work of dancing and singing of this brother and sister. Adele turned up wearing a hat – with her hair in curlers underneath.

'If Fred had been a woman,' said the writer, 'never in a thousand years would he have done such a thing. He would have been too worried what people would think.' Adele, however, just regarded it as a gas.

Bernard Sobel, one time press agent for Florenz Ziegfeld and later an important show business columnist, once introduced Fred to a group of chorus girls 'all in décolleté', as he put it. 'As is the custom in the theatre,' he said, 'I put my arm around one, thinking nothing of it. Astaire actually blushed!'

If he was frightened of what other people would think, he was equally difficult to please when it came to the art of dressing. London and the royal princes had taught him their idea of looking smart. Now, back in New York, he would spend hours choosing the material for a suit if he couldn't wait till he got back to London. He would mull over ten ties before he chose one. 'Yet,' said Adele in an interview in *Variety*, 'damn it, he always looks so casually gotten together.'

That, too, was the secret of his dancing – it always looked so 'casually gotten together'. After it seemed that everything that could possibly be done in *Lady Be Good* had been done, Fred decided to add more jazz steps – to accompany his song 'The Half Of It Dearie Blues'. Without them, he said, it 'wasn't much of a dance'.

If Astaire found *Lady Be Good* getting him down there was now something new in the field of show business to distract him. In 1924 Fred Astaire the song writer made his debut. He collaborated with Austin Melford in a tune called 'You're Such A Lot'. It was later sung by

43

Melford and Phyllis Monkman in the London production of *The Co-optimists*.

For a man like Fred who would jump to the piano whenever the mood took him, sometimes playing honky-tonk, sometimes more sophisticated music, in the middle of the night, it was probably a natural development of his musical talents. Just as he would devise his own dance routines, it seemed obvious that an extension into actual musical composition was the next step. It wasn't so much because he had studied composition in London, as a sense of the rhythm inside him just having to find an expression.

It was also the start of an aspect of his career that Fred was to say he enjoyed as much as anything he ever did in entertainment – and it does not take too wide a stretch of the imagination to think that perhaps he liked it a lot better than some of the other things for which he has become world famous. He was to go on to write some thirty songs.

Jock Whitney, the future publisher of the New York *Herald Tribune* and the man who would be the boss of the Technicolor empire as well as eventually Ambassador to the Court of St James's, was a close friend of both Fred and Adele. With them, he went to night clubs and to the race track. As far as Fred was concerned, the tracks were always the more tempting; no one was likely to ask him to dance in the paddock. Besides, he didn't like the sort of dancing they did on the night club floor. But the race track had a sort of magnetism for him that in the years that followed would become strong.

Just for a brief period, however, he did allow himself to take night clubs seriously – or at least one night club in particular.

The owners of the Trocadero wanted Fred and Adele to dance there each night, in competition to another club that was boasting its own team of ballroom dancers. The Astaires talked about it and said they could make enough money to buy themselves a Rolls Royce. They would do so only if they got five thousand dollars a week for it.

They got their five thousand, but voluntarily cut the figure to three thousand for the last two of the five weeks for which they were engaged. Business by then had begun to fall off and the rival club had already shut up shop. They had enough money to buy the car – but decided to wait for it. Soon, they would be in the most convenient place of all for buying a Rolls – London.

After 330 performances and a short tour, *Lady Be Good* was booked to open at London's Empire Theatre on 14 April 1926.

In between, they went to Paris for a short holiday, and had a try-out in Liverpool. When the curtains at the newly-redecorated Empire finally parted for the first performance of the show in London, the audience was ecstatic.

Changes were made for the *Lady Be Good* London production. Walter Catlett couldn't make the show in England and his part was to be taken by another American, William Kent. The order of some production numbers was changed and a totally new piece, 'I'd rather Charleston', for which Desmond Carter wrote the lyrics, was prepared for Fred. It summed up the new age and was as bouncy and as syncopated as anyone could dare to expect.

Adele arrived in London determined that when she did eventually get back to New York she would take something back with her – besides the Rolls-Royce which was already at the head of her shopping list. She thought the American theatre needed that traditional sanctuary of the British actor, the green room.

'Every London theatre has one where the players assemble after being dressed for the stage', she said at the time. 'It is like a drawing room in a millionaire's residence and there is a complete code which goes with it which is seldom violated.' And she explained the part about the room that impressed her most: 'No man, not even the manager of the theatre, would think of entering the green room without removing his hat.'

And they were both still head over heels in love with British manners outside the theatre, too – just as they had been on their last visit. Only this time, someone in America was listening.

'Americans are so full of hustle that they have no time to remember their manners and never say "thank you" or "please",' Adele repeated. 'I love English voices. They are so soft and melodious.' Fred laid it on thicker still, finding another source of inspiration. 'After wearing English clothes, I could not go back to American tailoring,' he declared. 'I was just about wearing my last stitch when we arrived here.'

The next day, the American papers were full of the statements, mostly without comment. But reporters told the Astaires that the Americans didn't like it at all, in fact, people were simmering with indignation.

So Fred issued a statement to the *New York Times* totally denying the things attributed to him and Adele and carefully ignoring what had been printed on their last London trip, he said:

'We adore our country and the people there. And in no case would we say such things in a foreign country.' Nor, he declared, did he state he wouldn't go back to American tailoring after wearing English clothes. But one of the first things he did after finally buying that Rolls-Royce was to visit Anderson & Sheppard in Savile Row and order a new suit.

At first, everything about this London tour was centred on the show. Again, Fred would rehearse until well past midnight, and occasionally Adele was working out on the sloping stage with him. When opening night arrived, the dividends of the usual Astaire ration of hard work came in the response of the audience and – as always – of the critics.

The Times used the sort of language it normally reserved for what it liked to call 'events of historic moment'. Said its anonymous critic: 'Columbus may have danced with joy at discovering America, but how he would have cavorted had he also discovered Fred and Adele Astaire!'

In the *Evening Standard*, Hugh Griffith compared them to the other performers in the show:

The play itself has no intelligence and no vitality. It is the work of too many authors, it is on too massive a scale, it comes from too stale a tradition to have any of either. On its own it seems to me to have no redeeming point . . . There is also a coloured gentleman who plays the banjulele, and, after singing songs telling how, 'I've found a noo baby. I've found a noo gurl', breaks into the most anguished series of animal noises in the throat. It suddenly struck me during this particular performance that if anyone had been present who had passed the last ten years in a civilised country where the latest achievements of the Blues and the Charleston are unknown, he would have taken one glance at the stage and the audience and then picked up his hat and run headlong to Bedlam for sane company.

And then came the Astaires. The Astaires, the dancers, would save any musical comedy, and I'm perfectly certain, no musical comedy could spoil them. They merely have to work much harder. (It is a mistake, of course, to imagine that they have any advantage from

46

being better than anything else in the show. They have to be on the stage twice as long and twice as often as they should and have to make up for leeway before they can begin.)

But they are the most attractive things on any musical comedy stage and Miss Adele Astaire is, I think, the most attractive thing on any stage. She dances as well as anyone, probably better. But she dances with an intelligence, with a gaiety, with a grace and delight in the mere act of dancing that are utterly irresistible. She is a comedienne in her toes and in her fingertips.

The *New York Times* informed the folks back home:

Probably the warmest welcome ever given by London to an American actor or actress was that accorded tonight to Fred and Adele Astaire. . . . Enthusiasm mounted during the highly successful progress of *Lady Be Good*. It conceived such a liking for them that their first applause tonight was a signal for a loud and long demonstration. *Lady Be Good* seems to be in for a long run.

It was. Even more important, the Astaires were in for a long run at the top of the social ladder in British society – with their mother coming along not merely for the ride, but with her own unique brand of criticism if she felt they were falling behind their own harsh standards.

They went to parties – although Fred still insisted that he hated them – and they went for rides in their new Rolls-Royce. On one of its first trips out, in Grosvenor Square, its wing was smashed in a collision with another car. The Astaires' car – it was the famous Baby Rolls model – once repaired, impressed their friends, like the constantly present Jock Whitney. He was seen so often in the Astaires' company that there were rumours that he and Adele were about to get engaged. 'Me marry Jock Whitney?' she chortled. 'Why he's still at school!' She did get to meet a lot of other people, however. Sometimes with rumours of romantic attachments, sometimes not.

People were mostly interested in the friendship they were building up with the Royal Family. While Fred cemented his admiration and liking for the Prince of Wales and Prince George, Adele appeared to be getting on very well with the Duchess of York, now the Queen Mother.

47

The Duchess invited her to tea one day at her Bruton Street house, in Mayfair, and suggested that perhaps she might like to come and see 'the baby'. The 'baby' is now Queen Elizabeth II.

Meanwhile, the Duke of York, who ten years later would become George VI, was sharing his brothers' fascination with Fred Astaire, the dancer and, reversing the situation, with Astaire the dresser. He thought it a marvellous idea that each pair of trousers hanging in Fred's wardrobe should have its own set of braces, instead of them having to be changed every time he put on a new pair of trousers. He was also fascinated as to why Fred kept his dancing shoes hanging upon the wall and not lying on the floor. It was, he explained, the best way to be sure that none of the mice which populated the Empire would nip the Astaire toes as he put on his shoes.

Princes, peers and mere socialites were making both Fred and Adele the toast of the town. At a London society ball, Gordon Selfridge the American millionaire boss of London's biggest department store, paid sixty pounds to dance with Adele. The profits of the ball went towards the Theatrical Ladies Guild and no one quibbled when Adele's services were auctioned and went up to the sixty pounds from a first bid of five.

'Mr Selfridge is really a good waltzer,' she declared. 'A rare thing nowadays.'

It was rare indeed. In fact, London was in the grip of Charleston fever and, Adele complained, was not doing it very well. In the *Sunday Express*, she shuddered at the thought of an 'All Charleston winter'. She said:

You have been dancing the original Charleston like two-year-olds and perhaps feeling awfully pleased with yourselves about it. But I was tired of it a few years before I came over here. It is the new kickless Charleston which will be all the rage this winter. Ankles will be safe and it will be the Charleston and nothing but the Charleston for a long time yet.

The Prince of Wales had now mastered the dance, too, and soon the Astaires would be responsible for teaching him a still newer step, the Black Bottom. It happened on the last night of *Lady Be Good*, the 326th performance of the show and the very last live production of any kind at the Empire Theatre.

Everyone knew that night in 1927 that the theatre was being pulled down and that this would be an important gala occasion. Celebrities from every branch of British life had bought tickets for the evening. The Danish ballerina, Adeline Genee whom Fred and Adele had seen so often as children, had taken a box for the evening. So had the Prince of Wales – although he hadn't taken the precaution to book in advance and only a personal call from the Prince to Astaire had done the trick. Fred had to ask the management to persuade another patron to give up his own seats.

As far as the Astaires – and the press – were concerned, it was fortunate that the deal for the box was made. The Prince and his party put a royal finish on an evening that has gone down in British theatrical history. The Empire, which started life as a Victorian music hall, shook with shrieks from the audience. The people in the stalls were as keen to see the Prince in full evening dress dancing at the back of his box as they were to watch Fred and Adele do the run-around on stage.

After the show, the Astaires and Jock Whitney followed the Royal group to a party at St James's Palace. There, Fred did a few steps himself, pulled Whitney on to the floor – and told him to demonstrate the latest dance craze. After his solo performance, the Prince asked Jock for a lesson. Whitney obliged and the Prince learned how to master the Black Bottom. As Adele recalled: 'And he had the bottom to do it, too. I'll tell you that!'

Funny Face

The biggest problem the Astaires had to face now was competition – the competition they alone presented to themselves. Every time they were pronounced sensational – and it seemed they constantly were – it meant only that the next time they were going to have to be even more exceptional. It is hard enough to have flops, but at least with these there is the satisfaction of knowing things can only improve. With a run of brilliant notices behind you, who can be sure the momentum will be maintained?

It was in that situation that Fred and Adele Astaire embarked on a new show called *Smarty*.

They had had the usual rapturous response from British provincial audiences in the short tour that followed the closure of *Lady Be Good* in London, and with it of the Empire Theatre. On the voyage home on the *Homeric*, they had taken life nice, easy and satisfied. Keeping them company on board ship was their Rolls, and for them this was the symbol that counted. It represented all the glittering success they had had in their short lives – after all, they were both still in their twenties.

Home again in New York, Alex Aarons and Vinton Freedley discussed their plans for the next show. *Smarty* would have a score by the Gershwins and a book by Robert Benchley and also the usual pre-Broadway tour. When it was ready, there was a brand new theatre waiting for them, the Alvin, formed from the first syllables of the names of ALEX Aarons and VINTON Freedley.

The trouble was that *Smarty* never looked ready. From the first dress rehearsal on the try-out tour, it seemed the Astaires were finally due to get the bird, and – to adopt the show-business parlance – that bird looked like being a turkey. Things appeared so bad at the Shubert Theatre in Philadelphia that Vinton Freedley called for a second dress rehearsal immediately after the first. When that ended about three hours before most people in the city were sitting down for breakfast, the co-producer announced the worst: The show only stood a chance if at least seventy-five per cent of it was thrown out of the window.

Everyone was downcast. Fred was worse than that. In *Steps In Time*, he has said he wished there and then that he could have been knocked down by a taxi.

Benchley scribbled furiously and then gave up – because he couldn't find the time to continue the rewriting job. Finally, Fred Thompson and Paul Gerard Smith were brought in to start almost completely from scratch – while *Smarty* in its original form played to abysmal business, first in Philadelphia and then in Washington.

The show finally was considered to be as ready as it could be. On 22 November 1927, Fred put on his red and green bathrobe and, as never before, hoped it would prove as lucky as it had been that night in Connecticut five years before.

Perhaps the robe *was* lucky. Or perhaps it was simply that the combination of the Gershwin songs and the sheer tenacity and brilliance of the Astaires' dancing couldn't make the show anything but a hit. Perhaps, too, the change of title had something to do with it. *Smarty* had become *Funny Face*, yet another of those titles that have come to symbolise Fred and Adele Astaire.

It took the *New York Times* more than two months to cogitate on the impact Fred and Adele made in *Funny Face*. It was, the paper finally decided, 'a type of our native product at its best'. The 'native product' it had in mind being the musical comedy, which, in their words, people 'who flock to the box office month after month' were always likely to underestimate.

The new Astaires' show was, however, also presenting the public with

The phenomenon of the dancer who can actually visualise music to an extent that is not achieved once in a blue moon in our more serious dance recitals.

To be sure, Mr Astaire would flounder hopelessly in Greek draperies to a Beethoven symphony for Beethoven did not write in dance measures. . . . All this is of no moment to a sheer dancer like Fred Astaire.

He gives through feet and legs, hands and arms, head and torso, the physical actuality of the music, warp and woof. And Gershwin, though he has written better scores, provides him with a rhythmic variety and some long and luscious phrases to play with.

The paper did not choose to name it, but those phrases were wrapped around one number in particular, a tune that time too has made a Gershwin standard, "'S Wonderful'.

Adele sang it in the show and of her the *Times* wrote: 'Style is the object with which she has crowned herself. Or more likely, she has not concerned herself with it at all, for such devil-may-care freshness is free of self-consciousness above all else.'

That indeed was Adele Astaire – to the proverbial 'T' and much to her brother's constant chagrin. While Adele was enjoying every moment of being a celebrity constantly courted by New York society, Fred was truly living up to his old reputation of being Moaning Minnie personified.

It was on the second night of *Funny Face* that Fred felt he was fully entitled to that attitude. Adele arrived at the stage door, 'half sloshed' as her brother has since described it. She had done something that was very rare for her – drunk more than one Martini, and it had got the better of her. She didn't like drinking, but the party she had been to was to celebrate the marvellous reception that had been accorded to *Funny Face* and at the time it had all seemed a very good cause. And Adele certainly wasn't feeling the least bit unhappy when she finally rolled up at the Alvin, something like a quarter of an hour before curtain time.

For an Astaire to arrive late was almost as unusual as one being sloshed. Even more unusual was for a member of the team to hit the other. But that is precisely what happened. Fred was out of his mind with worry – first at what might have happened to delay her and secondly, once he had seen her, to know how they were going to get through the performance.

They did the show, with Adele totally unaware that she wasn't up to her usual style and grace. Fred tried his best to get her to sober up.

He whispered from the corner of his mouth. But it was no good. Just as they returned to the wings, their routine finished, Fred slapped Adele's face.

All she could do in return was to repeat again and again, 'You hit me. You hit me.'

But she sobered up, and the show went ahead on schedule. And the next day, according to Fred, he gave her twenty dollars as a peace offering. Adele's memory of his remorse at slapping the sister he loved so much was of his being rather more generous. She says he bought her a diamond from Cartiers. Either way, both seem to agree that Fred was very, very sorry.

Funny Face was a smash by anyone's definition. But on the night when everything went right, without a single untoward event, that was the moment Fred decided to remain behind at the theatre. With no one around, and with that sole rehearsal light on the stage, he would try out yet more new steps or seek to perfect a routine he alone thought was less than it should be.

Adele's birthday always became an occasion for celebration at the theatre where she and Fred were performing. While in *Funny Face* Fred had his 'gift' sent round to her dressing room. This time it wasn't from Cartiers. The note at one end of a silk ribbon read: 'To Adele, from a devoted admirer.' A lovely thought? Not exactly. At the other end of the ribbon was a Tibetan mountain goat which Fred had persuaded a keeper of the Central Park Zoo to let him borrow.

The doorman admitted he had some doubts about the enterprise, but Fred assured him that it would be all right. The goat stood there at the entrance to the flower-bedecked dressing room while Adele let out something closely resembling a shriek. Since, should the occasion arise, she was never one to baulk at using the sort of language that sailors find familiar, she possibly said something else, too.

The long and short of it was that she told the doorman to turn the poor animal out among the Broadway crowds. Fred arrived just in time to put matters right. He told Adele that if he did not return the innocent goat to the zoo he would have to lose the fifty dollars he had deposited for it.

When Adele did get annoyed, Fred was usually able to smooth her down – and their show gave him a new name for her, 'Funny Face'. She called him 'Sap'.

At one time it seemed likely that the show *Funny Face* would also become a film, and with the Astaires in their original roles. They were tested by Paramount and had the deal come off, *Funny Face* would have been one of the first talkies – literally climbing on to the bandwagon of *The Jazz Singer*, the first sound picture which everyone thought would be the start of a whole rash of musical films. But the deal never did materialise and Fred does not to this day know why. It might simply have been a reluctance to accept those long angular Astaire features as sufficiently photogenic for the large screen.

Only a short time before that, Fred had contacted Ben Lyon, then on the threshold of an early brilliant Hollywood career, and asked if he could use any influence to get him on to the still silent screen. Fred presented Ben with a collection of photographs of himself and these were taken along to Universal. The response was not exactly encouraging. Lyon was laughed out of the office. 'Are you kidding?' said an executive who doubtless before long was eating his heart out, 'With that face?'

Tickets were hard to find for *Funny Face* but the attendants at Fred's Park Avenue apartment building could usually count on getting in. Astaire would always manage to squeeze a couple of seats out of the management for the people whom he knew – and sometimes he felt he got on better with those attendants than with most of the people who considered themselves his close friends.

In fact, he always was fond of the people with whom he came into regular contact, particularly the ones who had no pretensions about how Fred could further their own careers. When his chauffeur said he dearly wanted to learn to fly, Astaire advanced him the money for the lessons and said he would take taxis when the driver wasn't available.

And that got him friendly with the New York taxi drivers. When he heard that one of them was off work following a major operation, Fred sent a note wishing him a speedy recovery and enclosing a cheque. The note read: 'I'm so sorry I haven't done anything before. I've been so busy. You'll hear from me later.'

Only the Astaires could make the work that went into *Funny Face* look as easy as it did. And only the Astaires could perform 'The Babbit and the Bromide' in the run-around and somehow make the scene perfectly intelligible. Others have performed the number in which two people talk rubbish to each other – 'how are you: how're your

Adele and Fred.
The first steps.

National Film Archive

Fred and Adele.
Already looking like stars.

National Film Archive

Adele and Fred.
Toast of the Town. 1920.

National Film Archive

Adele and Fred.
In London – the black armband is for their father whose death marked the first sadness
in their lives.
Radio Times Hulton Picture Library

The Astaires with their mother – the real influence on their careers – in 1926.
Radio Times Hulton Picture Library

With Phyllis.

National Film Archive

On stage –
Fred with Claire Luce, *The Gay Divorce* at the Palace Theatre, London.

Radio Times Hulton Picture Library

Fred Astaire in typical pose.
The film – *Top Hat*, of course.

National Film Archive

Proving to Director Mark Sandrich just how hard hoofing on a film set can be.

Radio Times Hulton Picture Library

folks? What's new?' – Fred himself with Gene Kelly, and later, in a solo, Danny Kaye – but none gave it the zest that the Astaires did in *Funny Face*. When Ira Gershwin first produced the lyric, Fred said he understood what a babbit was but didn't have any ideas about a bromide. Vinton Freedley said he knew all about bromides but was mystified about babbits. All the audience knew was that it was a very good number.

"S Wonderful' presented a different kind of problem. One critic complained that it contained an obscene word – 'amorous'. Fortunately, the man's sensitivities were ignored and the word stayed in the song.

It was during the run of *Funny Face*, on 10 February 1928, that a moment which the people on the Broadway beat had been anxiously awaiting seemed to have finally arrived: the announcement of Adele's impending marriage.

William Gaunt, a Yorkshire wool manufacturer who also had an interest in the Shubert empire, said he was engaged to Adele. But although Gaunt had been seen at every performance of the show and had been hanging around her dressing room, Adele herself remained extremely quiet on the whole matter.

It seemed a strange romance. Adele told Fred she was frightened of him, but Gaunt issued a second statement to the press: 'Yes, it's true. We got engaged just lately.'

When would they marry? Gaunt was more cagey in his reply to that question. 'Well, whenever Adele can find the time.' And then he added: 'We will marry in England when *Funny Face* plays there.'

He was sure of one other thing, too: 'She will give up the stage then.' But he thought about that a little further. 'I'd better not say. She might change her mind. But we will live in England, of course.' He said he had known her 'a long, long time – perhaps a year. It doesn't take long to get married.'

It took rather less time than Gaunt imagined for Adele to tell him that she had no such intention at all, although for a while she went along with the marriage plans and actually made a public announcement confirming the engagement.

Gaunt was not alone in pressing his suit with Adele. Another was Mayor James J. Walker of New York, who told Fred that he was her new 'boyfriend'. Adele said she knew nothing about it.

Nevertheless, she and Fred were continuing to lead a very full life.

Particularly when *Funny Face* completed a successful run of 250 performances.

In July 1928, they were weekend guests of the former Princess Xenia of Greece and her husband, William B. Leeds, a millionaire playboy with an estate two miles from New York. As part of the weekend activities, her host took Adele for a jaunt in his shining new speedboat, *Fan Tail*. It was an idyllic trip, the weather was beautiful, the sea calm. Adele was enjoying everything about it immensely – until, quite suddenly, it all came to a frightening end. As if from nowhere, there was a violent explosion. They were out in Oyster Bay, off the coast of Long Island, when the boat's motor backfired at the same moment as a seepage of oil began dripping from the section of hull next to it. The explosion set the oil alight and Adele was in the midst of it all. Almost immediately, out of a blinding cloud of black smoke, she was pulled on to the open deck by Leeds.

A hand, her face and her shoulders were badly burned. Leeds, too, was burned – but less severely. He managed to get the boat to a landing stage and as soon as he had loosely tied up the *Fan Tail*, lifted Adele to safety. With some effort, he also managed to pull himself on to firm ground. Then from the stage, he untied the boat and pushed it out into clear water. He watched it glide slowly out to sea, smoke still belching from the cabin. A minute later, there was another, still more violent, explosion and the boat sank to the bottom.

A local doctor was called and looked over Adele's burns. He ordered that she be taken to Manhatten Hospital without delay. The burns, he decided were 'serious – but not dangerous'. They were serious enough, in fact, to keep her in hospital for several days. The talk on Broadway was that Adele Astaire would never work again. Yet, only a week later, her mother was reporting that she was recovering so nicely that she would leave soon for London and for the run there of *Funny Face*. And to everyone's surprise, she did just that. She arrived in London with Fred as though nothing had happened. Indeed, both were taken to the hearts of the Londoners now as they had been when they arrived for the openings of *Lady Be Good* and *Stop Flirting*. People were also convinced that they really were English – which, with the sort of clothes Fred wore, was not a difficult assumption. Both brother and sister blended as easily into London society as they had into the social set in New York.

People wanted to know their views on what made outstanding dancers. Fred said he thought he knew the answer: 'In a man, graceful dancing, the embodiment of smoothness, variation and a sense of rhythm. In a girl, the ability to follow where her partner leads, to melt into his steps, to harmonise with his every movement. . . .'

But, he added: 'There is one thing that strikes us very forcibly when watching Englishmen dancing and that is the bored expression on their faces while they are on the floor. We have heard people say that it is due to nervousness. Certainly, the Englishman is not so much at home on the ballroom floor as the American.'

Nobody had any doubts about the way the Astaires were going to be at home in *Funny Face*. They were going to have the top British comic Leslie Henson in the cast with them – taking the role William Kent had had in the New York production – and it all seemed to augur well. The only problem was that the idea seemed to get about that the show was to be called *Sunny Face*.

The opening at the Princess Theatre was a tremendous success.

The *Daily Sketch* said: 'There is no mistaking the fact that London is about to enjoy another outbreak of Astairia this winter. Adele's personality has still the same naïve and easy-going grace, humour and simplicity. Fred Astaire – that mild and intellectual-looking young man – is still the mind of the dance.'

Fred still adored anything British. He had perfected, too, his love of racing – racing, that is, English style. In Britain the turf seemed to be either really green or very muddy – and he loved being able to interpret the 'going', which was almost impossible to do in the same way in America.

Fred registered his own racing colours in London, a buff blouse and cap and a blue sash. He also bought his first horse, Dolomite. Actually it was half a horse, because the £500 he had paid only bought half a share. The horse had previously belonged to Mr Sidney Beer, owner of Diomedes, a top sprinter in its day. Felix Leach was training Dolomite and the day it made its debut at Brighton, Fred really felt like one of the 'racing swine'. The horse, though, was unplaced. But it didn't matter, as far as he was concerned, it was the start of an apprenticeship. Meanwhile, he told Leach to look out for at least two more nags – one of which he said he wanted to call '*Lady Be Good.*' But he never did give that name to a horse.

The management of *Funny Face*, Sir Alfred Butt and Lee Ephraim, understood this deep love Fred had for horses and presented him with a china model of a jockey and his mount. It became another permanent dressing room fixture like the bathrobe.

Funny Face ended its London run after 263 performances – 13 more than in New York, but 63 fewer than had been chalked up by *Lady Be Good* and 155 fewer than *Stop Flirting*. But no one suggested that this was anything but satisfactory.

The society friends they both seemed to accumulate as easily as good notices were as rash with their praise as ever. Among them was a young man to whom Adele had just been introduced, Lord Charles Cavendish, the younger son of the Duke of Devonshire. Adele told everyone she didn't find him particularly interesting and, like many a young female of the age, thought the right thing was to slightly overplay her indifference. 'I just didn't know he existed,' she said soon afterwards.

Adele went to Paris following the run of *Funny Face* while Fred stayed in London and visited his tailor. Officially, she was also searching for clothes, but when she joined Fred on the *Homeric* at Cherbourg for the voyage home she mentioned that she and Cavendish had met again.

It was as natural that someone as effervescent as Adele should be constantly courted as it was for her to want exciting young male company. She was also getting tired of a constant round of Broadway and London shows. When, however, a telegram arrived from Flo Ziegfeld, the most glamorous of all Broadway impresarios, she and Fred both agreed there was nothing to do but accept.

Ziegfeld loved sending telegrams. He also had a passion for Marilyn Miller, the girl who had even seemed to make dish washing sexy when she did it on stage to the tune of 'Look For the Silver Lining'.

His wire to the Astaires appears to have been written in a mood of sheer exhilaration: DEAR FRED AND ADELE: I HAVE WONDERFUL IDEA FOR YOU CO-STARRING WITH MARILYN MILLER – FLO ZIEGFELD.

Alex Aarons was not happy about their leaving the old firm, but Fred convinced him it could be good for them both. It turned out to be just about the most misguided assessment of his professional career. But it makes a good story. The Ziegfeld show was going to be called *Tom, Dick and Harry* and was to open what Flo (in his modesty) decided would be the most spectacular, the most magnificent, the most elegant theatre in New York. It would be situated slightly off-Broadway, but that did not matter. It could not matter in a theatre to be called the Ziegfeld.

Tom, Dick and Harry was also going to be the most expensive stage production ever to feature the Astaires. Its wages bill alone would total some $40,000 a week, a tenth of which would go to Fred and Adele.

It seemed that this show had everything going for it. Not only did it have the magic of the Astaires and the fame and beauty of Marilyn Miller – to say nothing of the appeal engendered simply by the name Ziegfeld – but it could also boast a score by Vincent Youmans and a book by Noël Coward. Coward's involvement made less of an impact than might be imagined. He had just scored a notable triumph with Bitter Sweet which was being produced very successfully at one of Ziegfeld's other theatres, but he was still a very young playwright who was feeling his way.

In the end, the great Ziggy, the man who believed he had his finger firmly on the pulse of Broadway – but whose biggest gift was really the ability to spend money extravagantly – decided he could do without Coward. Instead, he bought the rough outline of Coward's story of a Salvation Army lass – it evoked memories of The Belle of New York, a turn-of-the-century musical that Fred himself was to remake as a film nearly thirty years later – and handed it to one William Anthony McGuire. To say the least, that was not an inspired choice. McGuire had something of a reputation as a competent writer of Broadway shows, but his talent did not extend to writing Tom, Dick and Harry. The show went on its pre-Broadway run with only half a book and that half was awful. To make things worse, he did not care for the Astaires and they had scarcely any real affection for him. They told Ziegfeld that McGuire was up in the balcony making love to chorus girls when he really ought to have been busy with his typewriter or pencil.

Mr McGuire was not the only problem. Instead of spending his time on the piano stool with a sheaf of manuscript paper at his elbow, Vincent Youmans was more often to be found on a bench sleeping off the effects of drinking too much the night before. Added to all this was an unpleasant rumour, possibly confirmed by a subsequent event, that there was rather too much gangster money invested in the show – which now was reckoned to be costing about $600,000.

But Mr Ziegfeld couldn't afford to be too fussy about the source of his money, even when he was dealing with backers who more inappropriately than usual were called angels. He rarely worried about mere details like money – providing he could surround himself with beautiful girls; he told the press that the idea of getting the Astaires was all Marilyn Miller's. If he could convince the curvaceous young lady that he was simply providing her with another little indulgence, so much the better – and there was just the chance it would sweeten his hours in bed.

Once the show was due to move into Boston, however, even Ziegfeld had to admit that there was more at stake than just sex. The show was lousy and it seemed there was little that could save it. The title was even worse – but this at least did not present any insurmountable problems. *Tom, Dick and Harry* became *Smiles*. Smiles, however, were not the expressions seen on most faces.

The book was the first thing that had to suffer surgery. In the end, little of the original story remained. And the lyrics of many of the tunes needed to be changed – so Ring Lardner, one of the most brilliant writers of the age, was brought in to provide new words for the songs. But giving him the job was rather like asking a steeplechaser to plough a field.

The music was indifferent, no matter how classy were some of the lyrics. But one number at least should have stood out. Unfortunately, even in the miasma of *Smiles*, it didn't.

Larry Adler, then a seventeen-year-old mouth-organ protégé, was being given his big chance in *Smiles* and had a solo number called 'I'm Glad I Waited'. He had rehearsed the number for weeks, but just before the big try-out Ziegfeld sent a telegram asking him to come and see him immediately. They were both in the same theatre at the time, but the showman preferred using telegram boys to his own personal messengers.

Zeigfeld said he wanted to make young Mr Adler an offer: exchange 'I'm Glad I Waited' for a new number.

'If you don't mind I'd rather stick to the one I've got,' said Adler and Ziegfeld decided not to argue. The rejected alternative tune was called 'Time On My Hands'.

The solo seemed to be the only worthwhile thing in the whole production. In the early hours of one of those hard long nights of rehearsals and rewritings, lyricist Harold Adamson told Lardner:

'Christ, Ring, if we don't do something to save this show, it's going to be stolen by Larry Adler.'

To which Lardner replied in a *bon mot* that has lived after him: 'That would be petty larceny.'

Youmans, of course, was always too drunk to help in either the allocation of his music or the way it should be played.

When Ziegfeld decided that a new number might be the only answer to this desperate situation, another writer was called in. Walter Donaldson wrote the tune as a duet for Adele and the then very young Eddie Foy Junior, who, like the Astaires, had been on the vaudeville stage since he was dragged around the tank towns with his father and brothers and sisters as a tiny child, one of the Seven Little Foys. The song was called 'You're Driving Me Crazy'. It was to become one of those classic numbers that now always seem to turn up in a medley of tunes from the twenties. The trouble at the time was that neither Adele nor Foy could remember the words.

They were given just a day to learn the routine, which seemed an impossible task. Foy, however, thought he had the answer. He took some cardboard out of a newly-laundered shirt and on it scribbled Donaldson's lyrics. He then placed it firmly by the footlights. Adele knew of his idea and thought it was just sheer genius. The trouble was that the stagehands were not nearly so enthusiastic as they were – which was hardly surprising since no-one had let them in on the plan. As it was, when at seven p.m., they came on to sweep the stage, they took Foy's shirt cardboard with them.

At eight-thirty, on stage and in the middle of what was going to be the big number, Foy was enthusiastically in his stride. But he could see that Adele was trying to tell him something from the corner of her mouth. Exactly what, he couldn't tell. But there was a song to sing and he was looking forward to doing it. As for Adele, she was always kidding him as she did everyone else, and this time he wasn't going to worry about the risk of being her fall-guy.

The orchestra struck up the introductory music, Foy sidled up to Adele and looked down towards the footlights – and realised what his partner had been trying so hard to tell him.

Adele's answer to the problem was to start to laugh. Foy, ever a showman in the true theatrical tradition, found an instant answer. If he couldn't remember Donaldson's words, he'd invent his own: 'Oh, you're driving me crazy. What'll I do? What'll I do?' To which Adele, adept as she always was, countered: 'Oh, you're going crazy – and so am I. What can we do? What can we do?'

Donaldson was impressed. 'They're very good lyrics,' he told them. 'They're better than the ones I wrote.'

As Foy now says: 'Oh, it was an awful night. But these things happen in show business.'

What everyone hoped was that shows like *Smiles* didn't happen too often. When the piece finally opened on Broadway, the reaction of the critics was predictable.

Robert Benchley, who conveniently had forgotten he was less than sensational when he himself had tried to write for the Astaires, commented in the *New Yorker*:

'Considered as the Golden Calf brought in on the Ark of the Covenant, it was a complete bust. Of course, no show with Fred and Adele Astaire in it could be a complete bust.'

The saving grace as far as Mr Benchley was concerned was a routine that Fred himself dreamed up at four o'clock in the morning. He had jumped out of bed, picked up an umbrella, and visualised what he would do on stage for a number called 'Young Man of Manhattan'.

While Larry Adler played his mouth-organ as a street kid, Fred and a couple of a dozen chorus boys all dressed up to kill in top hats, white ties and tails, paraded on stage. The scene was the Bowery, with the Brooklyn Bridge in the background. At one stage, Adler called to Fred: 'Don't forget – a lot of big men came from the Bowery.' To which Astaire replied: 'Yes – and they're coming back, too.'

Eventually, the music gave way to the simulated sound of machine-gun fire with Fred first pointing his cane at the other well-dressed men about the Bowery and then methodically shooting each down, like victims of the recent St Valentine's Day Massacre or ducks in a fairground shooting gallery. Of that routine which was shortly to be recreated on film, Benchley commented: 'There are moments . . . when the back of your neck begins to tingle and you realise that you are in the presence of something pretty darned swell.'

There wasn't much about *Smiles* that was remotely swell apart from the Astaires and they had little with which to embellish their reputation. As usual, they made the run-around their pièce-de-résistance and as usual it was delightful and funny.

All the time that the show wended its unhappy way – there were eight weeks of solid advance booking from the ticket brokers but little more – Fred stayed at the theatre trying to pick up pieces and build something out of them. He kept to himself and rarely went out.

Fred had a black valet called Walter who not only used to lay out the Astaire top hat and tails but also shielded him from members of the public and the cast of *Smiles* alike. One of the few times Fred was seen out was when he and Adele escorted Marilyn Miller and Larry Adler to the famous '21' restaurant. The menu was impressive and the party went through it. The Astaires and Miss Miller chose caviare. Adler, much to everyone else's amusement, stuck to two boiled eggs – because he was still observing the Jewish dietary laws and decided that eggs were about the only kosher things available.

Larry Adler recalls that his relationship with Astaire was not of the happiest during the run of *Smiles* although Fred says everything they did together was in fun. Fred enjoyed playing the piano and thought he played it well; Adler thought that he himself played it better. The test, says Larry, came when Adele was due to appear on Alexander Woolcott's radio programme, and asked Larry, not her brother, to accompany her. Adler seemed to think that this was something of a victory – and didn't stop to wonder whether Fred would have wanted to be merely an accompanist to his sister. During rehearsal, Adele said: 'Larry, pick it up half a tone.' The trouble was that Adler had only one key in which he could play and that was that. 'Don't be silly, Larry,' she told him. 'You can do anything.'

Unfortunately, when the actual broadcast was over, Larry had proved he couldn't do anything of the kind. As a result, Adele was in tears and Woolcott refused to talk to him. When he got back to the theatre, he was told pointedly by Walter that 'Mr Astaire does not wish to see you.'

The next day, a letter was posted under Adler's dressing-room door. It was made up of headlines from the New York *Herald Tribune* and read: 'Larry Adler is a lousy . . . ' The last was a four-letter word of which Adler now says: 'If you think of the word aunt and change one of the letters, you get some idea of what it was.'

The language may have been unexpectedly earthy. But to anyone who knew the Astaires the sentiment was not. On another occasion, Adele sang on the Rudy Vallee radio show. One particular Broadway columnist didn't like her performance and said so. Then, he had the temerity to go along to the theatre and be confronted by Fred – who pulled no punches of his own. 'If you ever take a rap at us,' he told the writer, 'direct it at me, instead of Adele, will you?'

'Taking the rap,' he declared, was the least he could do in exchange for the gruelling work schedule he had imposed on his sister. Even now, she was still faced with the occasional last-minute impromptu rehearsal, called by Fred when he thought that perhaps a fraction of a step was out. She would have preferred to wind her way through the flower-laden admirers who nightly thronged the theatre alley like so many Stage Door Johnnies of the nineties, and gone out with one of them. But he insisted that the people who bought the tickets were entitled to perfection.

Both Fred and Larry Adler got over their altercation about the broadcast. Later, they worked together on a benefit performance which was regarded as an essential obligation to be fulfilled by any Broadway player.

When Astaire suggested that instead of using the theatre, he and Adler should rehearse at the flat on Park Avenue that he shared with Adele and their mother, the mouth-organ player was delighted. He thought they would simply work out the number they were doing in the show. But Fred had other ideas.

For three weeks, they rehearsed a completely new routine for that benefit performance. On the night of the show they were on stage for just seven minutes – and weren't paid for the privilege either.

There were gangsters hanging around the girls of *Smiles* all the time, and Larry Adler was aware of the dangers they could bring outside the stage door. With that reason alone in mind, each night he would escort home one of the girls in the show.

One night, the girl simply didn't turn up. He couldn't understand why. One show girl whom he asked – Virginia Bruce, who was before long to become a film star – just turned away when he broached the subject to her. Another burst into tears. The following lunchtime, he went out to buy a paper, and the headlines explained the girl's absence. 'Legs' Diamond, one of the gang-leaders of Prohibition-bound New York, had been found dead in her bed – despite the seventeen-year-old's efforts to protect the poor child from such evil wolves.

Nothing, it seemed, could protect *Smiles*. Marilyn Miller put the stamp of fate on the whole sad business when she went off to have an operation that still makes people's tongues wag. The official explanation was that she was suffering from sinus trouble, but in truth Flo Ziegfeld looked as worried about her as she was herself.

Meanwhile, Fred was trying at last to find solace outside the theatre. He could be seen going to night clubs – which he still insisted was not his image at all. At the Casino in New York's Central Park, he was in the company of a very pretty girl with hair that almost matched her name. It didn't take long before that name got out. – Ginger Rogers.

It was Alex Aarons who introduced the pair, although he had no thoughts of either professional or romantic entanglements. He was, however, staging a new Gershwin show called *Girl Crazy* and Ginger was his up-and-coming new star, a nineteen-year-old girl from Texas who showed an astonishing talent for making her feet appear weightless. There was, however, a problem. She was basically a Charleston dancer and was finding a number called 'Embraceable You' difficult to perform. Could Fred help? He decided he could and would.

They got on well together after that, and the occasional dates continued. But there was no thought of its blossoming into a full-scale romance. Nor had they considered working together as a team – 'A team? that sounds like a pair of horses,' Fred used to comment. When she later left for Hollywood, they said their farewells and neither had any thought of linking up on the West Coast.

Meanwhile, *Smiles* limped on for the length of the booking agents' commitments and then faded away after sixty-three inglorious performances – two less than had been 'enjoyed' by *The Bunch and Judy*.

It was not the end of the Astaires' interest in the show. They both liked Ziegfeld. Indeed, Adele said she 'just loved Flo'. But in July 1931, they both sued him. They claimed that Ziegfeld owed them $10,000. The money, they said, was salary they had not received. By 27 October 1930, when the show opened, they claimed they should have had a total of $12,000 between them. Instead, they only got $2,000. The case was put to arbitration, but the result was not totally satisfactory to the Astaires. They were awarded $4,000, just one week's salary. Money was important. Both Fred and Adele had lost heavily in the Wall Street crash. But for Adele, the money promised in show business was little more than peanuts compared to the prospects now offered by the future.

She was talking romance.

To a newspaperman, she confided that she thought a woman ought to look for a man who was younger than herself.

'Women,' she explained, 'gain wisdom more quickly than men. Their wisdom enables them to fend off old age with greater ease. To retain their independence and individuality, they should never tie themselves up to husbands older than themselves. That is an old-fashioned custom and should be discarded.'

What she did not reveal was that in the last few months, Lord Charles Cavendish, seven years her junior, had been becoming a much more noticeable feature of her life than she had previously been willing to allow. He had come to New York as a 'financial apprentice' to join the banking firm of J. P. Morgan and Company and had been seeing a very great deal of Adele. They had met again at a party given by Prince Aly Khan. The Manhatten Social Register set were laying heavy odds on an engagement being announced soon. They did, in fact, talk marriage. But it would mean retirement from the stage for Adele and *Smiles*, she considered, was not exactly the note that she would want for her swansong. If she were going to leave her career, she wanted it to be at her peak.

She told him she couldn't retire on a flop. There would have to be one more good show – and she knew there was one in the offing.

Lyricist Howard Dietz and composer Arthur Schwartz had seen the Astaires at the Ziegfeld Theatre and decided that they wanted to work with them. Max Gordon was anxious to produce an Astaire show and they were delighted to provide the raw material.

As for Fred and Adele, it was not a difficult decision to take. Even Moaning Minnie Fred could see that the show they were offering had alluring possibilities. It was to be called *The Band Wagon* and would be the most exciting of all the Astaire shows – and also the last.

But the night that the revue opened at the New Amsterdam Theatre the public had little inkling that their joint career would be going from anything but strength to strength.

Walter laid out the ceremonial bathrobe on 3 June 1931. The ritual now was that Fred would put it on just once and then hand it back. This time, the old magic that the gown used to possess, if superstitions mean anything at all, was back. It worked.

Dietz and Schwartz had achieved near perfection in a musical show and most of what they had planned came off in the way that they wanted

66

it to. As their work on the production seemed to be at an end, Dietz said he still needed a song to be used in a merry-go-round number. In a matter of seconds, he scribbled on a sheet of yellow paper the opening lines of a tune that was to show Fred Astaire at his most versatile best. It was called 'I Love Louisa'.

It was perfect for both Astaire the comedian and Astaire the actor. It was a mock German drinking song, with the kind of German used being particularly suitable for a man who had perhaps drunk a little too much: 'Och, when I choose them, I love a great boozen. . . .'

In another number, Fred danced, sang and played an accordion that had been strapped around him – all at the same time. 'I'll play my music box,' he sang, 'and keep playing my music box. . . sweet music to worry the wolf away.'

What few people realised at the time was that the wolf being worried away by *The Band Wagon* was precisely the one that seemed to be howling that Fred would never make it on his own. Everything he did was with Adele and the plots had to become more and more convoluted because brothers and sisters were not the easiest people to write stories for. But he was now busier on his own in this show than he had been before. The cast was smaller than in previous Astaire musicals and Fred had more character parts than he had previously attempted – while his sister happily looked on.

The big surprise of the show was just how wide his talents really were. He arrived at the Lambs Club one night after the show's opening to be greeted by a fellow member who shouted out to him: 'Boy, I hear you're an actor.'

It now seemed that his appeal was going to be broader than it had been before. Everyone knew that the debutantes loved Fred – but did the girls serving at Maceys feel the same way? Word was out that now they did indeed.

Fred was a man affected by mood. If he felt, as he put it, in a 'good humour', he was known to roll his elegant trouser bottoms up to his knees and do a dance to a girl sitting on a couch strategically placed on the stage. He thought he looked ridiculous. But the audience loved his now essential number in top hat, white tie and tails.

There was something more exciting and more elegant still in a dance without words in the show – although Dietz had written a set of lyrics for it immediately after picking up a book from his personal library called *Dancers in the Dark*. Dietz called his song after this title and told Schwartz about his inspiration. The composer rushed home in the early hours of the morning and played the melody he had devised for the title over and over again – because he had no manuscript paper handy and was frightened of forgetting it. The tune, he admits, took him a matter of minutes to write.

From the moment that Astaire danced it with Tilly Losch, 'Dancing in the Dark' became a classic.

If people marvelled at the ease with which he could turn numbers like 'Dancing in the Dark' into spectaculars of dance poetry, Fred would say it was simply a question of hard work. 'Dancing,' he declared, 'is as tough as stevedoring.'

But it didn't show. Brooks Atkinson reviewing *The Band Wagon* in the *New York Times*, declared that it was the start of a new era in the artistry of the American revue. 'When revue artists discover light humours of that sort in the phantasmagoria of American life, the stock market will start to rise spontaneously, the racketeers will all be retired or dead and the perfect state will be here.'

The New York *Sun* declared:

There is something utterly audacious about the two of them; there is a lightness and flexibility and dash in whatever they do; whether it is to chase a plump and bearded Frenchman around the revolving stage or to dance in black and white before an immense encircled drum. They may be chatty and intimate, teasing themselves and the audience. They may be bizarre, tantalising figures from a modernistic nightmare. They are in any case incomparable.

The public obviously thought so, too. Ticket sales were exceptionally good. Fred was so happy with the way things were going that he decided once more to try films. He had a test. The result was an appraisal by a studio executive who reported back: 'Can't act. Slightly bald. Can dance a little.'

As Fred has said: 'I was pretty well floored by that. And in addition I knew that any inventory of my face would disclose no feature which could be hailed as what the successful movie star should wear.' He conceded that he looked somewhat 'weird' on the screen and decided to concentrate on the stage.

Adele, meanwhile, contemplated the effect that the success of *The Band Wagon* was likely to have on her career. She decided that the time had finally come. This was the peak. It was the right moment to retire. The first person to be told had to be Lord Charles Cavendish – Charlie. At a party, after a single drink, she proposed.

He Loves And She Loves

It was just one drink at the '21' that signalled the end of one of the most successful Broadway partnerships in history. Adele and Charles Cavendish were at the club, which had by now become New York's most fashionable speakeasy, and the one drink had apparently gone to her head – she hardly ever drank at all and the occasions when she did seem to have gone on the record with some extremely notable consequences.

'You know, we get on so well,' she told him, 'I think we ought to get married.'

'Righto,' he answered. The following morning, Lord Charles rang Adele at her Park Avenue apartment: 'You proposed to me last night and I accepted. If you don't accept *me*, I'll sue you for breach of promise.'

The next person to be told was Fred – who reacted with a kiss and his best wishes. He always knew the moment was going to come sooner or later and he also knew that she was unlikely to marry another performer. The chances of her remaining as part of the team, and whether it sounded like a pair of horses or not, that is precisely what they were, were always remote. Now she confirmed it.

Both determined there would be no sad farewells. But Adele now admits her brother was frustrated at the thought of having to make it on his own. He had physically pushed his elder sister into the limelight to the extent that many reviewers had made her the senior partner. Now he was going to be put to the test. But Adele said she had little doubt he would make it without her. The way he and Tilly Losch performed together night after night in *The Band Wagon* in scenes in which she herself was not involved confirmed this.

Fred was not, however, going to be thrown in at the deep end immediately. Adele promised she would see out the Broadway run of the show and would start the road tour with the company, too. Fred liked the man she called Charlie and welcomed the match. A letter from the Duchess of Devonshire, her fiancé's mother, confirmed that the romance had his family's blessings, too. As for Mrs Astaire, she was delighted with how far the little Austerlitz girl had come.

The public heard about the engagement after an announcement made by Adele in her dressing room at the New Amsterdam, just before going on stage. She had arrived at the theatre, exhausted. It was in the heart of the Depression and all day long she had been helping to raise funds for the New York unemployed – but word had got out that she was even more concerned about a personal matter. A whole gang of reporters and photographers, all with press cards protruding from their hat bands, were waiting for her when she finally reached the stage door.

She decided that tired though she was, the time had come to reveal all. She went through the long history of her relationship with Lord Charles and told how 'we were very companionable and I saw a great deal of him'.

'Our friendship was renewed, 'she said, 'when he came to New York to serve his financial apprenticeship with J. P. Morgan and Company. When I was in England last year, his family received me very gracefully.'

She confirmed that now she had every intention of leaving the stage, but assured the reporters: 'My brother Fred will, of course, continue his theatrical career.'

The papers were full of just how well Adele had done by her match. Lord Charles, said the *New York Times*, was 'a mighty fine young fellow' – by which they meant he had money and position. He was the younger son of the Duke of Devonshire, who besides having completed a term of office as Governor General of Canada ten years earlier, was one of Britain's wealthiest men. If Adele had any worry at all about joining this branch of the British aristocracy, it was that she was going to be the first Devonshire bride who did not arrive on the scene as an heiress. Even the considerable fortune she had earned with her brother in show business did not begin to match the wealth to which the family was accustomed.

All the time that Adele recounted her romance with Charlie, the telephone in her dressing room rang with a succession of transatlantic calls – a rare thing in the early thirties.

Adele kept her word and stayed with the show throughout its New York run of 260 performances and saw it through the beginning of the tour, too.

But on an evening in March 1932 at the Illinois Theatre in Chicago, the big breakup came. With tears running down her cheeks, Adele left the theatre that night – and in more ways than one. It was the last time she appeared in *The Band Wagon* and also her last professional appearance on any stage at all.

Fred was contracted to continue in the show – so the day that Adele sailed the Atlantic with Charlie at her side, her previously inseparable brother was hoofing before an audience.

It is not difficult to imagine Fred's feelings that first night without Adele by his side. In all the years he had been in show business, his sister had represented security – even though he would never allow himself to slacken off. But audiences had a way of conveying their feelings to performers and it was no secret that Adele could win applause simply by being there. Her charm was as big an asset as her dancing ability. Now, suddenly, he was without her. He has always insisted that he was glad both that Adele was getting married and that he was able to go it alone but it was a bit like a small boy on his first bicycle – who suddenly realises no one is holding the saddle for him. He was on his own, balancing his career entirely by himself.

Vera Marsh took over Adele's role and found out just how difficult it could be to step into her shoes. She was a good little dancer, but the public couldn't accept anyone but Fred's sister teasing and dancing with him.

No date had been announced for the Cavendish – Astaire wedding, which turned out to be fortunate. Less than a week after the couple docked at Southampton, Charles was rushed to hospital and operated on for appendicitis. Two months later, the couple arrived with the

Duke and Duchess at their Derbyshire country seat, Chatsworth House, and the rumours of an impending marriage grew more persistent. But no one was saying anything. The local vicar, the Rev Foster Pegg, who always did what the Devonshires told him to do, was determined to keep the quietest of all. It was the organist who seemed to let the cat out of the bag. He said that he had been told his services might be required at any moment. And they were.

On 9 May 1932 Mr Pegg married Lord and Lady Charles Cavendish in the chapel on the first floor of Chatsworth House, which had been specially decorated with myrtle and acacia for the occasion. As they knelt at the altar, the choir sang 'O, Perfect Love'.

There had never been a marriage before at the stately home chapel – in fact, its only previous claim to fame had been a visit by Kaiser Wilhelm before the First World War. But that day in May 1932, the eyes of Britain and America seemed focussed on it.

Unusually, it was Mrs Astaire who gave her daughter away as she walked down the aisle in a dress of orange-trimmed beige satin. She had a cluster of orange carnations at the waist. Best man was Charlie's elder brother, the Marquis of Hartington who was heir to the dukedom.

It did not take long for Adele to be fully accepted as part of the aristocracy. Just a month later, the new Lady Charles Cavendish, complete with the required ostrich feathers, was presented at court to King George V and Queen Mary. The Princess Royal, the Duke of Connaught and a brace of princesses were on hand to witness the event. There was one titled lady who was not there – the Duchess. It had been announced that Charlie's mother would present Adele to Their Majesties, but where was she? The gossips were hardly satisfied when an explanation was given – the Duchess of Devonshire was ill with acute rheumatism. Or was she merely feigning a diplomatic illness? The surprise was heightened by the fact that the Duchess was Mistress of the Robes and virtually never missed a court.

When it became obvious that she had not turned her aristocratic gaze away from her new daughter-in-law – they were often seen together after that – the rumours died down. And there were other proofs of the Devonshires' approval. The couple were given use of Lismore Castle, a historic edifice built by King John in 1185 situated on the banks of the River Blackwater, for life. As far as Adele was concerned it was a magnificent present. But the castle had its faults.

Until she arrived on the scene to put matters right, it was extremely short of bathrooms. The story was that there was only one bath in the whole of the castle. A little while after that was published, Adele said: 'Since that got out, we've received a million letters asking what we do Saturday night!'

Very soon after the Cavendishes set up home at Lismore, Fred paid them a visit to offer personally his brotherly good wishes for their future happiness. He also had something to tell them. He was in love himself.

The quiet, hard-working business-comes-first Fred had spent a Sunday afternoon at the private golf course of a member of the Vanderbilt family. At lunch he had been introduced to Mrs Phyllis Potter, then at the tail end of an unhappy marriage to a Wall Street stockbroker.

He was enchanted by this twenty-three-year-old fragile beauty. Above all, it seemed he was taken by the fact that every time she intended to pronounce an 'r' it came out sounding like a 'w'. She was a Bostonian socialite and an heiress. Her fortune was reputed to be worth something in the region of twenty million dollars. Her father was a doctor. In New England terms, she was a 'Back Bay aristocrat'. She also shared Fred's love of horses. After her parents' marriage broke up, she was brought up by her uncle, Henry Worthington Bull, who was a famous bloodstock owner and was President of the Turf and Field Club. But any talk of marriage was slow to materialise because of her own problems.

She divorced her husband, Eliphalet Nott Potter the Third at Reno in January 1932 and was granted custody of her three-year-old son, Eliphalet Nott Potter, the Fourth – who happily was called Peter. But she only had the boy with her for nine months of the year. The rest of the time he had to spend with his father. Phyllis was not satisfied with this arrangement. She believed that the boy needed to be with her throughout the year, and until that was settled, there could be no new serious entanglement for her.

On his way back from Ireland, Fred met up with Phyllis again – but she held out little hope of marrying him. The problems seemed too big.

There was only one thing for Fred to do, both agreed, concentrate on the new show that was to mark the emergence of the solo Fred

Astaire, with the aid of a score by Cole Porter. One of its backers was to be Fred's old friend Jock Whitney. It was, Astaire decided, going to have to be a weather vane show, on it would depend the whole future of his career as a dancer and actor. This would prove whether he could exist on stage without Adele. It was a daunting proposition, but it had to be accepted.

Claire Luce, a delightful blonde dancer, was given the role that Adele would have had. The show was *Gay Divorce* – based on an unproduced play by Hartley Manners that had been scheduled for the stage many times but had never managed to get off the ground.

What convinced Fred that it was worth doing was the news that Cole Porter had signed the contract to write the score. He was even more impressed when he saw what that score contained. But there was one song which he looked at long and hard and started to sing only with considerable trepidation. It looked as if it were going to be one of the most difficult he had ever been asked to handle. All he knew was that it was very long. 'It didn't impress me at all,' he has long since said many times. But he persevered – and it became the greatest he ever sang: 'Night and Day'. It was appreciated by the audience both at the Boston try-out and at the New York opening at the Ethel Barrymore Theatre. But the show was not without its troubles.

The main one was that the audience was more interested in how Fred would get on without Adele than they were in either the story or the songs. The principal sufferer as a result of this was Claire Luce, who says now she felt more sorry for Fred than she did for herself. Despite her sympathy for him, she did have to suffer those comparisons which were constantly being drawn between herself and Adele. There was also the suffering that inevitably came from being on the receiving end of the Astaire search for perfection.

The dance routines they had together were harder than any she had ever had to do before – and were the hardest probably for Fred, too. They had to dance over tables and chairs – and more than once they fell over.

The press didn't know what to make of Fred Astaire as a single. Those who made up their minds were lukewarm, to say the least. One reviewer wrote: 'Astaire stops every now and then to look off-stage towards the wings – as if hoping his titled sister would come out and rescue him.'

That was precisely what Fred didn't want to read. Another described the show as 'dull and disappointing'.

There also seemed something significant about the title of one of the Porter songs that Fred performed, 'After you – Who?'

Ticket brokers were unperturbed at the indifferent press reaction, and were convinced that Astaire represented good business, whatever the newsmen's reaction. One ticket agency put up a banner declaring: 'Mr Astaire and Miss Luce are the legitimate successors to Mr and Mrs Vernon Castle.'

The story of *Gay Divorce* was, as usual, no more than an excuse for the dance routines. Fred played an author who when staying at a luxury British holiday centre is mistaken for a professional co-respondent. What more need be said?

One critic commented: 'Maybe if you've gone through a couple of divorces and stayed at one or two English seasides for your sins, you'll think it a lot funnier than I did.'

No Astaire show was complete without the most unexpected settings becoming backdrops for Astaire's rhythmic steps.

But in 1932 during the run of *Gay Divorce* real-life backdrops were just as likely to be used for routines of a different sort; routines strictly for fun. An eagle-eyed spectator might possibly have noticed Fred Astaire sailing down Park Avenue on roller skates – with two big wheels in the front and two small ones at the back. A friend had asked him to try them out and he was happy to oblige. There was no better place to do this, he thought, than the swanky avenue on which he lived – but in case anyone thought otherwise he did his skating late at night.

The only person who was actively concerned was his mother, who lived in the same building. It was not that she thought it was undignified – although she might – but she was concerned about the effect it could have on his career. Supposing he fell and broke an ankle? He'd never dance again. Fred assured her he would be all right and he was.

People thought *The Gay Divorce* was all right, too. After a time, even Brooks Atkinson, the principal Butcher of Broadway, offered what might have been thought a slightly back-handed compliment. He wrote: 'In the refulgent Claire Luce, Fred Astaire has found a partner who can match him step for step and who flies over the furniture in his company without missing a beat. As a solo dancer, Mr Astaire stamps out his accents with that lean, nervous agility that distinguishes his craftsmanship and he has invented turns that abound in graphic portraiture.'

Now, however, came the rub. Atkinson added:

'But some of us cannot help feeling that the joyousness of the Astaire team is missing now that the team has parted.'

So what price a pair of horses now?

The strange thing about Fred Astaire was that in *The Gay Divorce* the serious perfectionist could turn whatever he was doing into a joke at the most surprising moments. Fred was supposed to say to G. P. Huntley, Junior: 'I was lifting a forkful of chop to my mouth . . .' To which Huntley was expected to reply: 'They always cook these blasted chops too much.' It was an innocuous, stupid line that no one was supposed to notice. Fred certainly thought so. So one night and without warning – and certainly without Huntley knowing – he changed it. The astonished Huntley suddenly heard it become 'I was lifting a forkful of overdone ravioli to my mouth . . .' He was quick on the uptake: 'How would ravioli go without garlic?' he improvised – and the line brought the house down. As a result, at almost every subsequent performance, Fred was lifting a forkful of something else, sometimes bear, occasionally venison, more often corned beef or quail, all well-done, over-done, rare, medium, depending on how the mood took him.

This all became more than a private joke. Except that one night, and without telling Huntley, Astaire reverted to the original line in the script. Huntley couldn't think what to say: 'Cheerie bean,' he replied. 'Sure,' said Fred. 'Pork and Beans – my favourite dish.'

One joke developed into another. Almost in self-defence, the show's company led by stage manager Andy Anderson, decided to have his revenge.

It all started with the curtain call which players get fifteen minutes before opening. This was usually a polite tap on a dressing room door, and a soft-voiced statement of 'fifteen minutes, sir'. But Anderson wanted Fred to know that the tables were about to be turned. So he dropped a pile of tin plates and shouted 'Fifteen minutes' at the top of his voice. 'Louder, please!' called Fred, to which Anderson replied with a battery of stage revolver shots.

It was all good humoured and both sides regarded it as such. Fred rewarded Anderson by placing bets on horses for him. If the nag won, the stage manager got the winnings. If it lost, he just never heard there had been a bet in the first place. Fred could also make Walter, the valet, the butt of his humour. He would ask him for a glass of water and when it arrived, tell him: 'I didn't ask for that. I wanted a towel.' Of course, when the towel was brought that wasn't good enough either. Walter took it all in his stride, but he did once tell Astaire; 'Either you or I is just plain crazy. I don't think it's me and I'd hate to think it's you.'

Fred was not crazy, but 'Moaning Minnie' was concerned. 'The stage is beginning to worry me a bit,' he told the respected Lucius Beebe in the New York *Herald Tribune* in what must rank as the understatement of the age. 'Just why, I cannot say, only perhaps it's getting on my nerves. I don't know what I'm going to do about it, either. I feel that I ought to dance just as long as I'm able to do it and get away with it. Lots of people seem to like it and would be disappointed if I should turn to anything else.'

But he *was* thinking of turning elsewhere. He was also thinking more about his relationship with Phyllis.

On 11 July 1933 it appeared that things had come to a head. Phyllis left her home on East 62nd Street and went before Supreme Court Justice Selah B. Strong in Brooklyn. She declared on oath that she did not intend to marry Fred Astaire until she was satisfied she would be allowed to devote all of her attention to her child. In short, she was asking for full-time custody of Peter.

Both she and her uncle, Mr Bull, whose address was given as Islip, Long Island, testified. Asked about her plans with Fred, she said she had not given him any definite answer – because she was not sure that marriage would allow her to carry out her full duties to her child. Judge Strong was suitably impressed. The following day, he granted Phyllis custody of Peter for eleven months, instead of nine, and she was allowed to take the boy anywhere she liked. The father could visit him whenever he wished, too.

The decision reached, the Judge just took off his robes. Then, when they went into his private chambers, Phyllis told him: 'I've decided to marry Mr Astaire right away, now that I know that Peter's future is assured.'

There was a hurried discussion and the Judge put on his robes once more. In the court library he performed a wedding ceremony. Phyllis was wearing a light coloured summer dress and Fred, who had taken the precaution of procuring a licence just in case, a grey business suit.

Mr Bull gave away his niece in marriage. The witnesses were Supreme Court Justice Thomas Cuff, Phyllis's lawyer, Fanny Holtzmann and the attorney's brothers Jacob and David Holtzmann who were also lawyers and happened to be about the building.

After the ceremony, Mr and Mrs Astaire posed for photographers in one of the court building's corridors, and went back to Fred's apartment at 875, Park Avenue – where he immediately buttonholed the doorman. 'Aw gee,' he shouted ecstatically, 'she's married me,' and then he thumped the unsuspecting man in livery on the chest. They couldn't afford to take off more than that one day because Fred had commitments on the West Coast. He had finally decided that he was now going to worry less about the stage and would try his luck in Hollywood. More important, Hollywood had decided to try Fred Astaire.

The Sky's The Limit

Any discussion of Fred and Phyllis leads inevitably to a mass of clichés. They were the happiest couple in Hollywood. Their's wasn't a film-land marriage. They knocked on the head the old adage about the inevitability of divorce among anyone in the showbiz set. It was all true. And one reason was that they went to Hollywood because it offered not a new way of life, but just a new career prospect. Neither dared speculate that Fred had made his last Broadway appearance, but he had.

Their one-day honeymoon was spent cruising down the Hudson River in the yatch *Captiva*, lent to them by a friend. The following day they went flying down to California to make a movie called *Flying Down To Rio*. When they arrived in Hollywood after a twenty-six-hour flight – it was Fred's first time in a commercial aircraft – the film city was as anxious to meet the wife of the Broadway star as it was to see Astaire himself.

One writer observed that Phyllis was 'undeniably pretty – not in the Hollywood manner, but rather in the manner of those tailored-hat ads in the smart fashion papers. She's smaller and slighter even than Fred, about Adele's size – but with none of Adele's gay insouciance.' Mrs Astaire doubtless dismissed the writer in one of her favourite words 'dweadful'.

The contract for *Flying Down to Rio* was with RKO Radio pictures – recently formed by an amalgam of the old Keith-Orpheum Circuits which Fred and Adele had known so well in their vaudeville days. As far as RKO were concerned, it was a gamble, which they desperately needed to come off. The studio was mortgaged up to its collective eyeballs. In fact, there were two Wall Street bankers who were acting as receivers for the company. One false step and it was ready for final liquidation.

If Fred could come up trumps, the wolves could be sent scurrying from the door.

Before work on the picture got under way, Fred had a chore to do. It amounted, in fact, to a dress rehearsal for *Flying Down to Rio* and for his entire Hollywood career. MGM had offered him a guest appearance in the new film they were preparing for Joan Crawford and a rather awkward young man with big ears, Clark Gable. It was called *Dancing Lady*. His name in the film was – Fred Astaire. He played the star of the Broadway show in which Miss Crawford was being given the big break – later Claire Luce was to claim that she saw amazing similarities between the story and her own history of breaking into show business. Gable was the hard-bitten producer of the show, Franchot Tone his rival for Miss Crawford's romantic affections, Robert Benchley was a newspaper columnist, and also in the cast were Eve Arden, the Three Stooges and even Nelson Eddy singing at the film's end.

Gable didn't like being made subordinate to La Crawford in the billing and had a row with Louis B. Mayer over it. The result was that Mayer decided to punish him – by handing the erring star to the run-down studio operating from an area of Hollywood known as Poverty Row. The company was Columbia Pictures. The film was Frank Capra's *It Happened One Night*, which literally became over-laden with Oscars.

In *Dancing Lady* Fred danced in top hat and tails and when he made his first entrance he told Phyllis he thought he looked like a knife. But she told him he looked lovely and that was praise enough. His scene lasted just four minutes fifty seconds, but there could never have been a more important four minutes fifty seconds in his entire career. They proved that not only could Fred be a dominant film personality, but that he liked the medium, too.

Fred did more than just impress Phyllis.

Motion Picture Daily said: 'Fred Astaire links an attractive screen personality to ace dancing and should go somewhere in celluloid.'

He went where he was supposed to go in the first place – to the RKO lot, where he surprised a lot of people by the seriousness with which he regarded his work. No one had ever seen such effort before from a mere musical comedy artist – and those were the days when people were chosen to dance in films rather more for their faces than for their feet. If an elephant had a pretty face and could be suitably trained, someone would have had him in tap shoes.

He was also the quiet gentleman performer, the well-dressed actor who amazed everybody by turning up on the set chewing gum and with his trousers held up by a tie. Both were soon to be recognised as trademarks of Astaire at work.

He wasn't the star of *Flying Down To Rio*. In fact, no one could be sure for long who were the stars. Helen Broderick, then a light comedy favourite, was first mentioned as a star. So was Arline Judge. Joel McRea was listed, too. But they all dropped out. Finally Dolores Del Rio and Gene Raymond were brought in.

As the juvenile female lead, the studio selected . . . Ginger Rogers, and to play opposite her, Fred Astaire. But they forgot to tell either of them about it. Fred said he was delighted to meet Ginger again, but was totally taken aback when the announcement was first made. Ginger just heard he was on the lot, but knew nothing more.

The girl who began her career when she was spotted by Eddie Cantor – and then sent by him on a tour of New York theatres – had gone on to unexpected heights in *Girl Crazy* and then had a $1,000-a-week role in Pathe's *The Tip Off*. Now, she saw she was already an important Hollywood property. But she was plainly not important enough to be told with whom she was to play.

Fred said he just happened to hear someone say: 'Let's get Fred and Ginger together.' Certainly, neither of them imagined it would blossom into anything more.

They were helped by a score by Vincent Youmans, who seemed a lot happier than he had been in *Smiles* and rightfully so. His most inspired part of the score was the big production number 'The Carioca' in which Fred and Ginger showed how a couple could dance, not cheek to cheek, but forehead to forehead.

Astaire and Rogers were very much the second leads in the picture – Fred playing merely the best friend of Gene Raymond, a band leader and pilot who was in love with the beautiful Miss Del Rio. Ginger was the vocalist in Raymond's orchestra.

To quote them both, Fred and Ginger had a few laughs on the set and by the time the film was over, were good friends once more. But Ginger told Pandro S. Berman, a top RKO producer, that she didn't want to make another like it. She had nothing against Fred, she just didn't want to make any more musicals of any description.

Miss Rogers, who was, after all, essentially a Charleston dancer until Fred had come on the scene, was plainly going to be a box office smash.

The director of *Flying Down To Rio* was Thornton Freeland. Early on, during one of Fred's solo numbers, he carefully drew a chalk line on the studio floor.

'Whatever you do,' he instructed Astaire, 'don't go beyond these lines. Otherwise, you'll be out of frame.'

Fred had only gone through half his number when he was completely carried away by the experience. He concentrated so hard on the steps he had to do for the routine that he completely forgot about the chalked line.

'That was a helluva lot of good work for nothing,' Freeland told him. 'Didn't you hear me call "Cut"? You kept crossing that chalked line so many times that you might have been having a skipping game. Now, when you're ready, we'll take it again. . . .'

'The Carioca' took, it was estimated, a hundred hours to rehearse and lasted about four minutes on screen.

By the time the film was over Fred did some careful reckoning. He now worked out he had danced a total of 100,000 miles in his career.

Fred was to say that he learned a great deal about filming techniques when he made *Flying Down To Rio*. Possibly his biggest single gain from the production came with a lanky young man who bore an astonishing resemblance to Fred himself, in build and appearance, in voice and in dedication to the dance as not merely an art work but as a serious labour.

He was Hermes Pan – the surname, an abbreviation for the Greek Panagiotopulos. He was six years younger than Fred and had been born in Tennessee, which as far as the casual listener was concerned, was responsible for the only real difference in their accents. A dancer himself, he was now working on the RKO lot as an assistant dance director. When Fred was finally installed in the company, the two were introduced to each other and Pan was asked to give Fred any help he could. He not only helped on the dance floor, but it was to be the beginning of a lasting friendship between them.

Now, with the filming over, Fred had an obligation to meet – two obligations, in fact: Phyllis had not yet had the real honeymoon he had promised her. And he was contracted to do *Gay Divorce* in London. He decided that both commitments could be fulfilled together, and with a visit to 'Delly' thrown in at the same time.

Fred left Hollywood for London in one of his less contented moods. He was convinced that *Flying Down To Rio* had been a career interlude that hopefully he would one day forget. Both he and Phyllis enjoyed being fêted by the Beverly Hills set, but all Fred could see when the first rushes were run off was that 'knife' again.

Once their bags were packed, the Astaires ran round to their friends' houses, saying goodbye.

Fred told Ginger that it had been a useful experiment, but dancing would never catch on on the screen. In a studio executive's office, he suggested that perhaps it wouldn't be a bad idea if the dance routines were cut out completely. No one could be found who did agree – so Fred suggested remaking them. This time, he was shown the door and told to come back when he had finished in London. The men at RKO had ideas that might make him feel better.

He was still unhappy, but his contract specified he had to be in London and there was no time to argue.

Adele actually heard Fred before she saw him. Soon after arriving in London, the BBC invited him to do a radio show – something that he avoided whenever he could, because he considered himself principally a visual entertainer. But the BBC shared the view of the top song writers of the age that Fred could sing their work more faithfully than almost any other performer.

Adele heard the broadcast, broken up occasionally by the odd burst of static, as she, her mother, and Charlie Cavendish sat in the principal drawing room of Lismore Castle. As she recalled years later, 'Fred started to sing. He went on. Why, he was even hitting those high notes that used to scare us. It was grand. We cried a little.' Adele had reason to cry. For despite her happy marriage, she was desperately miserable.

She was not in the audience the night the show opened at the Palace Theatre on 2 November 1933 because a few days earlier she had given birth prematurely to a baby girl. The baby died almost immediately. Adele was both heartbroken and ill for some time. Her mother had come over for the confinement, but events had overtaken her too. By the time Mrs Astaire arrived at Lismore, it was all over.

But the people in the theatre the evening of the London opening knew only that it was yet another great occasion. Among those in the stalls was Prince George. When it came to the routine in which Fred and Clare Luce had to dance over the furniture, the thing Astaire feared most of all happened, they fell.

Miss Luce fell so badly that she damaged her hip. It was eventually to lead her to a lengthy stay in hospital and before long mean the end of her dancing career, but she got up and in great pain did the dance again. What is more, she kept on doing it throughout the run of the show.

Fred had no idea how serious her injuries were, although he was very solicitous about her well-being. His main concern was whether or not he had made a fool of himself. Nobody mentioned the fall. It wasn't even reported in the following morning's papers.

The *Morning Post* certainly was not affected:

The word 'welcome' could coldly describe the riotous delight of last night's audience at the Palace Theatre over the return of Mr Fred Astaire, the jollity and charm of Mr Cole Porter's music and the lilt that Mr Felix Edwardes, as producer, has brought into a certain and brilliant success.

The magic element which inspires the whole thing is Mr Astaire's dancing and comedy combined. In this piece he raises tap dancing to a high art. He dances through his part with a skill absolutely on a level with that of a fine ballet dancer. As a matter of fact, he uses quite a number of ballet steps – cabrioles and brises and so on – in a way that has never been attempted before.

As before, Fred was saying how much he liked London and Phyllis was saying the same sort of thing, too.

'When tired of dancing I imagine Mr Astaire will come and live in London,' said the *Daily Express*. As we have seen Fred has been saying much the same thing for years.

Several weeks after the opening, Adele was well enough to see the show at the Palace. She was treated regally – flowers, speeches and a mass of adoration for 'Funny Face' from 'Sap'. It was the first time she had ever seen him from the other side of the footlights, a chastening experience. It was also, she said, the first time she realised that her brother had sex-appeal – although in many ways the worried look on his face reminded her of the wrinkles that drooped from one of her pet dachshund's eyes.

She told people that night that she now knew why when the two of them had danced together, all eyes were always on Fred. It was not completely true. But in *Gay Divorce* in London, the eyes were all on Fred, and whatever he did. People watched him not merely in the theatre, but waited outside the house in John Street, Mayfair, which he and Phyllis had rented – just for a chance to see him go in and out and possibly get his autograph.

They watched him on the racecourse and studied with concern the progress of his latest horse, Nick the Greek, named after one of the gamblers who was making American front-page news most days.

Fred, however, would never believe anyone who assured him he was a great success. He worried that he wasn't doing well enough in *Gay Divorce*, and when Walter promised him that the people out front were not applauding simply to be polite, he worried that there might be another fall on stage.

Nothing bothered him more, however, than the thought of what was happening in Hollywood. Before leaving for London he and Phyllis had started settling down to life on the West Coast and were enjoying the relaxed way in which even stars were able to have something resembling a private life. At that stage, Fred certainly did not feel committed to a career in films, but he was, as always, committed to doing a satisfactory job. And he did not yet know just how satisfactory *Flying Down To Rio* had been. He hadn't seen a preview because he left the country before the film was ready. So now every message from America seemed as if it might be a potential threat to his whole career.

Every time a cable arrived from the States it was Phyllis or Adele who would have to open it – in case it contained a message of doom to Fred Astaire, film actor.

When the prognosis finally came, it was greeted with undisguised relief. Pandro S. Berman whose first name was an abbreviation for Pandrovich sent Fred the wire which confirmed he had more than made the grade:

FLYING DOWN TO RIO COLOSSAL SUCCESS STOP OFFERING SEVEN YEAR CONTRACT STOP MAKE SURE FILM RIGHTS GAY DIVORCE STOP REPRESENTATIVE WITH NEGOTIATIONS RIGHT ON WAY TO YOU.

Berman, son of Russian-Jewish immigrants, was still in his twenties, but was already regarded as one of the top whizz-kids in Hollywood. He was to RKO what Thalberg represented to MGM, the boy genius whose ideas just had to be followed through.

As Berman confessed later, it was not until he saw the preview, that he had any idea himself of the impact Astaire and his young partner had made in *Flying Down To Rio*. The story was flimsy and never allowed to interfere with the musical spectacles. The Hays Office, which the film industry had set up under the Chairmanship of a former Postmaster General, was soon to get much tougher and more sanctimonious, but near-naked girls were still allowed to prance on the wings of aircraft.

Despite the girls and the scenic effects, it was principally Astaire and Rogers who had made the impact in the film and Berman wanted to be sure that there would be more. With Ginger, there were no problems; she was under a long-term contract to the studio and had to do what she was told, despite her ambitions as a straight actress. Fred, however, was the lynchpin. He had to be brought firmly into the studio's orbit and he had to be assured of his importance to the operation. It was not so much a case of flattery as of making him realise his own value. Finally a deal was struck. Fred would get the seven-year contract with a guarantee of complete control over all the films he would be asked to make in the future.

In addition to that, the studio insured the famous Astaire legs and made them the most expensive set of limbs in the world. The value placed on them was a million dollars. It would take a war and the arrival of Betty Grable to equal that record. As a result of the insurance policy, the studio was protected from loss 'through any exigency which deprives the said Astaire of the full and complete use of the said Astaire's legs'.

Once more, too, the gossip columnists were studying the Astaire family as a part of society. They drooled at Adele's presence at the Grosvenor House Derby Ball and noted the number of dances she had with Prince George.

And they were fascinated that Adele was going back to show business – of a kind. She had agreed to play one of the 'Chattering ladies' in the Pageant of Parliament put on by members of London society for a few days in June 1934. Claire Luce need not have worried about that sort of competition.

Adele herself, however, worried rather more about the rumours that were now being spread about her marriage to Charlie Cavendish. When Mrs Ann Astaire returned to New York from London, she had to go out of her way to 'emphatically deny' stories of their imminent splitting up.

'It is utterly stupid,' she told reporters. 'I have never known a happier couple. I've been with them for the past year in London and at Lismore Castle, Ireland. The report is utterly absurd.'

Not so absurd as it seemed was an advertisement Fred had inserted in the papers asking for the return of a pair of dancing shoes. He said they were a lucky charm – although they hadn't yet taken the place of his talisman, the bathrobe. He also sent a long letter to Hollywood asking RKO to see if they had turned up at the studio by mistake. They hadn't.

There was talk in London that Fred was about to make a film with the darling of the British musical comedy stage, Jessie Matthews. Isabel N. Gordon wrote to the *New York Times* from Mount Vernon, New York, protesting.

'I want to say, as one of the vast American theatre-going public, that the present Fred Astaire–Ginger Rogers suits me to a T. Moreover, I imagine my choice is representative of the majority of the film-going public in this country.'

There had been only one Astaire–Rogers film so far, but RKO had insisted there were going to be more and Miss Gordon wanted to be sure they kept their word. Fred, the studio announced, was going back to work just as soon as the London run of *Gay Divorce* ended. But London was making it very clear that it did not want the run to end. It was Fred's first show in the British capital for five years and the citizens of the city were treasuring every moment of it.

In the tailor shops in Savile Row – which were as much artist's studios as workrooms – Fred was not confining his acquisitions to mere clothes. He was picking up snatches of dialogue which he was determined one day to use in an act – and he did, on radio. One of his new trouser legs was too long. 'We shall have to nip them up just a sensation, sir,' said the tailor as he looked at his handiwork. Fred did his best not to collapse in a heap on the spot.

As for himself, he was delighted with the response of the London audiences, not just to himself, but to the players in all the theatres in the West End. When he left New York, half of the houses were shut and of four straight plays on the boards there, two were English.

But the end of *Gay Divorce* had to come. After 108 performances, the curtain closed for the last time – both for the show and for Fred Astaire. He would never appear, full time, in a live theatre again.

I'll Be Hard To Handle

Fred was still in London when a newspaper revealed that his next film partner was going to be the British actress Diana Wynyard. The picture was going to be the screen version of *Gay Divorce*.

The story, like so many about stars who were the public idols of the day, was only partly right: *Gay Divorce* was such a success that it was indeed going to be filmed, but Diana Wynyard had not been selected for the role.

RKO, in fact, couldn't get Fred back to work quickly enough, and that meant back to work with Ginger. Miss Rogers was less than ecstatic about being told to make another musical and Fred thought he was being saddled with the inevitability of always being part of a 'team of horses' again. But he relented.

Gay Divorce appealed to him as much as it did to Pan Berman. He had developed the same sort of affection for 'Night and Day' now as had the audiences who cheered it both on Broadway and in London. But he did have those reservations about co-starring with Ginger. And not just simply because he didn't want a regular partner. She wasn't English and without an English girl to sing and dance with, he thought, *Gay Divorce* wouldn't work. Berman's view of this was that the audiences 'didn't give a hoot'.

Astaire and Rogers could be persuaded. Louis Brock, the producer of *Flying Down To Rio*, could not. He didn't like the story and didn't want to make it into a film. 'Right,' said Berman, 'if you won't make it – I will.' And he did, and as a result was to be credited with the biggest success RKO had yet had.

Another beneficiary was Hermes Pan. Now Pan was the dance director on the film in his own right; meticulously working with Fred, then chalking the routine on the blackboard as though it were a military operation and every twirl by Astaire and Rogers an intricate battle plan, with the attack matched by an appropriate defence.

This was the big difference between Astaire the stage hoofer and Astaire the film dancer. No one could have been more of a slave driver to himself in his Broadway days, more of a perfectionist. But once he had established a number, he had an audience on which to try it out. If it didn't work on the pre-Broadway run, then it was discarded and conveniently forgotten. If it succeeded, it stayed virtually unchanged for two years as well as on the London run that seemed inevitably to follow. But once it was on film, there could be no second chances. So Fred worked harder than ever, and Pan often worked with him – and satisfying either was an almost impossible undertaking.

Some of the best routines took shape as Fred stood in the studio listening to the music. His arms would droop, and then his feet began to trace a step or two. Before long an idea became a reality.

The story of *Gay Divorce* was basically the one that the theatre audiences had seen, with Erik Rhodes repeating his stage role as the mistaken professional co-respondent and Eric Blore as the waiter in a Brightbourne (you took your pick as to whether it was supposed to be Brighton or Eastbourne) hotel. The differences came in the score and in the title. The Hays Office didn't approve of a divorce ever being considered gay – it was just that Mr Family Man American was expected to regard a divorce as a tragedy that was a solemn occasion for all concerned. But an alternative title was found without too much difficulty and the clean-up campaigners were immediately satisfied. If it were called 'The Gay Divorcee', they reckoned, there would be very little difference in the box office appeal – few of the people who had either seen or wanted to see the show would notice the difference – and, strangely, no one could see any moral objection to a divorcee being gay if the action itself remained tragic. British audiences were not

91

considered to be so sensitive. In England, the title remained *The Gay Divorce* – without the extra 'e'.

Of the music, only 'Night and Day' was considered memorable enough to be repeated on film. So it stayed, with Fred using most of the original steps he had done with Claire Luce. But Cole Porter was not involved in any of the other numbers. The rest of the score which now only amounted to three songs, was provided by Con Conrad and Harry Revel, with lyrics by Herb Magidson and Mack Gordon.

Apart from 'Night and Day', which in early talkie terms was a sensation, there was only one really big number in the *Gay Divorcee* film – 'The Continental', which had Astaire and Rogers sweeping through a chorus that managed to turn a black and white film into a riot of colour. The first male dancers to be seen were in white tails, while the girls with them wore black. Behind these was another group of about twenty dancers with the men in black and the girls in white. At the back of these was still a third group where the colours, this time, were mixed. The male chorus dancers wore white jackets and black trousers while the girls had white dresses with black trains-cum-sashes. The effect was stunning. And so was the dancing of 'The Continental' by Astaire and Rogers.

Usually, the music in a picture was closely guarded until the film was ready for release – that way it could be relied upon to do some good, publicising the film. But 'The Continental' escaped. Somehow, the dance bands got hold of it and it was being played all over America before the film was released. In the end, it served to whet the public's appetite for the picture.

The number started – as did most feats of inspiration – with a casual couple of steps on the studio floor. 'I've figured out a new routine,' Fred said to Pan, 'tell me how you like it.'

All very simple – except that Pan has described the work involved on the number as 'blood, sweat and tears'.

Fred was determined to do each routine straight through in a single take. That did not mean, however, that it was shot once and that was that. The number could be photographed many times before Fred was happy and for each of those times, every single step was repeated.

Astaire would turn up early in the morning in a sports shirt over his slacks and with the inevitable tie around his waist. He would plan the number, pace out the steps and then change – for the first time. A top hat, heavy tail coat and stiff white shirt were not exactly conducive to filming in the heat of arc lights. After perhaps only two takes, the shirt would wilt with its owner. Fred had to call for a break and the now soft, sweat-sodden shirt was replaced. Only years later was Fred convinced that sometimes he could look even better if the dance were, after all, broken into takes – to say nothing of the saving in terms of time, energy and sweat, and the occasional tears from the female members of the cast. Fred once had the temerity to say that when the girls cried, he had finally got things as perfect as they could be.

Astaire was certain that his face looked much thinner in the dialogue scenes than it did in the dance numbers. And he was right. The gruelling routines were always got out of the way first and by the time it came to film the other scenes, he had already lost a few pounds. When everyone was finally happy, Astaire and Pan would say they had a 'good deed'. It was the most important phrase of all. It meant that all was well.

The big problem was selecting the chorus – who collectively were only just a little bit easier for Pan to handle than a single Fred Astaire. Fred himself pondered the problem of the chorus in an article in *Picturegoer Weekly*. He said, 'Believe me, picking dancers for the stage is as simple as scrumping an apple off a tree, compared with selecting them for the screen. For a film dancer has got to be a show girl as well as a chorine.'

The work on *The Gay Divorcee* was worth every dripping shirt and each salty tear. The public loved it, and Adele said it made her realise that she must have been holding Fred back all the years they had worked together.

If there were difficulties with the dance numbers, there were few problems in the humour department. Edward Everett Horton added a slice of comedy in his quite unique style – the first of a whole succession of important appearances in Astaire films – and he even did a dancing bit, 'Let's K-nock K-nees', with a young lady who escaped the attention of most critics at the time, but who was to go on to become that symbol of World War Two morale boosting, Betty Grable.

The *New York Times* described the film as 'an entirely agreeable photoplay which sings, dances and quips with agility and skill. . . . Fred Astaire is an urbane delight and Miss Rogers keeps pace with him.'

Variety's celebrated Editor, Abel Green, who rightly believed everything he wrote was going to be preserved for posterity as part of the history of show business, commented: 'All through the picture there is charm, romance, gaiety and éclat.' As for Fred, he was a 'new marquee satellite. The picture unquestionably will set the musical comedy star for the celluloid firmament.'

Immediately after *Gay Divorcee*, Ginger Rogers was assigned to other pictures. She was told, however, that there would be more Astaire vehicles on the way – and, like it or not, she was expected to do them. She didn't like it, but the choice was not hers; it is frequently forgotten that throughout the whole period in which she and Fred were working together, she was making other films in between, sometimes as many as three a year. They were, however, eminently forgettable.

Fred managed to take time off in between pictures – playing golf with Phyllis, who proved to be a player of championship standard, and going deep-sea fishing with her. She could bring in a giant marlin more than three times her own ninety pound weight as easily as lesser mortals could carry shopping baskets.

In the evenings, they would relax together at home or in a retreat they had rented for a vacation. A host of publications by now had voted Fred the world's best-dressed man, but that didn't stop him on one notorious holiday being refused entry into the Catalina casino for not wearing a tie.

Fred's growing international fame only served to increase interest in his now aristocratic sister. Would Lady Charles return to work? Fans and gossip columnists alike wanted to know. Would she make films herself? Adele said she would not, but now it seemed a somewhat unconvincing denial. To the people who knew her, she was still too extrovert a character to be content with spending all her time in the rather foreboding surroundings of Lismore Castle.

And there were times when certain members of British society wondered whether perhaps she was not just a little too extrovert. In a staid, dignified London courtroom and before robed and bewigged judge and counsel in January 1934, Lady Charles Cavendish put her thumb to her nose and wiggled her fingers. It convulsed the court but disturbed the peerage.

Adele was giving evidence on behalf of her friend and fellow dancer Tilly Losch, soon to become the Countess of Carnarvon. Tilly was being sued for divorce by her husband Edward James, who charged her with infidelity – which occurred, he said, with the Russian Prince, Oleg Obolensky, in a cab on the way to the Empire State Building.

Adele said that she had been in a cab driving parallel with Tilly's much of the time and could see inside it. She said they were so close that she thumbed her nose at her friend on the journey – and showed the court exactly what she did. The building dissolved into hysterics. Anyway, she said, 'There's no such thing as a fifty-block kiss.' Miss Losch and her companion had been accused of making love throughout the whole journey.

Mr Norman Birkett – one day to become one of Britain's most eminent judges, a man who sat at the Nuremberg war crimes trials – asked Adele whether a gift of a sable coat had anything to do with her evidence. 'I've always made a lot of money,' she told him. 'And nobody has to buy me any furs.'

Tilly lost the case and had to pay about £12,000 in costs.

Fred, meanwhile, was back at work at RKO with Ginger, with Pandro S. Berman as producer and Hermes Pan as his dance director, and working harder than almost any other performer would have thought possible. He was now so fussy about everything working out perfectly that he did not even trust other people to nail the taps on to the toes and heels of his dancing shoes, so he did this bit of cobbling himself.

The new film was *Roberta*, an adaptation of the stage play which had marked the big-time debut of a young comedian called Bob Hope. It was centred around a fashion house. In the film Fred played Hope's part. He was a band leader, Ginger a secretary. Astaire's real life close friend Randolph Scott was on hand too, as a country bumpkin who takes over the couturier's establishment.

The strange thing about *Roberta* was that, despite the overwhelming success of *Gay Divorcee*, Astaire and Rogers were no more the stars of the new picture than they had been in *Flying Down To Rio*. Berman decided to use the elegant Irene Dunne in the film as the principal brains behind the fashion house – because at the time she represented even bigger box office pulling power than either Fred or Ginger.

In one scene, Miss Dunne had to lean forward to examine a button on the dress worn by a model. Fred thought she was showing too much cleavage and asked her if it was really in the best of taste. 'I thought he was too stuffy for words,' she says now. 'But afterwards I thought he was right.'

An important plus in *Roberta's* favour was the score – this time by Jerome Kern. Another, which seemed a lot less notable at the time, was the appearance of a young lady called Lucille Ball.

Few of the songs in the original Broadway show were transferred to the screen – with Kern's finest number sung first by Irene Dunne and then reprised as a dance routine in all its considerable glory by Astaire and Rogers. It was 'Smoke Gets In Your Eyes'.

Two other tunes were added by Kern himself, both of them important in any song history of the century – 'I Won't Dance', and 'Lovely To Look At' which was to become the title of a later remake of the *Roberta* story. That song presented a few worries to Pandro Berman who said it was much too short. 'That's all I have to say,' replied Kern, leaving absolutely nothing more, in fact, to be said.

According to the Hays Office, Broadway audiences were made of much stronger stuff than the people who saw movies. The censors insisted on a number of changes in lyrics that hadn't brought a single blush to a theatre patron's cheek. For the song, 'Let's Begin', the worries of the purists were appeased. The line 'no reason for vain regret' was substituted for (horror of horrors) 'necked till she was wrecked'.

Fred danced both on-camera and off- for his incredible taps had to be heard as well as seen. It was the hardest and least rewarding part of his screen work, but recording the sound of his dancing had to be done and as usual he had to do it the Astaire way. Other dancers might have been satisfied with their taps recorded by a drummer using coconut shells, but Fred had to do his as though there were a thousand people in the studio watching him. If he could spot a single beat that failed to match the action on screen, that and all the other taps would be repeated until everything was perfect.

Ginger, however, was not quite so fussy. Nobody expected her to be able to work with that sort of precision, so nobody asked. As a result, every Rogers step was later repeated by Hermes Pan. With a pair of earphones on his head and his loudest tap shoes on his feet, Pan repeated each step that Ginger had done on the screen. So whenever Ginger is seen dancing in those films, it is Hermes Pan's shoes you hear, not hers. It was rather like a vocalist dubbing a tune for a non-singing actor, except that there was no optical illusion about her performances. Certainly, the effect of seeing Pan dance with Fred wouldn't have been anything like as stunning.

If the amount of work put into a number had any bearing on the results, *Roberta* had to be brilliant. There was a solid nine-week period of rehearsals before shooting started – much of it all by Fred on his own; he didn't take off a Saturday, a Sunday or even a public holiday. Rehearsals covered the days of Thanksgiving, Christmas and New Year. On each of these, he telephoned Hermes Pan in the morning and suggested they get together for a couple of hours that afternoon 'to rehearse some more'.

For *Roberta*, he rehearsed dance routines that came to him before he had any idea of the music they would accompany. The steps were planned two weeks before Kern delivered the score.

The songwriter, who was not usually given to ungrudging admiration of another man's capabilities, was stunned by Fred's innate musical sense. On one occasion, to prove a point, Fred danced through Kern's Beverly Hills house as the composer watched the procession from room to room, wide-eyed and incredulous.

Every step was rehearsed day after day from nine in the morning until six in the evening – with Ginger turning up for work in slacks and Fred dressing as informally as he always did at these times. It was difficult to imagine how different everything would be when she was in her flowing ball gown and he in his white tie and tails. But Fred and Pan knew – and Ginger took their word for it.

Filming complete, Fred took off as usual with Phyllis to play golf and then went deep sea fishing in the Lower Gulf of California with their friend Randolph Scott. All the time that Fred was away, he seemed to be worrying as much about his newly-finished picture as he was about getting a hole-in-one or catching a 150-lb marlin.

Early on Fred set a pattern to which he would religiously keep: he avoided going to previews of his pictures and there were, in fact, some films he couldn't bring himself to see until years after they were made. If he had gone to see *Roberta* at the preview stage, 'Moaning Minnie' might have stopped moaning. No one could pretend it was a great film; the plot and much of the acting was pedestrian. But Astaire and Rogers stole it for every minute they were on the screen.

The press had no doubts whatever.

Said the *New York Times*: 'The Kublai Khans at RKO have erected a bright and shimmering pleasure dome. The work is a model of urbanity in the musical films and Mr Astaire, the debonair master of light comedy and the dance, is its chief ornament.

'To watch him skipping on effortless cat's feet across a dance floor is to experience one of the major delights of the contemporary cinema.'

The only fault in the production was that Fred 'and his excellent partner, Miss Rogers, cannot be dancing during every minute of it'.

It was enough to make anyone connected with Fred Astaire feel marvellously contented. But not Fred Astaire himself.

Top Hat

RKO and almost everyone else in Hollywood were by now convinced that there was an Astaire–Rogers bandwagon in full motion and with nothing to stop it. Fred, however, needed a great deal more convincing. Not even the record-breaking box-office figures assuaged his concern.

And when there was nothing to worry about, he created causes for anxiety.

It would be years before he made a movie in colour, but already he was worrying how he would cope. He had heard that chorus girls were being sprayed with make-up so that they would photograph better in Technicolor. For a man who changed his underwear four times a day under the heat of the studio lights that was a fiercesome prospect. But much more seriously, he worried just how far he or the kind of films he made could be expected to continue.

As for himself, he had promised his mother he would retire at thirty-five but his income-tax bills had persuaded him that that was an unreasonable goal. His mother had to understand and so did Phyllis, who had no interest at all in show business and whose occasional visits to the set were much more gestures of wifely devotion than fascination with his work.

The future of the sort of films he was making was even more difficult to predict. Just how long would audiences accept the slightly abrasive Miss Rogers constantly mistaking Fred's true intentions?

The dancing was more difficult to plan every time. He and Pan had learned a number of lessons, particularly as far as placing the camera to the best advantage was concerned. You couldn't photograph dancers in the way you could other performers – audiences had to see their feet as well as their faces, but not always at the same time. The art was being able to decide which camera angle matched which beat of the music and which tap of the stars' feet.

But those routines couldn't be repeated from one film to the next. There had to be a new *way* of dancing every time Fred and Ginger changed numbers and not just for each film.

He told an interviewer soon after making *Roberta*,

Filmgoers will not stand for the same stuff over and over again and this is to a great extent responsible for making film dancing such damned hard work.

Since being in Hollywood, I have come to the conclusion that screen acting is no job for a lazy person at the best of times. I know dancing isn't. I just happened to take it up before I knew any better.

In another interview, he went into greater depth:

It's often a slow and painful process and I try to work out the general pattern and feeling of the dance and then fill in the outline step by step. Sometimes, the ideas and steps come rather easily. Again, I have, figuratively, to sweat blood. In the main, it's plain hard work.

A dance to be effective in a picture should be more than a combination of intricate steps. It should mean something definite, do its part in developing characterisation and telling a story. It falls short of its purpose if it is a mere exhibition of dexterity and technical skill.

All that dexterity and technical skill was going to be needed when a small, desperately shy man with shiny black hair walked on to the RKO lot and started pounding on an upright piano as though it were a punchbag. Every now and again, he would reach for a lever under the keyboard and attempt to play the tune again – always entirely on the black notes.

His name was Irving Berlin, and playing the piano in the key of F sharp was the only way he knew. He had to use a battered upright – he called it his 'Buick' – because that was the only one that could be fitted with a lever which would automatically change key for him, like a gear stick on a car.

What he was pounding out for the stars and the assembled company of RKO executives was a score that he figured summed up Fred Astaire to the bottom of his impeccably pressed trousers. To match Astaire's dancing, the studio had retained the most successful songwriter in musical history, the Russian-born Jewish cantor's son who with the name of a German city had become the unofficial American poet laureate in song. The film was going to become Astaire's trademark, the archetype vehicle for what was to be regarded as a typical Astaire performance in a perfect Rogers–Astaire mould – *Top Hat*.

Berlin has said he would never have written some of his most successful numbers if he hadn't had Fred Astaire to write for. Certainly he would never have written 'Top Hat, White Tie and Tails'. Neither would we probably have had 'Cheek to Cheek', 'Isn't This A Lovely Day' and the sort of number the public hoped would return in *Top Hat* – the new dance performed by Fred and Ginger as part of a spectacular which this time was called *The Piccolino*.

Irving Berlin, like most of the big songwriters of his age, composed to order when there was a deadline to meet. Years later, Sammy Cahn was to say that neither the words nor the music came first when he himself wrote a song. What came first was the phone call commissioning it. It was much the same with Berlin, except that when he had an idea that didn't quite jell, he would file it for use another time. With Astaire no filing cabinet was needed. In Fred he had a man who could put on to the huge dance floors of the studio sound stages exactly what he had buzzing round in his own genius head.

For *Top Hat*, Astaire resurrected the one really bright spot in the otherwise disastrous show *Smiles* – the 'shooting' down of a gang of chorus boys with his evening dress cane. The moment of inspiration that had had him up at four o'clock in the morning, proved its worth once more in the film. But the blood was sweated as fast and as furiously as usual.

Before the filming started, the studio prop department worked out, as they always did, exactly what would be needed to make the picture complete. Among them, a hansom cab, a street light, a sword and a collection of canes.

'How many do we need?' asked the prop manager. 'About a dozen,' Hermes Pan recommended. To be on the safe side he ordered thirteen. As the day went on, no one was sweating more blood than the props man. Fred was unhappy with the way the number was shaping up. Every time he felt really depressed about it all, he snapped a cane.

During this sequence he was joined by a man who was fairly used to appearing before the cameras himself, if usually with a somewhat more lethal weapon in his hands. He was James Cagney. Cagney watched one cane after the other being snapped – one, two, three . . . he was actually on cane number eight, when Fred finally decided he would be happy to see the rushes. The take he chose was the first of forty in which he had performed, long before any of the other canes were brought into use. He decided to dedicate the scene to Cagney – and to suggest that before long they should make a film together. If they waited till they were too old, they would both regret it. They both have.

The *Top Hat* number was not the only one to bring problems. The innocent-sounding, romantic, beautiful and feathery 'Cheek to Cheek' was much more difficult. And it was the feathers that gave everyone who had anything to do with the scene the biggest headache of all.

As always, the dance routine for 'Cheek to Cheek' had been meticulously rehearsed. Berlin saw it, so did Hermes Pan and so did the rehearsal pianist Hal Borne. All the other people involved in the picture were banned from the sanctuary of the Astaire–Rogers presence during rehearsals.

And as always, too, Ginger, in slacks, sat in her chair watching Fred and Pan chart the dance numbers on the rehearsal room blackboard. Just occasionally, she might make a suggestion of her own, but she didn't pretend to be technically minded and left the work of planning the 'battle' to Fred and his choreographer.

Nobody, however, anticipated what would happen when Fred – wearing the first of his stiff shirts under his thick black tail coat – and Ginger in her ballgown, came on to the studio floor and started dancing before the cameras.

To coin a phrase, the feathers flew. They flew into Fred's eyes, on to his shoulders, into his mouth and lodged unhappily, in his ears. Fred kept sneezing, much to his and everybody else's amusement. The names he called the dress and its feathers hadn't been heard coming out of the Astaire lips since his days on Broadway.

David Niven, who was on the set with Phyllis, recalled Mrs Astaire describing Ginger that day as looking like a 'wooster'.

Once the commotion had died down, Fred and Pan laughed themselves into composing a parody to Berlin's 'Cheek to Cheek' lyrics – a rare indulgence on the songwriter's part if he ever knowingly allowed it: Berlin, who used to print instructions on his sheet music forbidding parodies, has been known to take people to court for less.

On this occasion, the Berlin line beginning 'Heaven, I'm in heaven. . .' became 'Feathers, I hate feathers . . .'

The feathers finally came home to 'woost' – after the designer had stayed up all night on the job. Those that remained were more securely fixed to Ginger's dress, the floor was swept clean and not a flying feather was seen on camera.

What *was* seen was the perfection of Astaire married to the equally perfect Berlin score. All of it was under the streamlined direction of Mark Sandrich, who had been responsible for *The Gay Divorcee*. He was now firmly set to be Astaire's personal director in all but name.

The story was as weak as ever, but who cared whether or not Ginger did think Fred had an affliction that made him dance on the floor of his hotel suite – which conveniently just happened to be above hers?

The big white sets that became an RKO trademark almost as recognisable as Fred and Ginger themselves, were in evidence and so were the huge ultra-modern settings for the big production numbers. In *Top Hat*, Astaire and Edward Everett Horton fly to Venice and land their seaplane at just the spot where Ginger is waiting for someone else.

The usual case of mistaken identity combined with the usual insults from Ginger. And as usual, too, they dance off at the end in each other's arms. Once more, there was also Lucille Ball in a now-you-see-her-now-you-don't role.

Fred and Ginger always went their separate ways outside the studio. They had not socialised with each other since those early dates at Manhattan night clubs. Once in Hollywood, Fred and Phyllis had set up a home that intentionally excluded as much of the show business world as possible. They rarely went out to parties and if they did, it was with their own small coterie of friends, which included David

Niven and Randolph Scott but few other actors. Fred and Ginger got on well together, but they were content to say goodnight to each other at the end of a day's filming and then, when a picture was finally completed, *au revoir* until the next one – always with Ginger for her own reasons hoping there would not be a next one.

Top Hat opened at New York's Radio City Music Hall – which gives some idea of the importance of the picture – to an incredible reaction from the public. Almost every performance was greeted with thunderous applause from the audience.

The Press were equally enthusiastic. The *New York Times* said of the picture: 'Irving Berlin has written some charming melodies for the photoplay and the best of the current cinema teams does them agile justice on the dance floor.'

The critic Andree Sennwald, said that Astaire performed 'his incredible magic' and Ginger showed herself to be 'increasingly dexterous' and the whole lot provided 'the most urbane fun that you will find anywhere on the screen.'

The welcome was equally warm in London.

The *Daily Express* said it was,

> much better entertainment than *Roberta*. . . . Saint Vitus is a Karl-offian portrait of Frankenstein's monster compared with Fred as Jerry Travers, top-hatted musicomedy star who declares his passion for the unknown blonde (Ginger Rogers).
>
> He sprinkles fire-bucket sand on the floor of the room above hers and shuffle dances her to sleep. He makes terpsichorean advances to her in a lonely bandstand when she is caught in the rain. . . . If a more diverting variation of the old musical love-chase theme has ever been done, I can't recall it. Ginger Rogers is more charming than ever as the prey and the contributory antics of Edward Everett Horton, Helen Broderick, Erik Rhodes and Eric Blore could hardly be bettered. Irving Berlin's music and lyrics are as fresh and hummy as only Irving knows how. The most perceptive statement was in the tail: Fred Astaire is by a few thousand miles the ace musical comedy personality of the hour and you will never see him in better form.

Top Hat looked like being an expensive film by 1935 standards and there were worries about ever getting back the $600,000 the studio had invested, particularly since both Fred and Irving Berlin were on ten per cent of the profits. (Ginger had her more modest contract salary and was about to be directed to another film.)

In the end, the picture grossed three million dollars. RKO were ready to get to work on their next film for the duo, but Fred first wanted his customary holiday with Phyllis. Along with them they took Peter, who was being brought up as much a part of the Astaire household as if he had been Fred's natural son.

Meanwhile, the family was due to expand. Both Phyllis and Adele were pregnant.

In September 1935, Adele gave birth to twin boys. But again, both died. This was now the saddest point in her whole life. The happy-go-lucky clown of the family was distraught. She now knew that she would never have what she wanted most, a child.

While Phyllis waited for what Reuter's newsagency described as her 'happy event', Fred was trying out a new medium and was not over impressed. He was the link-man – cum-singer in a radio series for 'Lucky Strike' cigarettes called the Hit Parade. It was a superb opportunity to plug *Top Hat*, to sing Irving Berlin's songs and the other numbers that were selling in the record stores. He also danced a bit, too – at the end of the show on a tiny dance floor with a special mike at foot level to pick up the taps. The only trouble was that he had to do the taps at the end of the show, because had they come any earlier, he would not have had enough breath left to sing and introduce his guests.

Possibly to his sponsors' chagrin, it was the effect on his breathing that made Fred give up smoking more than the occasional cigarette.

'An athlete can puff all he wants to, a dancer may not', he explained at the time, 'he must appear graceful and at ease while dancing. The microphones are very sensitive, and would pick up hard breathing. I smoke very little. Just a cigarette every now and then by way of relaxation.'

Fred was much happier relaxing playing golf, going to the races or – a regular diversion this – studying the American criminal. Detective stories were his favourite reading matter, but he took his interest rather further than that. He made more than one visit to the local police headquarters, watching witnesses attending identification parades.

It was while relaxing, but doubtless not at the police station, that he thought up his own music. He had worked on a number of tunes since his first was published in 1924. Several of them were published and had sold quite well. For 'Tappin' The Time' in 1927 his old friend Jock Whitney had written the lyrics. 'Blue Without You' and 'More and More' came in 1930 and 'Not My Girl' in 1935. But in 1936 was the real block buster songwriting year. He had 'Just One More Dance, Madame' (for which the very experienced Dave Dreyer supplied the lyrics with Paul Francis Webster); 'I'll Never Let You Go', (Dreyer again with Jack Ellis), and what was to prove the biggest success of his life – 'I'm Building Up To An Awful Let Down'.

Johnny Mercer collaborated with Astaire on that and the result was a vocalisation of the sheer poetry Astaire had previously seemed to reserve for his dancing. The song got to the top of the hit parade and for Fred it seemed to justify the membership he had taken out some time before in ASCAP – the American Society of Composers, Authors and Publishers.

The success of 'I'm Building Up To An Awful Let Down' had a predictable effect. He told a film magazine that it had turned him into a 'fugitive from melodies'. He explained: 'I pick up my morning coffee and I hear racy sharps and flats pounding in my ears. I go to swing a tennis ball and a host of notes swarm over me. It's a wonderful malady.'

But it didn't affect him to the extent that he no longer appreciated the full-time songwriters, some of whom had become millionaires as a result of their talents.

Irving Berlin had to be at the top of the list of Astaire's favourite songwriters. After the almost unbelievable success of *Top Hat*, Pandro S. Berman booked him for the next Rogers–Astaire film, a movie in which Fred wore bell-bottoms as well as the expected top hat, white tie and tails.

The picture was *Follow The Fleet*, a remake of a musical filmed only six years before as *Hit The Deck* – which itself had been based on a 1925 vintage silent movie called *Shore Leave*. In this new version Randolph Scott appeared with his old friend.

The film wasn't Fred's usual image at all. He could actually be seen chewing gum, and when he gave the embarrassed little bronchial laugh that turns up in all the Astaire films – and, indeed, in any conversation with Fred, even today – it was usually in the midst of a diction that sounded totally strange coming from his mouth. Not at all the sort of thing that had endeared him to London society.

Ginger is a dance hall queen and Fred the fellow she used to dance with, who decides to join the Navy and who in reality would rather lead a band – to coin a title of one of the songs in the film. He also leads the chorus in singing 'We Saw The Sea', all about the joys of world travel.

But although 'We Saw The Sea' went to the top of the 1936 hit parade, it was the numbers with Rogers which, as usual, were the show stoppers – including 'I'm Putting All My Eggs In One Basket' and 'Let's Face the Music and Dance'. That was yet another classic which easily could have been a new signature tune for Fred any time he wanted to discard 'Top Hat, White Tie and Tails'. But this was also to give Fred problems – it was shot about fifteen times yet it was the first take that was used.

His affection for Berlin grew the more they worked together. In January 1936, Phyllis went into hospital to await the birth of her baby – and Fred moved in with her. But there were times when they could not be together and these were the moments when Berlin proved himself to be particularly good company. In Fred's private room at the hospital, the two played gin rummy while Berlin hummed a tune that he thought Fred might like.

'Say what do you think of this?' he asked Astaire.

'Yeah, I like it,' said Fred.

'Good,' Berlin replied chuckling. 'Gin.'

His good tune had turned to a good hand, and if Fred were the beneficiary of one, he wasn't expected to mind being the loser on the other. Phyllis, on the other hand, was doing very well. She presented Fred with a son. For days, gossip columnists speculated on the baby's name. Finally, they were told. He was going to be Fred, Fred Astaire, Junior.

Lucille Ball had yet another microscopic role in *Follow The Fleet* and the singing trio included the blonde who at the time seemed destined to do nothing more than smile in Fred Astaire–Ginger Rogers pictures, Betty Grable. No one had yet begun to guess at the potential those legs of hers offered for cheering up the boys in World War Two.

In the midst of the escapism of *Follow The Fleet*, which was still an important ingredient in the life of Americans who had just emerged from the Depression, there was also a certain amount of realism. Hermes Pan wanted dancers in a public ballroom to be real kids who paid to go to a real dance, so he toured the local halls to get characters who were used to 'cutting a rug'. When they appeared on screen, it was obviously a wise move.

There were nearly as many costume problems in *Follow The Fleet* as there had been in *Top Hat*. Except that in the new film, the feathers were, by some kind of poetic justice, replaced by what appeared to be lead weights. Ginger wore a metallic skirt for the 'Let's Face The Music And Dance' number, a garment that looked much better than it felt – certainly to Fred. Every time she swirled, the skirt swirled, too, even when the rest of her stopped. As it did so, Fred's legs felt as though sharp blades were slicing into them. A beautiful delicate hand movement would end up with his getting slapped in the face by a sleeve which was a mass of sequins with fur cuffs but which felt as though it were made of solid steel. Each sleeve weighed thirty-five pounds.

Take after take of this number was shot and again it was the first one that was used.

Of course, the public were never aware of the problem caused by Ginger's dress. Nor did they know that when Fred was supposed to hit Randolph Scott in the film, he did just that. The gentle dancer for whom movement was an art hadn't learned how to aim a punch without hitting his 'opponent'. When Fred took a swing at Randolph, he actually drew blood.

Which was almost what some of the critics did. The *New York Post* declared that *Follow The Fleet* did not 'come within hailing distance of the glamorous and shining *Top Hat*, even though it does confirm the endlessly amazing talent of Fred Astaire.'

The public were less condescending. The box-office take was as high as was now expected of an Astaire-Rogers film and few complaints were heard from the paying public. Berlin made another small fortune from his score.

In London, the critics welcomed the film warmly.

The *Daily Telegraph's* Campbell Dixon said: 'The Fred Astaire–Ginger Rogers partnership is revived with the happiest results. *Follow The Fleet* has ideas style and charm ... Mr Astaire and Miss Rogers have never danced better or acted half so well.'

As well they might, everyone seemed to be more than happy at RKO, too. Or were they? Suddenly there was talk of bitter disagreement between the studio and Fred. There were rumours that he was going to court and was likely to leave Pandro S. Berman and everyone else at what was colloquially known as Radio Pictures.

His original contract with RKO was hardly the sort of document that was boasted about by superstars of the Astaire bracket. In fact, it was still basically the same one he had signed after taking those first hesitant steps over to the RKO lot for *Flying Down to Rio* – $1,500 a week with options of additional weekly sums of $500 while actually making a film.

Fred said he wanted more money and discussions were begun with the studio – at first amicably and with everyone saying there was plenty of room for talking. But a new lawyer entered the fray on the Astaire side and the fight became altogether more bitter. Neither Fred nor the studio took to the change of tactics kindly. RKO thought about teaching a lesson to the man they considered was getting too big for his dancing shoes. They considered simply sitting back without offering Fred any more work for the time being. That way, they reasoned, they wouldn't even be obliged to pay him an extra $500 a week.

The row burst open – and with it came the first public news that perhaps things were not so good between Fred and Ginger either. Fred had let slip that he didn't think it wise for him to go on making too many pictures with Ginger.

'Ginger and I have made several together and have done almost every variety of dance,' he said at the time. 'People will begin to wonder if we aren't doing the same thing all over again.'

It was his old fear, that the public would soon get tired of both of them and of the vehicles that still had people lining up for blocks outside the theatres.

RKO quickly announced that they had no dissatisfaction with either star – the fact that Ginger had been making the same sort of noises almost from the beginning would not be allowed to interfere with a convenient policy line. Fred, too, denied he had any difficulties on that count. It was one of those private things that he wasn't willing to talk about. More frankly, he admitted that he wanted at least six months off so that he could visit Adele and Charles at Lismore Castle. He desperately wanted to be with his sister again. They hadn't had one of their heart-to-hearts since long before she had lost her twins, and the old intense feeling for each other was as strong as ever. If he had to go from one new movie to yet another, there wouldn't be time for a reunion.

A statement issued in Fred's name declared: 'The studio has violated my contract on several counts.' There were reports that he had been offered $400,000 for each of eight new pictures, and was still turning the studio down. 'He is legally sulking,' said the RKO men.

But before long, everyone in the affair announced they were happy. RKO said they had a new deal with their unlikely problem boy, and out of deference for the privacy of Mr Astaire, didn't tell anyone how much it was worth – although the previously mooted figures were close to the final amount. What was stated was that Mr Astaire would not be required to make more than two pictures a year. Ginger came on to the scene again now with the rather obvious announcement that she wouldn't be required to make more than two pictures a year with Fred. She was, however, going to do a total of four films a year, and the other two would be starring vehicles for her alone.

If it was an amicable settlement, Fred was a lot less friendly when he heard about *Esquire* magazine and a jewellery firm who were advertising in that sophisticated journal. The firm ran a picture of Fred which clearly gave the impression that Astaire wore their jewellery. It was captioned: 'As inspired by Fred Astaire in *Top Hat*.' But he didn't wear it. In fact, Fred said the advertisement 'humiliated him and exposed him to ridicule.'

He was angry – more angry than he had been in public for a long time, and he sued.

'In the last year, I've refused more than $40,000 offered to me to sponsor hats, coats, ties, shoes and every other article of wear,' he declared. 'I think this is the silliest form of advertising there is and that is why I object to the advertising in *Esquire*.'

Adele, meanwhile, decided not to wait for Fred to cross the Atlantic. She went to America herself and so was able to visit Fred and Phyllis and see their new son. She was immediately asked her view on Fred's name being taken in vain in the *Esquire* ads. 'He has been like that all his life,' she said. 'Anyone who refers to him as a well-dressed man becomes his mortal enemy.'

Astaire won his case. He was awarded $25,000. Supreme Court Justice Rosenman declared that the use of Fred's picture was 'clearly unauthorised' and had been published for 'the purpose of trade'. The magazine was ordered to get back every copy of the January 1936 issue that might still be on the stands.

The first thing Adele did on arriving in New York was to watch the city's policemen at work. 'I love policemen,' she declared as her luggage containing, she revealed, sixty pairs of shoes was brought ashore. She stayed in America for just over two months. When the holiday was over, she told reporters: 'It gives me the weeps to think of leaving America.' But she wasn't going to be away from her brother for long. He and Phyllis were now planning that holiday in Britain and would be away for all of the six months Fred declared he was taking at the time of his wrangle with the studio. First, however, there would be one more film with Ginger.

Shall We Dance?

Fred wasn't thinking of just six months' holiday. At thirty-six he was wondering whether the best of his dancing days were behind him.

No one could venture that it had all hardly yet begun; that the real Fred Astaire, the man with the unique quality of dancing like a youth while always acting his age, had still to etch himself a permanent place in history. So he felt he had to plan for every eventuality.

'If I cease to act and dance,' he said in 1936, 'I'll continue to compose and write.' But that could never really be a viable alternative for Fred Astaire. As if to reassure himself, he said:

I don't want to do anything, but I think I'd like to have a stable of race horses. I like to play golf, too. Aside from that, I can't think of anything I really want to do. I'm just naturally lazy. I like dancing with Ginger – she's developed into a fine little dancer. I think, though, I do too much dancing in films. I know that musical pictures are in vogue just now, but that won't last. People will tire of them and if they think of me as nothing more than a dancer, they'll tire of me too. So I want to do more acting.'

Nor were these the only reasons. He couldn't really understand his popularity on the screen.

'Personally, I feel like breaking down and weeping after I've seen one of my films,' he told the *New York Post*. 'I can't bear to see a picture in a projection room and it's only after I've witnessed a finished film several times with a theatre audience that I begin to think it's not so bad.'

So he had to be convinced.

New Theatre magazine did its best to impress upon him the sheer devotion in which he was now held by the film-going public. It wrote:

Fred Astaire is not only a remarkable technician in a field of spectacular tap-dancing, where tap, however complex, is to be heard and not seen, but also he has an extremely personable manner.

He is always the brilliant amateur dandy surprised into a demonstration of such a bravura technique that few, if any professionals can match.

But his mask of top hat, kid gloves and white tie and his other identifiable minor disguises do not diminish one's pleasure at his performance – though they keep him from the scope of irony or even tragedy with subsequent intense rewards.

And it was precisely that philosophy which did govern RKO's thinking. They didn't want more acting and less dancing. Pandro S. Berman was convinced that the box offices would before long all but sink into their concrete foundations – through the sheer weight of coins avidly being handed over by the movie-goers.

Fred, who now had the full right of refusal, was persuaded once more to look to his true value. Ginger, who had no say whatever in the matter, simply turned up on the lot at the right time and went to work on the new picture. It was, she was told, going to be called *Never Gonna Dance*.

For all the seemingly inseparable bond that had existed between himself and Adele, Fred had always been a lot tougher with her than he was going to be with Ginger – and in her own way, Ginger was a lot more co-operative. When Fred said rehearse, Ginger rehearsed, until both of them were exhausted but satisfied. It was a props man who discovered, before most people gave it a thought, just how hard Ginger did rehearse. He was mopping up the floor after yet another repeated take of what was then the title number 'Never Gonna Dance' when he noticed it was covered with a film of what looked suspiciously like blood.

At the time, Fred was out changing his shirt yet again and Ginger was hobbling to a corner of the sound stage, clutching a very red foot. The props man didn't realise that she was still wearing her shoe, but the blood had soaked right through the sides and sole of the satin dancing slipper and it all looked like a solid red mass. Despite Ginger's injuries, Fred called for yet another take – and he was still not satisfied. When it was shot again all looked perfect – until Fred himself spoiled everything by tripping up. In the end, just one more take was called for and everyone seemed content.

The picture was eventually given a new title, *Swing Time*, but there was little that was new about the story. It was the usual Astaire–Rogers mixture, with Fred playing a gambler and Ginger the girl who takes a hundred minutes to fall as hard for him as he did for her in the opening reel. Again, the principal ingredient in what served as the plot – apart from the comic relief supplied by Eric Bloore, Victor Moore and Helen Broderick – was deception; Fred pretending this time, of all things, that he couldn't dance. Ginger was a dancing teacher – which explains why. As usual they danced to a completely new set of routines. The policy of never repeating a dance step was followed as closely in *Swing Time* as in all the other films. The plot could be vaguely – and often, not so vaguely – similar from one picture to the next; the dance routines never.

And just as the dances were different, so were the tunes. Jerome Kern was the composer on the set once more, and for *Swing Time*, he created two new classics – 'A Fine Romance' and 'The Way You Look Tonight', both of which reflected the strange moral code that Astaire insisted upon for his pictures.

People had already begun talking about the way Astaire and Rogers conducted their film love affairs. No one minded that they were never seen in bed together, but they didn't even kiss. Absolutely never.

In 'A Fine Romance', lyricist Dorothy Fields emphasises it is a love affair 'with no clinches'. They don't kiss, so the story in the movie goes, because Fred is still engaged to the girl next door. In fact, he would have been married to her already had he not bothered so much about the turn-ups on his trousers that he made himself too late for the wedding.

Ginger has always said they never kissed on screen because she thought Fred was frightened Phyllis might get the wrong idea. As for himself, he has maintained he simply tried to avoid the 'mushy love scenes' adopted in every other film.

The treatment of 'The Way You Look Tonight' was another attempt at avoiding embarrassment. While the script called for Fred to sing to Ginger as she washed her hair in the bath, he was safe behind a locked door all the time. And just in case someone, somewhere, still got the wrong idea, Ginger was covered by a sea of opaque bubbles.

There was one other particularly notable number in *Swing Time*. For 'Bojangles of Harlem' and for the first and only time in his career, Fred worked in blackface, in a number inspired by Bill 'Bojangles' Robinson.

Kern worked hard on his numbers for the film, punching out tunes that sounded like magic from the keyboard of a proficient musician, but which from him resembled a collection of cowbells rung on an off day. It was Kern who kept a bust of Wagner staring down at him from the top of his piano – and who turned the head away when he felt he was disappointing the 'master'.

As for Fred and Ginger, there were rumours that they were about to disappoint the public. Ginger, it was reported, was getting more and more difficult to work with. She had banned visitors from the set while filming was going on. There was a sense of unease which was not helped by the constant change of title for the picture. *Never Gonna Dance* had become *Swing Time* and was then going to be called *Stepping Toes*; finally, and to most people's relief, it became *Swing Time* once more and stayed that way.

Was the Astaire–Rogers partnership going to last or had it really bitten the dust, never to recover again? Did the new contract make no difference, after all? Even Pandro Berman was forced to make a statement: 'I realise,' he said, 'that very soon I've got to face the certainty of breaking up my team.'

The talk now was that Fred and Ginger were both so determined to sever the partnership that RKO had to find ways and means of hinting at the inevitability of its happening sooner rather than later, if as painlessly as possible. The studio even revealed that Fred's next partner would not be Ginger, but Harriet Hoctor, who had appeared in *The Great Ziegfeld* and was about to go into the next stage production of the Ziegfeld Follies. But this turned out to be a kite that need never have been flown. Berman realised that Ginger was still safely in the bag for at least one more film. There were some critics, however, who were not sure whether that was a good or a bad thing.

For the first time there was less than unanimous approval for an Astaire–Rogers film.

Howard Barnes was totally committed to Fred's and Ginger's performances in the picture. 'They have never performed with more exquisite finish,' he reported in the New York *Herald Tribune*. But, he said, 'It is high time that Fred Astaire and Ginger Rogers were relieved of the necessity of going through a lot of romantic nonsense. The vast success of *Swing Time* is more of a tribute to them than the material of their latest song and dance carnival.'

And in London, the *Daily Telegraph* ventured to say:

Fred Astaire and Ginger Rogers are so firmly entrenched in the affections of their public that a little criticism is not likely to affect the success of their latest picture *Swing Time*. I thought parts of it rather dull. The plot is even more inconsequential than usual; the situations and dialogue not so funny.

In two important respects, however, *Swing Time* is well up to standard. There are a number of songs surely destined to haunt the ear for months to come and the dancing is as brilliant as everything even this gifted pair has ever done.

So what more could anyone ask?

RKO, for their part, wanted no more doubts. The next Astaire film would be with Ginger Rogers and that was all there was to it. The press, however, were not so easily convinced. Ginger's unhappiness with her fate as an also-ran to Astaire was not easily hidden. The two 'starring' vehicles that she was promised for her appearances without Fred were not even sops to her disappointment. Every one of them looked like being forgotten the moment 'The End' had flashed on to the screen. The rumours of dissent in the ranks were out in the open again. So RKO decided it had to despatch emissaries to deny the very idea.

Any suggestion that the film partnership between Fred Astaire and Ginger Rogers may be broken either by Mr Astaire or Miss Rogers is as fantastic as anything even in the films can be, [declared the studio's top writer, Dwight Taylor, who had worked on *Gay Divorce*, *Top Hat* and *Follow The Fleet*.]

In temperament, [he agreed,] these two players are strongly contrasted, but there is a terrific artistic affinity between them. The moment they start to work together, they bring out the very best in each other and they both know it.

You can discount all the stories about professional jealousy between Mr Astaire and Miss Rogers. No such thing exists. They are the most complete team in Hollywood.

Mr Astaire is greatly concerned over what people think of his work. In spite of his enormous success, he suffers from the fear of failure. He worries.

He considers every detail of his work over and over again with the genuine apprehension of a sensitive artist. Miss Rogers, on the other hand, is more like the traditional trouper, concentrating every energy on her work. Not ignoring what people will think of her, but being satisfied that they will think the best of her if she does the best that is in her. Very few stars of her fame, ability and beauty are so conscientious. She works herself completely out, sees the results in the studio projection room, says 'I must do better than that', and begins all over again.

As for Fred, before anything else, he was going to take his holiday and this one was going to prove profitable. On his way to England with Phyllis, he stopped off in New York and did six fifteen-minute radio shows – at $4,000 a piece. When he finally arrived at Southampton, he contented himself with: 'There is not a word of truth in (the rumours). We shall, each of us, make films on our own, but we shall also make films together.' It was the first intimation that Fred did, indeed, plan to make films without Ginger in the future.

But he emphasised, 'Any idea that we are jealous of each other or have quarrelled is simply silly. We are the best of friends.'

Back in London, he was being treated as a local boy made good. It was his first visit to the capital in two years and that, he declared, was at least twelve months too long. 'I have never liked to be away from England for more than a year' – and he was sure that went for Phyllis, too.

Reporters and photographers gathered around him, but uncannily

117

let him escape – while they tried to get the latest word from Hollywood via the lips of fellow voyagers Ethel Merman and producer Joseph Schenck. The fact that Fred had his hat pulled down over his eyes might have had something to do with it.

'Just a moment, Miss Merman,' shouted one reporter. 'One word more, Mr Schenck, please.' And no one noticed either Fred or Phyllis.

Safe into the customs hall, the Astaires hid behind a massive pile of luggage. Outside, it seemed Fred was only interested in one thing – the date and place of the next race meeting. It would give him a chance to catch up with Jack Leach again.

And racing they went. If Fred won on the course, both cheered. If he lost, Phyllis comforted her husband with the knowledge that she, too, thought that the horse had behaved 'dweadfully'.

Fred was no longer an owner himself. He had sold Nick the Greek after it had won the Glasgow Plate for him, and the rest of his British stable because he realised that escaping from Hollywood was getting more and more difficult. But he did have racing ambitions for when he got back home. He was spending more time with horses in the States than he had before, and he loved every moment of it. One day, he promised himself, he was going to establish his own stable at Santa Anita.

Everything he did on this English trip he did in a hurry – whether it was buying a couple of new suits, a dozen ties or giving an interview to C. A. Lejeune, the celebrated critic of *The Observer*. He talked to her in just three-and-a-half minutes flat. Miss Lejeune, who was one of the most respected film specialists in Fleet Street, had been waiting for that interview for more than two years. She had kept watch on the sailing lists week by week in the hope of finally catching up with Astaire. Eventually, she spotted his name and discovered that he would be staying at Claridges. On the day they met, she found him in the hotel lobby as he was about to rush through a side door, his coat-tails flying.

He was restless, she discovered, but 'charming and courteous, too'. He could not understand why people were interested in mobbing him, he told her. 'That sort of thing's silly and embarrassing. I've been in shows since I was seven. They could always see me. I've not changed.'

Was he limbering up for a new film? No. Work was always a matter of 'practice and thinking about ideas'. But he didn't like practising in public – because it was like reading a book with someone looking over your shoulder.

'I can't sing,' he told her. 'So why should I worry? It's all part of the routine and a new routine is the only thing that matters. I'm no better than I was when I was seven. Only more people see me.'

The strange thing is that Astaire was about to experience the biggest single audience of his entire career – and almost nobody would see him at all. He was having another go at radio.

This development had begun at the tail end of Fred's holiday. He and Phyllis had gone over to Paris and were enjoying themselves immensely – mostly because they were able to keep out of the gaze of over-enthusiastic fans and newspaper men. But Johnny Green, who had conducted the orchestra for Fred on his records of film tunes on the Brunswick label, managed to reach him.

Green had been working with Jack Benny on the Jello programme, which was beamed from New York through the Young and Rubican advertising agency. The firm was now anxious to land Fred Astaire for their Packard motors show. Green, a dashing young man who never had any doubts about his own abilities, said he could achieve what Young and Rubican had hitherto failed to pull off: contact Fred Astaire.

Green found out the name of Fred's hotel – which in itself was no mean feat – and arranged a meeting at the Vendôme a few days later. 'Come for lunch,' said Fred.

Over that lunch, Green told Fred about the Young and Rubican offer, and then handed him a piece of paper. It was a contract giving Green the option to play on the programme if Fred accepted. Fred did accept and signed.

Again, he was going to have to dance on a small floor in front of two microphones and because, as he has said, he 'likes to cover ground' that was going to be as limiting to him as any one of the other problems faced by a dancer in sound broadcasting. To complicate matters still further, he and Ginger were about to start yet another new film, *Shall We Dance*.

But he went into the radio show in the same spirit in which he embarked on any project, by treating it as the most important thing in his career and as if his whole professional future depended upon it – which, in a way, it might have done. Had he made a mess of the shows the disapproval of millions would have shown itself instantly.

But he didn't mess up anything. Astaire's own unique personality pulled him through. As John O'Hara has said, it was the trust that people always had in him that came to the fore during those weekly hour-long shows.

O'Hara wrote years afterwards in *Show* magazine:

All you got was what you heard – although what you heard was Charlie Butterworth, Johnny Green's music and the nimble beat of the feet of Fred Astaire.

Nobody was troubled by a nasty suspicion that the sounds were being made by a George Wettling or a Dave Tough or any other trap drummer. We the people just took for granted that Fred Astaire was dancing, that every precise click we heard was made by Astaire's feet on a studio floor, and not by my friend Wettling with a pair of sticks and a wood block.

If you were acquainted with Astaire you knew that he could pick up a pair of drumsticks and beat out a steady daddy-momma or an accurate rim shot any time he chose; but the radio programme advertised his dancing, not his drumming and we trusted him.

Variety left no doubt that Astaire was making its duty of recording show business history a lot easier. It had something to report:

Astaire, of course, is Astaire, which means he gives out with heaps of personality. A lot of his charm comes across the kilocycles.

His manner is easy, his reading of lines clear, his singing voice bouncy and likeable. When he dances, the hoof beats become a new form of radio entertainment.

This was an almost unanimous verdict. But the *New York Post* took their time to succumb to Fred Astaire, the radio star.

After a long interval of inattention, [wrote their radio critic] we tuned in last night to the Fred Astaire Show.

At last hearing, fairly remote from the past, we came out of the hour with a rather lukewarm reaction . . .

Mr Astaire is now being given material which is a good fit for his informal manner of delivery.

No performer is equal to speaking awkward phrases in a glib manner and last night's script was as easy as its delivery.

Green and Astaire, meanwhile, were getting along like a studio on fire. They laughed a lot together and seemed to spend as much time kidding about linguistic acrobatics as they did on dancing and playing the piano.

A feature of the series was Astaire singing and reciting in dialect – 'I Love Louisa' in German: 'Christopher Columbus' in Italian and a couple of numbers featuring Englishmen and Scots thrown in for good measure. Green has described him as 'like a sophomore playing his first part in a high school dramatic play'.

He was hilarious and successful. But again and seemingly from nowhere, all his uncertainties crept back. Suddenly, he would complain that he was no dialectician and scream that he was just not good enough at it. Then finally, when he had cooled down, he'd sidle up to Green and ask him if perhaps it was quite as bad as he had feared. Green's assurances that he was as brilliant as ever consoled him only up to about an hour before transmission time. Then, all the old nervousness would re-occur. But no one listening would ever guess.

He could be just as disarming to Green himself – in play. When the conductor had finished a particularly ornate arrangement of 'The Piccolino', Astaire could comment dryly: 'Why don't you give yourself something that you can play?' To which Green replied: 'I'll have to remember that next time you practically break your ankle.'

One writer described Astaire's mastery of these antics as 'charming and insouciant', but at the end of the thirty-nine-week series, Fred called a halt. He had had enough. Phyllis preferred him knocking his brains out working on the routines for his films – if he had to work at all. She hoped that before long he would be able to give up show business and lead a more gentlemanly existence, but if he did have to work, the films were much more rewarding than standing in front of a microphone.

Radio was, however, *the* medium of the day. People who couldn't afford the price of even a suburban cinema ticket, could gather round a battered old radio set in their homes. But he had made his decision, and, although he would occasionally regret not carrying on with the work, he never again had his own regular radio series. One of the problems was that all the time he was rehearsing and broadcasting on the Packard Hour he was having to add on to the day already cut out for him on the set of *Shall We Dance* – which again had Pandro Berman producing and Mark Sandrich, who by now had established for himself almost a divine right to sit by the camera on an Astaire–Rogers set, directing.

The big songwriting team this time were the Gershwins. It seemed to be an unwritten law that the music on these films had to come from one of the big four – Porter, Berlin, Kern, or George Gershwin (with his brother Ira writing the lyrics).

For *Shall We Dance*, three out of the six Gershwin numbers became standards, 'They All Laughed', 'Let's Call The Whole Thing Off' and 'They Can't Take That Away From Me'. Of the other three, 'Slap That Bass' and '(I've Got) Beginner's Luck' were better than most of the songs heard in films of that time, and only the title song ever sounded less than strong. The story was, as usual, as weak as Hollywood tea. But that mattered no more now than it ever did. Fred this time was a ballet dancer who strangely enough looked just as good in top hat, white tie and tails as he did in a leotard.

The sensation in the film – and there always had to be one of those – was the sight of Fred and Ginger dancing on roller skates. They did this to the tune of 'Let's Call The Whole Thing Off' and the whole production number took an estimated thirty-two hours in preparation and four days in shooting. The pair covered approximately eighty miles in the process. The finished number lasted precisely two minutes forty seconds on the screen.

The roller skating trip through Central Park was Hermes Pan's idea. The notion of Astaire doing a dance in the engine room of a ship came from Pan, too – after noticing how Fred danced instinctively to the rhythm of a cement mixer they passed together on the street near the studio.

Shall We Dance itself was performed by the chorus, all wearing masks of lifesize photographs of Ginger's face.

There was one other important dance routine that Fred had in the picture – but it wasn't with Ginger. RKO had decided to bring Harriet Hoctor into *Shall We Dance* after all, even though she wouldn't be taking Ginger's place. In the picture's finale number, 'They Can't

Take That Away From Me', it is Hoctor not Rogers, with whom Astaire is dancing.

It was, however, all Fred's and Ginger's picture. Ginger told *Picturegoer* magazine in October 1936: 'Having Fred as a partner and Hermes Pan for dance director has been a tremendous help to me. I know that I was better when dancing with Fred than I have ever been by myself. So he must get the credit. Fortunately, however, my style of dancing fits in perfectly with his. It's a sort of feminine Fred Astaire style, if you know what I mean.'

This was a time for people to do some sums. A cartoon feature syndicated in American papers at the time noted that Fred and Ginger spent an average of 450 hours dancing together when working on each of their films. Another writer accepted the already published fact that they had covered 100,000 miles together, but said that when the rehearsal time was also taken into account, this had to swell to a massive 350,000 miles.

People wrote to Fred worrying about the cost this must involve, since no pair of shoes could last a fraction of that. No, he agreed, they could not. He paid $16 a pair for his size 8½ dancing shoes and he reckoned they could stand up to no more than ten miles of the use to which he subjected them. That, he estimated, was about a week in real terms. Needless to say, he always wore an old, worn-in pair for rehearsals, shoes that would match the old slacks held up by one of those old ties.

But the statistics went on. Since Fred and Ginger spend approximately a fifth of their time off the floor, said one expert, 'they have been in the air together for nearly four weeks'.

But how much longer? Finally, the announcement was made: In the next Fred Astaire picture, he will be without Miss Rogers.

Who's Your Lady Friend?

The way had been paved by the rumours, the counter-rumours and the leaks. But when the decision was finally announced that Ginger Rogers would not be in the next Astaire movie, it was still a shock to their fans.

The film was going to be an adaptation of the P. G. Wodehouse story, *A Damsel In Distress* and would be set in contemporary England, but filmed, of course, on the RKO lot. The man who wrote Jeeves had a story that the studio wanted to handle but RKO decided to put its own scriptwriters on to the job. When finally, even Pandro S. Berman agreed that their screenplay bore little resemblance to the Wodehouse story, he asked the expatriot Briton to have a go himself.

To an Anglophile like Fred the tale set in a quaint stately home seemed to be perfect. But with the certainty that Ginger wouldn't be in it, who could possibly take her place? It was a question much more easily asked than answered.

The filling of the vacancy almost reached the dimensions of the search for a Scarlett O'Hara two years later. One report said that Astaire would have five dancing partners in *Damsel In Distress*, which was something of an exaggeration – although, as it turned out a little later, if you included a few brooms as partners it was nearer the mark.

When it was realised that the new leading lady would probably have to be English – Mr Wodehouse let it be known he wouldn't have it any other way – all sorts of other names were mooted. Jessie Matthews was one – she had been busy dancing over counterpanes and singing with such a perfect upper-class English accent that she now seemed an obvious choice; specially since British critics had been trying to get her together with Fred for years.

In a moment of sheer panic, even the name Ruby Keeler came up, but she wasn't English either.

As the names were tossed about like press cuttings in a Hollywood office, stories about the possible rift between Fred and Ginger reached a crescendo. There could only be one reason that the pair had split up, the gossips decided. They hated the sight of each other and couldn't bear to be in one another's company. Matters were hardly helped by the intervention of Ginger's mother. Mrs Leila Rogers told pressmen, 'Ginger never had anything against Fred, nor has he against her. But she will be glad to get away from the team. Ginger is not only a dancer, but a screen personality and an actress.'

Fred said he was sure that the next film after *Damsel In Distress* would be with Ginger but it was getting harder and harder to find new stories. 'The more our films succeed, the more we have to live up to, and it seems the longer we have to wait till the right story comes along,' he declared.

Mark Sandrich was less certain that there could be a continuing relationship between Fred and Ginger. 'You see,' he told Paul Holt, of the London *Daily Express*, 'the snag we're up against is that we have to keep to the same story formula, not because we want to, but because at the slightest deviation, the public squawks. I don't think the public wants new things half as much as the people who advise the public.'

And Astaire and Rogers just couldn't be put in any other kind of movie. 'They are unique in this way – they are superb at supplying their own comedy. Generally, you get a character comic supporting to put in the fun. But these two can beat them every time.'

Yet, asked Mr Holt, was there truth in the stories that they really did hate each other?

'Just this much,' replied Sandrich. 'They're scared of losing their identities. Every time they see that group of letters 'Astaire–Rogers' in a headline, it makes them sick in their stomachs.'

Fred, he decided, was 'an ole worryguts. The only difference between his worrying in a stage show and his worrying in a film studio is that with films he's only got his dancing feet to fret over. Rest is none of his darn business.'

Which might have been summed up with a comment of 'So there!'

As for Ginger? 'She's a darling. She's just a hardworking little girl as genuine as they come. Her only fault is an inferiority complex. She doesn't know how good she is. That's a strange thing in a star. Generally, when they get famous, they dig up ancestors and an intelligence that nobody ever dreamed they had.'

Fred was very plainly unhappy about that piece. He ringed in red pencil the passage in Holt's article about the two stars being scared of losing their identities and sent it back to the writer with a covering letter.

'Ginger Rogers and I,' he wrote, 'are the best of friends and there has never been anything but COMPLETE HARMONY ever since we have done our pictures together. The only reason we are doing separate films at present is because of story material.

'We, at the moment, have not got a satisfactory story and, therefore, have decided that until one is prepared to our liking, each of us will do a picture with other co-stars.'

He was almost as angry about that rumour as he was about another that said he was knock-kneed. 'Here,' he told a reporter. 'You can't push my knees together, if you tried. Try it.' The newspaperman could not.

Having proved that Fred's legs were as perfect as the insurance company believed, the reporter asked him about the rumours concerning Ginger. Particularly a recent one that said they had thrown pots of make-up at each other. 'That's just as true as rumours that I'm knock-kneed,' he declared.

'This back-fence talk about Ginger and me not getting along is one of the most ridiculous rumours that ever came out of Hollywood. There's never been the slightest difficulty between us.

'I'd like to say that she's the nicest person in the business.'

The stories seemed to die down after that – particularly with the announcement that, really, Fred would have no new partner in *Damsel*. Instead, he would have most of the dance routines entirely to himself. He would, however, have a co-star – but she wouldn't do any dancing at all, apart from an occasional stroll with Fred.

And she wouldn't be English either. But the aristocratic Joan

Fontaine, sister of Olivia de Havilland, cousin of the British aviation pioneer and a descendant of one of the Norman conquerors of Britain, seemed to measure up to most people's requirements at RKO.

There were the usual misunderstandings and traumas in the film. Fred was an American dancer who helps Lady Alyce Marshmorton (Joan Fontaine) escape from a fate worse than death.

There was also George and Ira Gershwin. They provided two classics for a film which, in retrospect, really didn't deserve them – 'Nice Work If You Can Get It' and 'A Foggy Day', the latter sung by Fred in full evening dress, sitting on a farm gate and contemplating life as the mist swirls around him. For that number, Fred demonstrated as perhaps he never had before, his signal art of handling a song's melody and lyric as though they had been fashioned precisely for his own vocal chords. Neither he nor Pan considered devising a dance routine for this number. It was a singer's song and Fred showed yet again just why the leading composers rushed to have him perform their work. He respected what they wrote for him.

Ira had particular reason to be pleased: he wrote the lyric in just twenty minutes flat.

Fred showed much the same devotion to his work singing probably the strangest Astaire song of all – 'The Jolly Tar and the Milkmaid'. It was an Elizabethan style madrigal for which he joined Jan Duggan, Mary Dean, Pearl Amatore and Betty Rone. Constance Collier hovered in the background.

But what about the comedy, that ingredient which Mark Sandrich had said was so well supplied by Fred and Ginger themselves when they were together?

Here, Pandro Berman had a stroke of genius. He borrowed George Burns and Gracie Allen from Paramount. The zany vaudeville act of Burns and Allen was one of the great joys of American entertainment of the period. On radio, George would ask Gracie why she insisted on putting salt in the pepper pot and she would reply: 'Everyone takes the salt when what they really want is the pepper. This time when they take the wrong one, they'll be right!'

The idea was that George would play Fred's press agent and Gracie, his secretary. Berman rightly believed it would be great casting. So did George Stevens, the director. It was up to Fred to decide as he had the final right of approving the cast – and particularly who was to dance in the pictures. There were plans for comedy dance routines with Burns and Allen. This worried George and Gracie, who were getting $10,000 a week for six weeks work – if Fred gave the scheme his stamp of approval. With Gracie, there were few problems. She came from a long line of Irish dancers and felt sure she could cope with anything Astaire wanted, particularly since he didn't have her in mind to replace Ginger.

The trouble was George, who seemed to be nothing more than one of the funniest men who ever trod a stage; who even pointed his cigar with great wit. But dance? As he says himself, he was a 'right-footed dancer'. He could hop a bit with his right foot, but his left foot had to be seen to be believed and after giving up his vaudeville dancing act, he preferred not to let anyone see it.

'My left foot always lays off.' If Astaire saw the way he danced, he'd be out of a job. And that would have been tragic for him. He not only liked the idea of making $10,000 a week, he greatly admired Astaire and the way he dressed.

'It used to take three neckties for me to keep my pants up. He made me ruin a lot of ties, that guy.'

Eventually, he remembered a team of two vaudeville dancers with whom he and Gracie had played on the same bill a couple of times. They had a routine with a pair of whiskbrooms – brushing each other off in syncopation, with the brooms in effect becoming additional legs. Burns invited the surviving member of the duo to come and stay with Gracie and himself so that they could be taught the routine. The man stayed and got $500 for his trouble. It was $500 well spent.

Burns asked Fred if he would like to see a new dance he had devised. Fred said yes, he would – and he loved it. The whiskbrooms would be ideal for the film.

Just as always, Fred adapted and tailor-made the routine to his own requirements – in a room surrounded by mirrors, so that every step would be watched from every possible angle and the right moment recorded by the camera. And, as he danced, Hermes Pan watched intently – so that he could then copy and put on paper what Fred might very easily have forgotten.

The whiskbroom dance was embroidered to include a dance seemingly done by empty suits of armour that had stood inside the baronial mansion.

With Burns and Allen and the three brooms, Astaire had his five partners.

'It's a hell of a dance,' Fred told George – who now comments: 'So instead of Fred teaching me to dance, I taught him. At the finish of the picture, I took the whiskbrooms home. I didn't want him to use them again in case I could work up a routine with Gene Kelly.'

Fred worked as hard on that picture as any other he had ever been engaged in. He would get to the studio and go over the same steps for hours until they looked as good as when he had first improvised and paced them out.

When others gave suggestions, he considered them kindly. But, as Burns recalls, 'he didn't baby anybody. He's the nicest, kindest, most considerate man. You'd never know he was the star. But you've got to do it his way. When Fred Astaire makes a step that's the step you've got to do.'

And that was precisely what the public paid their money to see. In *Damsel In Distress*, they saw another side to Fred Astaire – Astaire, the drummer. He had for years had a way with drums, being able to make the sounds as nimble as those he produced from the taps on his shoes. But now he was showing audiences how he could co-ordinate the drumsticks with what he did with his feet.

At one stage, he was working so quickly that the microphone couldn't cope with it all. So he had to slow down the beat. To the people who paid money to see films in 1937 it was a fascinating sight – Fred Astaire in white tie and tails playing the drums as excitedly as a musician in a smoke-laden Harlem jazz club.

It was all very much set in England, Hollywood style. Fred sings 'Nice Work If You Can Get It' in a fog-laden street. The only problem was that the fog was patently finding it difficult competing with the bright and obviously very hot Californian sun shining above.

Reginald Gardiner, as the family butler (up to no good) was the typical stage Englishman, who despite his real British nationality did nothing to discard every cliche that the plot demanded. Miss Fontaine looked elegant. But it was Fred's film – and Burns and Allen's too. And with the sort of score they provided, also the Gershwins'.

It was to be the last film on which George Gershwin ever worked. In July 1937, five months before *Damsel In Distress's* release, he died.

Was starring Fred in a film without a partner a good idea? The man for whom a team sounded like a pair of horses was never again to try going it quite so alone in a musical.

'The missing link between a smash Astaire hit and just good film fun,' said the *New York Journal*, 'is Ginger Rogers.'

Pick Yourself Up

It was a situation that couldn't last. Both Fred and Ginger – not to say Pan Berman and the other executives at RKO – realised that to make money, the team had to stick together. With that thought in mind, the studio announced that the next Astaire picture would be Astaire–Rogers again. The title would be *Carefree* – which, as anyone who knew Fred could testify, was hardly an appropriate description of his attitude to life.

One writer commented at the time: 'He doesn't relax worth a darn. Even while he's phoning, his hands move and he crosses and recrosses his feet.'

The way most people relaxed in Hollywood was to go to parties where the singers would vie with each other to get to the piano and try to stay 'on' the longest; the dancers would require no persuasion whatever to show what magnificent artists they were.

But, as George Burns remarked, 'You expect marvels when you see Fred Astaire. But at parties, he didn't get paid, so he just did what everybody else did on the dance floor.' That never ceased to disappoint all the other guests, but Phyllis, who liked to keep her 'Fweddie' to herself, was delighted.

The few occasions that Fred did accept party invitations gave them a rarity value among the Hollywood set. For hostesses, it was a magnificent game of one-upmanship that you failed to win at your peril. For her social background alone, Phyllis was a catch at any time but she played along with Fred – going when he wanted to go, staying away when he preferred to remain at home. It had to be a top-flight band, Benny Goodman was a finishing touch for anyone's function, to get Fred to open up and even join in the festivities.

Bosley Crowther of the *New York Times* wrote: 'Somehow, you have the feeling when he walks into the room that at any moment he is going to swing into a dance. He has the "swingy" grace of every musical comedy hero he has ever played.

'His smile spreads all over his boyish face and he tilts away back on his chair when he sits down to talk. To look at him it all came natural.'

This reluctance to perform on private occasions didn't mean that Fred was not prepared to have fun with his own little circle of friends. At one time, his favourite gambit was to dress up as Stan Laurel – the resemblance was quite amazing.

The day after *Damsel In Distress* was shown and there was nothing more Fred could do but worry about it, the Astaires and Randolph Scott took off for Mexico to go quail shooting. But they found it hard getting past the border because they didn't have enough pictures for their passports. They had the wrong sort of permits for their guns. And to make things worse, even if they had the right guns for the job, the bullets didn't fit.

In a local photographers' studio, Fred sneaked in unrecognised and had his required six passport pictures taken despite the fact that he hadn't shaved for two days. No-one gave any hint that the man behind the crude camera recognised his subject. But on the way back – with bullets bought and used on the quail safely in the bag – Fred saw that he had been wrong. A bewhiskered Astaire, looking more like a refugee from a gangster movie than the star of *Top Hat*, was staring out from the window of the photographer's shop in six life-size poses.

Where he really unwound was on the racetrack and racing was just about the only thing that could possibly take his attention away from complicated dance routines in the studio. More than once he was spotted leaving the set to make a phone call to his favourite bookmaker. Probably second only to the track in Fred's affections was the golf course which fortunately, was also high up on Phyllis's list of recreational priorities.

Carefree enabled Fred at last to combine business with pleasure.

In the film, Fred did a golf routine that is now remembered as nostalgically as the shooting of the men in *Top Hat* and the dancing of 'The Continental' in *Gay Divorcee*. While an off-screen orchestra played 'Since They Turned Loch Lomond Into Swing', Fred swung his golf-clubs with the precision of a surgeon doing open-heart surgery. It wasn't a dance in the conventional sense, but Fred made the clubs and balls swing rhythmically at his command. As usual, it was the result of dozens of takes over a period of two weeks – and was achieved only by the loss of over six hundred golf balls.

Part of the success of the number was due to the composer of the score, Irving Berlin, the only writer whose name habitually appeared on film credits in type either as big or even bigger than that used for the stars.

Carefree was not vintage Berlin, but the little man who only played his upright piano on the black notes, produced some pleasant enough numbers. One of the best was 'I Used To Be Colour Blind' which, in typical Berlin style, was written to Doctor Astaire's prescription. No other songwriter has ever been able to provide songs that so perfectly match the requirements of a certain artist. Berlin made a profession of doing just that – right from the time he wrote Al Jolson's crie-de-coeur 'Let Me Sing And I'm Happy'.

He wrote 'I Used To Be Colour Blind' because he was told *Carefree* was going to be the first Astaire–Rogers production in colour. But the disappointing income from *Damsel In Distress* – it hardly came near the Astaire–Rogers productions – made Pan Berman and the men who controlled RKO's finances think again. It was one reason for Fred deciding that, before long, not only should he and Ginger part permanently, but he and RKO should go separate ways, too.

Carefree was, however, a *very* notable production. For in this film, at last Fred and Ginger actually do get to kiss – and seemingly for a very long time.

All sorts of new rumours had gone round as to why the two stars never did do that huddle. Ginger's feelings of embarrassment at possibly upsetting Phyllis had become magnified into tales of Mrs Astaire positively insisting that her husband should never kiss another woman. Fred constantly denied they were true. So for *Carefree* he decided to end the speculation for good – especially since a fan magazine had headlined a story 'Why Won't Fred Kiss Ginger?' And added four question marks to emphasise the importance of the query.

The historic clinch came at the end of the 'Colour Blind' number.

The dance was done in slow motion and the kiss with it, with an additional few seconds ordered by the director Mark Sandrich – who was back in what many considered to be his rightful position – so that the scene could dissolve comfortably.

When the rushes of this historic number were ready, Phyllis decided that it was one moment when she ought to remember her responsibilities as a wife. She went along to the studio with Fred, which in itself was cause for speculation. At the end of the viewing session Phyllis looked at her husband – and said she noticed just how much he seemed to have enjoyed the experience.

Audiences especially relished it. People could be heard actually saying as they left the theatre, 'Fred's finally kissed Ginger.'

If the women were particularly captivated at the idea, the men could rejoice that Ginger never looked more beautiful. Since in *Carefree* she actually falls in love with Fred before he is smitten with her, the brittle front she adopted in the other films is softened as much as were the skin tones captured by the camera.

Berlin's one real hit tune of the film, 'Change Partners', seemed to have a symbolic ring about it after all the rumours of a split between the two stars – although the impact was reduced by the fact that *Carefree* did represent something of a reunion. 'Change Partners' stood on its own simply as a good song, which was more than could be said for most of the other numbers in the picture.

People didn't go round singing 'I Used To Be Colour Blind' as they had almost every number in the earlier Astaire–Rogers films and 'The Yam', the speciality piece in *Carefree* was more notable for its intricate steps than for its hummable qualities. It was a perfect example of the precision that Astaire insisted upon for all his routines. Every step had been considered and weighed against possible snags at least three weeks before filming began.

'It's a simple step,' Fred told the *New York Post* in August 1938. 'Just a little shuffle. Any amateur can do it. I'm pretty sure the kids will pick it up' – and then he demonstrated what he meant.

'Steel springs seemed released in his legs as he took a series of long steps and did the little shuffle,' said the paper.

Now Fred was telling people that he consulted Ginger before finalising routines. 'I've grown to rely on her judgment,' he told the *Daily Mail* in London. Certainly, changes grew out of chats between dances with Ginger and frequently entirely new routines developed from these floor conferences.

Carefree had no rapturous reception from critics or audiences. But it took money at the box office and the men at RKO were quick to talk about there being yet another Astaire–Rogers vehicle soon.

Life magazine said: 'The seven previous Astaire–Rogers pictures all had plots as light as featherdown. *Carefree,* the eighth, is scarcely any heavier, but it does give its dancing stars a chance at the straight acting they both enjoy.'

But what now of Adele?

All the time that show business writers were chronicling the Astaire–Rogers story, Lady Charles Cavendish was not merely sitting at home at Lismore Castle with her memories. She and Fred were as close as ever and corresponded as regularly as they could. When she heard on short-wave radio from the States that Fred was in bed with 'flu and a temperature of 102, she made a transatlantic telephone call to find out how he was feeling.

It was just an example of how she still worried about him. As he crept towards being Hollywood's most popular male star, so his self-confidence seemed to diminish. The better he got, the less sure of himself he became.

He told Adele about this time: 'You'd think after all these years, my whole life in show business, I'd have achieved some form of security, that I'd have earned at least that. But no, I've got less now than when I started.'

She knew he worked hard, but the old trouper in her couldn't resist offering a few words of occasional criticism to her younger brother when she thought it was needed. But he didn't always like it. 'You give him one little criticism and he grows mad,' she told *Variety.*

Fred's temper could be very hot at times, but it usually stayed at boiling point just briefly, and quickly he was his cooler, more analytical self again. 'Yes,' he would say on reflection. 'You're right. It stinks.' Then it was back to the physical drawing board of the set.

Meanwhile, Adele was secretly wondering whether she ought

135

to get back to work herself. And almost everybody in the business who thought they might have some influence was itching for her to do so.

Her first tentative steps in that direction came in a short radio broadcast she did in 1938, for RCA. One writer commented: 'This broadcast by Miss Adele Astaire should not be taken too seriously, in as much as it is extremely doubtful if she has any air, film or stage intentions. Yet this brief appearance was sufficient to indicate that any decision on professional resumption will be hers.'

She finally did make that intention known. Her decision was, finally, to go back to work.

René Clair, the French director who had had such a sensation with the Robert Donat picture *The Ghost Goes West* signed Adele to co-star with Jack Buchanan in his next film, *Break The News*.

Buchanan now revelled in the title 'the British Fred Astaire' and, indeed, there was still a similarity in their styles. Buchanan was older and taller than Fred, but he played the same sort of role and, like Astaire, looked as though he had been born in a tail coat and had worn a top hat in his pram. When he danced on the London stage, there was always a cane in his hand. When he sang, his distinctive voice was as light and almost as lyrical as Fred's.

In *Break The News*, he was going to get away from his dancing image and the film was to be a comedy without music. Indeed, it was said at the time that Adele had insisted that if she were to do the picture, a condition would be that she would not be asked to dance.

'It will be a gay comedy,' said Clair, 'planned to present two attractive personalities as they are, rather than to show what two clever players can do.'

After just two days on the set, Adele decided to break some news herself. She wasn't going on with the picture.

'I felt it was not the right part for me,' she declared. 'It was really a straight part and I didn't like the idea of not having dancing and singing to do.' So much for conditions. Finally, she added: 'Then I thought of my brother Fred and how disappointed he would be, and of the stage audiences who remembered me and the young people who have never seen me – and I imagined them saying: "So that was what she was like!" I felt I couldn't go on with the part.'

The news was disappointing to more than just Fred – who had an obligation to RKO to make at least one more film – and probably one with Ginger at that.

He did, however, have enough time between shooting schedules to think of the world in general, and away from the hurly-burly of Hollywood. Fred was one of a group of movie stars who signed what was termed a 'declaration of independence' – calling on President Roosevelt and Congress to sever all economic relations with Germany. A boycott, the declaration said, would last 'until such a time as Germany is willing to re-enter the family of nations in accordance with the principles of international law and universal freedom.' The document was agreed to at a meeting of the stars and other Hollywood personalities at the Beverly Hills home of Edward G. Robinson.

Astaire's was a voice to listen to. In September 1938, for the first time, he was listed in *Who's Who In America*. He was also stated to be one of America's richest men – *the* richest was William Randolph Hearst, whose year's salary cheques had been worth $500,000. Fred came fifth in the list of best-paid actors – trailing Mae West, Bing Crosby, Charlie Chaplin and Will Rogers – after earning $127,875 in 1935, the year for which figures were now available. The money didn't necessarily impress Fred's fans, who were now constantly bombarding him with requests for old top hats, dancing shoes or anything he no longer had use for.

It was estimated that 70,000 people wrote to him every month.

Fred himself was always amused by these requests. But what interested him was the future, and apart from the dressing gown which still gave yeoman service at every preview of an Astaire film, there was little thought for souvenirs in his attitude. As he was to go on saying, he didn't like living in the past.

However, he would have been forgiven if perhaps, just once, he might have dreamed of going back to that past. *Time* magazine, without any warning, came out with the unbelievable statement that Fred Astaire was 'box office poison' and printed his photograph alongside their story as if to underline the fact. If that was Fred Astaire's 'present', then his 'past' seemed altogether more attractive.

The magazine picked up a list of stars which a major American theatre owner had published in a paid advertisement in one of the Hollywood trade journals. The strange thing was that Astaire's name was not on the original listings, although *Time* – for reasons that have never been properly explained – chose to add his name to all the others.

RKO called in their lawyers and were about to demand an apology when they decided to let the whole thing simmer down. Few people whose business was selling seats to Fred Astaire films thought he was anything like poison. Give them an Astaire–Rogers film every week, and the box office would look after itself.

Everyone now knew that wouldn't happen. Finally and with no punches pulled, RKO made the big announcement: The next Astaire–Rogers film will be the last.

The Passing Show

Nobody really expected it would ever happen. There had been too many false alarms in the past. Surely, this was just an example of how a 'final retirement' would be followed by another still 'more final retirement' a year later?

There *was* more to it this time. The Astaire–Rogers films were still making money, but the pair were not succeeding in making every step they took seem as brand-new as it really was. It was not exactly a tired look, much more a growing suspicion that audiences were asking: 'So what are you going to do to impress us next?'

What they were, in fact, going to do as a final burst was to make a film about the couple who years before were such an influence on Fred and Adele – the Castles. Looking back, it seemed almost inevitable that Fred Astaire would one day feature in a film dedicated to Vernon and Irene Castle. In the days when he and his sister were just getting going in the big time, it was the Castles who were constantly being held up to them as the couple to follow. At one time, it seemed that *Variety* would bring the Castles' name into every piece they published on the Astaires.

Now, in 1938, if one looked for a couple who were closest to the Castles in contemporary terms, it could only be Astaire and Rogers. But that very factor presented a whole host of problems. For one thing, there could be no single composer brought in at ridiculous expense to write a complete score for the picture – as there had been for all but two of the films Fred had ever made.

The music in *The Story of Vernon and Irene Castle*, just had to be old – melodies to which the Castles themselves had danced all those years before. There would be a veritable feast of hotted up nostalgia, ranging from 'Oh You Beautiful Doll' through 'Waiting For The Robert E Lee' right up to 'It's a Long Way to Tipperary' and 'The Missouri Waltz' – this last tune played as Irene Castle 'dances' with the ghostly image of Vernon soon after he is killed in the Royal Flying Corps during World War One.

And that was the second difference between 'the Castles' – as invariably the film is now known – and the fluffy, near-plotless Astaire-Rogers films that had gone before it. No longer was there the silly young man who inevitably got his wires crossed trying to date the pretty but slightly aloof young lady. Gone, too, were the big white sets that made everyone wish he lived in a house that seemed to be a cross between a palace and an operating theatre; where never a speck of dust could be allowed to intrude, or a piece of furniture get out of place.

Now there was a true story, full of all the problems people in real life have to face and culminating in the biggest problem of all – death. Neither had ever played real characters in any of their joint films before and one of the weaknesses of the picture was probably a desperate attempt not to put a dancing foot wrong on or off the ballroom floor. It was almost like the clown playing Hamlet.

The picture's progress was anything but smooth, thanks to the rather formidable Mrs Irene Castle, now Mrs Irene McLaughlin, who had been retained as technical adviser on the picture. Every item of Ginger's wardrobe had first to be approved by Irene. Every dress had to be identical to the dress Irene wore and Ginger had to wear it just as she had. The fact that Ginger was much shorter than her subject – and had to wear four-inch heels even in the other films with Fred – was not allowed to interfere with the styles that made Irene so attractive. Or which she thought had made her so attractive.

Ginger always wore a high neckline on her dresses because she felt her own neck was too thick to be exposed. When Ginger explained this to the lady, she was careful to be polite. 'Yes, I know,' said Mrs McLaughlin, 'but I never had that thick neck.'

In the *Castles* film Ginger had trouble with the riding hat she was supposed to wear, so she discarded it. But Mrs McLaughlin had other ideas. 'I wouldn't have been caught dead riding without a hat,' she told Ginger in no uncertain terms.

She even tried to get Ginger fired from this last film of the partnership and replaced by someone else. But neither Fred nor Pandro S. Berman would accept that – and doubtless the public would not have done so either. One man even wrote a letter to Fred and Phyllis threatening the life of Fred Junior, if the split with Ginger finally materialised.

Even in her young days, Irene Castle was known as 'hell on wheels' and the now matronly Irene McLaughlin was doing little more than keeping up her old reputation. She was one of the first women in public life to dare to talk about the right of girls to show their bare legs. 'Women,' she declared, 'should show off their leg lines because that is their best point.'

As for her own legs, she had dared to show them up to the top of her ankles in the best known of all the routines she did with her husband – the Castle Walk.

Irene Castle was the first girl to bob her hair and sent every other American girl – and a few in Britain too – to the hairdresser for a carbon-copy job.

Matters were not helped when Ginger decided she did not want to have her hair bobbed, although a compromise was worked out fairly soon afterwards. Neither did she want to have her hair dyed brown.

Mrs Castle was well aware of all the difficulties she was causing. 'I'm sure the studio would rather I had been dead,' she said at the time the film was being made. 'They even waited two years for me to kick off, I suspect, after I had sold them the story. But when they found that I was indestructable, they went ahead and made it.'

She was, in fact, given $40,000 for the privilege of letting RKO film her written memoirs. She was offered more money still if she took a role in the film, playing her own mother. She turned that down.

The problems with Mrs McLaughlin came to a sudden end, thanks to a brilliant idea cooked up in Pandro Berman's office. It was the year California was debating whether or not to end vivisection a – subject about which Irene was known to care even more passionately than the dresses worn by Ginger Rogers. A secretary in Berman's office casually brought to her attention the news of a referendum on vivisection, with the sound advice that her views on the matter could sway the state's decision on the matter one way or another. The former ballroom queen was duly impressed and took off for the hustings immediately; leaving the entire production crew of *The Story Of Vernon and Irene Castle* to breathe very pronounced sighs of relief.

It was not to be the spectacular film that Fred, at least, would have liked to have seen. It would have been altogether more lavish had it been in colour, instead of in black and white. But there were moments of glory that deserve to be remembered just the same – chief among them the giant map of the United States painted on the studio floor on which the Castles seemingly danced their way across the country.

Some of the events in the true Castle story were changed, although much of the flavour of their lives was retained – and Fred looked as immaculate as only he could in his Royal Flying Corps officer's uniform.

To add a touch of authenticity, Lew Fields, one of American vaudeville's great old-timers, relived a sketch he had performed 'on the boards' with Vernon Castle which must have rekindled some of Fred's own vaudeville memories.

The reaction of the press was highly predictable, with almost every writer commenting on the change in the joint Astaire–Rogers appearance. It may have been too late to matter, but they really did still seem like a single person – or, at the very least like a pair of inseparable Siamese twins.

The *New York Times* commented: 'Rogers and Astaire have been so closely identified with light comedy in the past that finding them otherwise employed is practically as disconcerting as it would be if Walt Disney were to throw Mickey Mouse to the lions and let Minnie be devoured by a non-regurgative giant.'

As if to apologise for its 'box office poison' slur, *Time* magazine let it be known they were laying out a red carpet for Astaire–Rogers and their new look.

'To say that Fred Astaire and Ginger Rogers are well fitted to fill the Castles' dancing slippers is an understatement,' the magazine commented. 'Astaire and Rogers symbolise their era just as completely as the Castles symbolised theirs.'

If the film *was* different for them, Fred's approach was not. At the first preview of the completed film in the studio, which against his usual policy he agreed to see, he developed one of his temper tantrums. The dancing images, he said, were at least two frames out of synchronisation with the soundtrack. So a delicate editing operation had to be performed – to make the taps that Fred and Hermes Pan had so carefully recorded match the Astaire–Rogers feet perfectly. No one else would have noticed it, but Fred wouldn't allow the film out of the lot till the matter was rectified.

Fred and Ginger were still saying that they would make more pictures together – even if the RKO studio was more quiet than usual on the subject. But to show that both were still crazy about each other, the studio invited the press to meet them and get a few ideas about modern dancing.

Ginger said she didn't like jitterbugging. 'It's exclusively for kids,' she declared. 'It never was meant for adults. It's far less graceful than any other dance crazes were, even the Charleston. And unless you're still in your teens, it's too strenuous for real enjoyment. I think the jitterbug is already dying. And when he dies, he's never going to be revived.'

Fred on the other hand, was not all that unhappy about it. 'Sure, it's screwy,' he declared, 'but this is a screwy age. I've always been a swing fan and to me jitterbug dancing is visual swing. It's unrestrained and youthful and – well, it's got something. I like jam and jive and stuff. I think it's swell.

'It'll surely stay as long as the jive boys stay hot. And I hope they don't ever cool off.'

In later generations, people were to be even more critical of a twenty-year craze called rock'n roll – and Fred Astaire would be one of its defenders.

'I can't do the rhumba or any other "hip" dance,' he declared in his usual self-deprecating way.

He was much more interested in going racing – and seeing England and his 'Delly' again.

Something's Gotta Give

The end of the twilight was approaching. Chamberlain had come back from Munich waving his piece of paper and when Fred and Phyllis paid their last pre-war visit to England in May 1939, the euphoria of 'peace in our time' was beginning to wear off.

People still kidded themselves that there wouldn't be another major conflict and besides having a vacation, this was Fred Astaire's way of showing he had faith in human nature.

As the liner *Georgic* docked at Cork – Fred was introducing Phyllis to Ireland and making a stay at Adele's castle the first part of their itinerary – he said: 'We have chosen a European holiday because we like Europe and we don't believe that the folk here are so silly as to go to war.' Then, wearing a bright yellow scarf, and with Phyllis in a fur coat, they drove off with Lord Charles Cavendish in the direction of Lismore.

Fred was equally determined to show that he hadn't changed as success had followed success and his annual bill for income-tax reached the $60,000 mark. When a few days later in London, he held a press conference at the Savoy, he arrived twenty minutes early and looked, as one writer reported, 'as gay as Charlie Chaplin doing the Ocean roll in the party scene of *The Gold Rush*'.

The *Daily Express* said it was Astaire's chin that made the biggest impression – 'it goes on, like a Rolls Bentley engine mounted on a Morris Minor body'.

He told the newsmen he could dance as well in his bare feet as he could in expensive pumps. 'I love it.' he said.

Phyllis was showing great restraint. A girl who never liked to involve herself too deeply in Fred's business affairs, she was now having to suffer the one thing she always tried to avoid – answering questions posed by a nosy Press. While Fred tried to brush away the trite questions, Phyllis sat demurely in a corner of the plush room, wearing a velvet hat to match her pink lipstick. She sipped a cocktail while she tried to bury most of her face in her fur collar. When she thought no one was looking, she slipped out. 'I think she got lonely,' commented the *Express*.

When writers did get to her, they asked what one of them freely admitted was the hack question – the inevitable one about Fred and Ginger.

'It is vewy simple,' she declared. 'Miss Wogers wants to play more dwamatic parts and who can blame her? If she can star in pictures without having to do those endless wehearsals of dance woutines, she'd be cwazy not to.'

Ginger was, in fact, currently making a picture with the Astaires' close friend, David Niven.

One thing Phyllis would not allow was a picture of herself. All she had were family snapshots, and these had to remain with the family. She made no secret, however, of one fact: that best of all she liked going trout fishing and hoped to do a lot of that while in Britain. She had managed to catch a number of trout while at Lismore and Fred had tried his luck at salmon fishing – without any notable success. As Fred said at the time, he was very 'in-e-fish-ent'.

Phyllis wasn't particularly proud at having more luck in the River Blackwater than her husband. 'I'm not a perfect wife,' she said modestly. 'I can't cook. I can't sew. I hate housework. I can't look after Fwed's business affairs. All I can do is sit and look pwetty.' Which she always managed to do.

Fred himself was once more musing about the future. 'After three more years, I shall be finished as a dancer. I may begin acting in dramatic films then, I don't know.'

As usual, he and Phyllis went racing and then, leaving her behind at the hotel, he went to play golf – borrowing Douglas Fairbanks Junior's clubs in order to go round the course at Addington, Surrey, in an hour and fifteen minutes – compared with the 'par' of two hours and a quarter. On the eighteenth tee, he gave a demonstration of the 'Carefree' routine which by now had become something of a golfer's dream number – a constant subject for discussion in clubrooms where it was spoken of in hushed reverential tones. They also knew that Astaire could get round most courses in between 77 and 80. He had a handicap of five.

Some of his other fans, meanwhile, were feeling less enthusiastic towards him. The rumour had got around that he refused to give autographs – and since he calculated he had just signed something like a thousand of them, he was unhappy at the suggestion.

'After all,' he declared, 'we are merely what the public makes us and I feel we are at their service over anything like that.' Being asked to sign an autograph was always flattering.

Most of all, Fred wanted to go racing. Jack Leach was training a two-year-old called Crosswire and he wanted to see it perform.

It was in Fred's and Phyllis's judgement their first real holiday in five years – and the first without a contract with RKO. As he and Ginger finished *The Castles*, he had also finally severed his links with the outfit which had given him international fame.

What would he do when the vacation was over? MGM had signed him to make *Broadway Melody of 1939* and for some three years there had been talk of starring Fred in another biographical picture – this time as Nijinsky. Phyllis approved of that one – probably because she thought that it gave some proper recognition of his true dancing worth. But Fred was not so sure. 'It would take me three years of rehearsals before I could approach him.' The idea, he said, 'scared me stiff.'

He didn't consider himself a new Nijinsky either, simply a hoofer who enjoyed doing what he did for a living more than anything else. Now, on holiday, he was trying to spend all his time racing, fishing and playing golf. He did venture, however, that he missed being with Fred Junior and Peter, Phyllis's elder son, who was now away much of the time at boarding school.

'There's no secret about married happiness,' he declared. 'It's fate. We are the happiest couple in the world.' In the words of the press handouts that bombarded every show business writer's desk on both sides of the Atlantic, 'we're made for each other.'

Meanwhile, he was also delighted to be back once more with Adele – 'She's definitely retired. And she looks as well and happy as I've ever seen her.'

They seemed to be talking every night away with memories of the past and their thoughts on the present and future.

Hardly a day passed by without each receiving letters, telegrams and transatlantic telephone calls begging them to name their price and return to Broadway. But this team seemed as unlikely to get together again as the firm of Astaire–Rogers.

Adele admired her younger brother and loved talking about him. She was certain now that he had sex appeal. 'All the women I know tell me about it,' she said. 'In England they say they want to mother him, to nestle that funny face of his on their chinchillaed bosoms.'

What he really had, she determined, was 'sympathetic appeal'.

When the holiday finally came to a halt, Fred had to settle down to *Broadway Melody of 1939*, which was so long being discussed that it had now become *Broadway Melody of 1940*. There had been ten of these annual tributes to the street that was the real cradle of transatlantic showbiz and, although no one knew it at the time, this was going to be the last.

But who would dance opposite Fred in this magnum opus? There were no doubts whatever that it wouldn't be Ginger. But who else was there? It was MGM who finally resolved the question. They would co-star Fred – but *not* 'team' him, it was stressed – with probably the finest girl dancer of the age, Eleanor Powell. When the news of the possible partnership first broke, newspaper columnists wondered if two already established stars like Astaire and Powell could possibly work together – particularly on the terms Fred invariably imposed.

Fred, who always kept abreast of the market, greatly admired Miss Powell. He conceded that she 'danced like a man' – by which he didn't mean that she had lost any of her femininity; simply that she had the same sort of stamina and, more important, discipline that he expected of himself. But he *was* worried about her as a partner, and it was the same worry that constantly cropped up whenever a new dancer's name was considered in the context of facing him on a stage or a film set: was she too tall?

Fred, as it happened, measured 5 ft 9¾ inches and Eleanor was two-and-a-quarter inches shorter. But he couldn't be sure and he let his doubts be known to the MGM bosses.

It was Louis B. Mayer himself who suggested to Eleanor that she should make the film, but even he was worried about the height problem. It called, he decided, for a confrontation – and the scenario he adopted could have fitted beautifully into any matrimonial comedy of the period being made by his studio; he suggested that she come to his room at the same time that Fred was there – but without letting him know. While Mayer and Astaire were talking, he said, Miss Powell would be hiding behind the large wood-pannelled office door.

That was precisely what happened – although, unlike a film story – she didn't hear anything she shouldn't. The conversation was extremely complimentary to the lady. Finally, the mogul put Eleanor out of her misery and revealed to Fred that she had been with them all the time – and wouldn't it be a good idea if, once and for all, they stood back to back with each other? They did – and everything looked just fine. But with Fred what 'looked' fine was not always good enough. He had to see how they danced together before he committed himself. In the rehearsal room at the studio, specially fitted for him with long mirrors, Astaire pronounced himself content.

Mirrors played an important part in the picture itself. For the 'Begin the Beguine' number, which alone would have made this *Broadway Melody* a notable film, Fred and Eleanor danced before a sixty foot mirror that had been fixed by the engineers to a moving track. As it rotated, the mirrors had the effect of changing the backgrounds for the routine.

It was not like other dance numbers – certainly it was unlike almost any other version of Cole Porter's 'Beguine'. It was a syncopated dance to a roller-coaster speed rhythm. The tune had been written five years earlier, but neither before nor since had there been an interpretation of it quite so stunning. It was a moment to savour.

The film was in black and white, and this superb joint performance was somehow enhanced by not having colours to distact the audience's attention away from the artistry of their footwork, or of the rhythmic use of Fred's hands, which seemed to dance as much as his feet. It was probably never to be equalled.

All the music and lyrics in the film were by Porter and in one of these, 'I've Got My Eyes On You', Fred accompanied his own singing on the piano – showing another facet of his many-sided talents which was all too rarely seen by the general public. Fred's affection for the piano has also not always been appreciated. He generally had one in his bedroom and many of his own songs had their first airings on that instrument in the middle of the night.

In 1940, there were two such tunes. One was 'Sweet Sorrow' for which Gladys Shelley supplied the lyrics. The other, which he wrote with Willy Shore and Morey Amsterdam was 'Oh, My Aching Back'. Two decades later, Amsterdam was to be one of the stars of the Dick Van Dyke television show.

There was not much to be said about the story of *Broadway Melody* – no more, in fact, than there had ever been for an Astaire–Rogers picture. It was about putting on a big Broadway show, with Fred as the hard-working dancer who achieves a well-deserved success near the end of the picture. If it all seemed vaguely reminiscent of *Dancing Lady*, perhaps no one ought to have been surprised. It was in that picture at MGM that Fred had made his debut. Now, as the studio said, he was home again.

George Murphy, a song and dance man who went on to become a United States senator, was one of the other stars in the film and there were a few delightful moments too, from Frank Morgan, fresh from the title role in *The Wizard of Oz*.

But it was Astaire and Powell who made the picture – with generous help from Porter's music. One of the numbers he wrote especially for the film was the celebrated 'I Concentrate On You'. Another was 'I've Got My Eyes On You'. Which was precisely what the critics had on Astaire and Powell, wondering whether there would ever be another joint venture. As it turned out, there never would be – but the studios could have done a lot worse.

One critic wrote, however: 'Despite her funny face, funnier figure and wooden acting, Ginger Rogers found herself as Fred Astaire's dancing partner. Can Eleanor Powell follow in her footsteps? No threat to Ginger appears in the face and figure of the Broadway musical comedy star pictured at the left below.' And at the left below was a picture of – Miss Powell.

The London *Daily Express* was not much kinder.

Its critic commented:

Remember that little fellow with the scull head, dangling arms, the tiny feet that step delicately like Aggag, the narrow trousers and the crooked smile? The little fellow who danced so delightfully among the kitchen furniture? Mr F. Austerlitz he was to your Mum and Dad. Fred Astaire to you.

He's back and succeeds in making this a film to go to, a film against fearful odds. There's no Ginger.

Eleanor Powell is his dance partner. She's a nice, good-tempered girl from out of town, who keeps superb time. But she looks so strong and confident on her own, you just don't care whether Fred gets her or not – and because he dances so well around the parlour sofa, they've given him acres and acres of black glass and silken drapes and phoney twinkling stars. Even so, the Astaire charm gets through. I swear the little man could make you feel matey in a morgue.

Picturegoer magazine put it like this: 'When you see Fred Astaire in *Broadway Melody of 1940* with Eleanor Powell as his new partner, you need not feel that the little lady is just a sort of substitute for Ginger. We ought to put that straight in the first place. Already, the gossip writers are trying to drag from Fred an answer to the question: "Do you like Eleanor, as a partner, better than Ginger?" '

Neither the gossip writers nor *Picturegoer*, in its attempt at shifting responsibility for a question it dearly wanted answered itself, came up with a solution.

The film arrived in the theatres soon after Fred's optimism about the world situation was finally shattered. Europe had been 'silly enough' after all, to get embroiled in a new war. To an Anglophile like Fred, sitting at home in Beverly Hills made him feel almost isolated. Adele was still in Ireland and Astaire knew they were unlikely to see her this side of the peace settlement, whichever way that went and in 1940 no one could be sure which way that would be. Civilian overseas travel for all but the people most concerned with the war effort was an impossibility. And Fred was brooding.

'It makes me very sick to think of "my" beautiful London and England being outraged by bombs,' he wrote in October 1940 – and sent off a cheque for $500 to the American ambulance fund.

With thoughts on less weighty, but undoubtedly equally important

With Ginger.
The film is *Swingtime*.

National Film Archive

Reunion with Adele – at London's Rainbow Corner.
Associated Press

The family at home.
National Film Archive

With Triplicate.

National Film Archive

Fred and Judy Garland.
The tramps number that might have ruined an image.

National Film Archive

With Ginger again after ten years apart – in *The Barkleys of Broadway*.
Associated Press

'Triplets' – the 'other babies' are
Nanette Fabray and Jack Buchanan. (From *The Band Wagon*)
National Film Archive

With Cyd Charise, rehearsing for *The Band Wagon*. Fred's genius was to persuade people to
take their eyes off her fabulous figure.
National Film Archive

With Ava at her coming-out ball. That was the evening when they were the only ones out of step. The other couple are Anthony Quinn and his daughter.
Associated Press

Adele and Fred in 1972 – at the opening of the Uris Theatre in New York. Adele insisted on taking her own pictures.
Associated Press.

Fred Astaire in 1975.

matters, Fred sent off another note to his old friend Jack Leach. The Newmarket jockey was now in the army, but Fred was certain he still had his mind on the turf. Fred told him he had a new and infallible betting system – worked out carefully by himself and based on the form books of several years past. It was impossible, he reckoned, to put a foot wrong. Like all other systems it had its weaknesses – which he admitted in another letter to Leach about a week later.

He had tried out the system with Bing Crosby and a group of other friends, and it had proved disastrous.

'In fact,' wrote Fred, 'on the last sixteen times it hadn't picked one winner.'

Bing and Fred had been racing companions for some time. They represented a strange contrast – Fred as immaculate as ever seemingly always about to accept an invitation to the Royal Enclosure at Ascot; Bing as casual as the bales of straw in the nearby stables. When he visited the Del Mar Turf Club – 'Where the Turf Meets the Surf' as Bing describes it in the song still played at the opening of race meetings there – Fred 'brought class to the track'. Screen actor Pat O'Brien, who with Bing was one of the owners of the club, put it that way and he had to be right.

During those early days of the war, Fred kept in close touch with all his English friends. Letters went in both directions across the Atlantic, between Fred and Delly; Fred and David Niven and Fred and George Griffin, who had at one time been his valet in London.

From his house on the White City estate in West London, George began his letter: 'Dear Sir,' and told him about his recent leg injuries and about the incendiary bombs falling outside his house. 'If they had been proper bombs, 'he wrote, 'well, I would not have been writing this letter. . . .'

Niven's reminiscences were of a different and slightly more sophisticated sort, although the message was much the same. He wrote from his club, Boodles, in St James's.

His letter began: 'Dear old Fred,' and went on:

Since Dunkirk, we have been reinforcing the battalion and being one of the old boys with some experience, I was taken away and put into a special job with M.I. (don't laugh) military intelligence. Naturally, I can't tell you anything about it as I have not yet been intelligent enough to find out what I am trying to do. At least, I have managed to be in all the worst Blitz we have had, including three months in London without a day or night off during the worst period . . .

Things are getting pretty interesting again right now and we are all set to be invaded. I think he is bound to have a crack at it and if he does he will use gas and everything else that has been thought of . . .

He is apparently quite happy to lose a million men trying it, and he may be able to get considerable forces loose on the island; and enormous damage may be done before they are rounded up. . . .

It's going to be a pretty little tea party once it starts, but we are all ready for it and it can't start too soon for our liking.

That was the kind of talk Churchill had got people into the habit of using. There would be fighting on the beaches, fighting in the streets, but the old bulldog was going to win.

Niven was determined to come back to the States as soon as things sorted themselves out. 'Anyway, I hope it won't take too long as all this bombing has aged your old chum quite a bit – C. Aubrey Smith parts if it lasts much longer.'

As for show business, Niven was involved with troops concerts. He gave Fred this typical example of Army humour:

'I can't, you can't, Hitler can't.'

'Can't what?'

'Milk chocolate.'

Niven concluded:

'Well, as housemaids say when they finish a letter – I will close now – hoping this finds you as it leaves me. Best possible love to Phyll. God knows I miss you both terribly.

Yours aye,
David.'

Adele's letter came from the Mayfair Hotel in London's Berkeley Square, a plush oasis in the midst of the blackout, although even there austerity was cutting out many of things that made up the style to which people like the Cavendishes had become accustomed.

Darling Fred,
Well, a nice blitz was staged for me last night. I know what it is

like now. This is my first and I must say I have never had such an opening night in my life. Really, Fred, it was hell!

I arrived in town from Derbyshire and dined with Foxie, Dotty, Averill, Tony and an American journalist named Greig. We had our dinner in a private dining room on the ninth floor of the Dorchester and, in the middle of eating, a waiter came in and said that if we would like to see some fireworks, to look out of the window.

So we switched off the lights and at first I thought it was a fourth of July display – the flares first and the red glows in the distance. Then explosions. Anti-aircraft guns booming and the whole works. But when two or three huge fires were started – enormous red glows in the sky – I began to get jittery. And even more so when one of those suction bombs exploded nearby and my ears went funny. That all took place between 10 and 12. So we all decided to go below.

. . . So Foxie, Dotty, Greig and myself got in a car and middled down to Lansdowns House – where your little Delly (scared silly) lay on the floor in the corridor of Dotty's flat from 12 until the all-clear sound about 5.30 in the morning. Honestly, Fred, it was terrifying. Incendiary bombs fell on this roof and on Berkeley Square a bomb went off before and the lights went out. Those screaming bombs are the most maddening things. I have never heard anything like them. You know how I even hate to hear a stage gun go off.

I finally got into bed, being too stunned to venture out (just around the corner to here) where I'm parked. And anyway, its no fun in a 'blitz' alone. It isn't fun at any time, but you know how misery loves company. Those lice made a wreck of things in this part, Ritz, St James's etc – I guess it was a reprisal for our work in Berlin recently . . .

I was supposed to go to the dentist today, but I'm too jumpy to sit for teeth. Don't think I'll stay here long – but it has been so quiet for the last few weeks, I thought it would continue. Well, so long and will write later – just wanted you to know about my first raid. And I hope my last. Love to Phyllis and you,
Your
Delly.

Fred was so moved by these letters that he had them published almost immediately after receiving them.

153

Delly was not quite alone in war-time Britain. She not only had Lord Charles, who was an Army officer, but her mother was with her too. Fred sent Mrs Astaire Senior, parcels of Californian dried fruit.

'Delly' wrote to him on their mother's behalf. 'It is marvellous. Food is going to be scarce here, so it's grand to have such luxuries.'

In the States, luxuries came in more costly packages. One of these was a Fred Astaire film that might have benefited all concerned if it had been part of an economy drive and just never allowed to happen.

Second Chorus marked Astaire's entry into Paramount Studios. It came at a time when Hollywood considered its main task to be making a declaration of normality. Fred was desperately worried about England. His friend David Niven and a few of the other members of the film town's English colony may have decided their duty was to go home, but for almost everyone else in Hollywood, Europe was a long way off. Normality was escape and *Second Chorus* should have been allowed to escape without trace – but it didn't.

It was a symptom of the disease that doctors might have called Gingervitis – had they not already used a similar word for an entirely different malady.

With Ginger as a 'natural' opposite Fred, and with Eleanor Powell unavailable for more films in the forseeable future, studios seemed to develop a mental blockage when it came to completing an Astaire cast list. They refused to accept that he could more than adequately hold a dancing picture on his own and insisted, instead, on giving him a starring partner. For *Second Chorus*, Paramount chose a beautiful, dark-haired girl who could be a stunning actress; she and her husband also lived near Fred's Beverly Hills home on Summit Drive. The girl was Paulette Goddard, fresh from the triumph with her husband Charles Chaplin in *The Great Dictator*, she was not known as a dancer and *Second Chorus* hardly provided her with that additional qualification. Yet dance she did in this film – if to no one's great pleasure.

Hermes Pan did his best with her and Paulette's long legs clad in the sheerest black tights that those pre-nylon days could offer, were enticing. But she never looked like a professional dancer. The studio – as seemingly did all studios – insisted on a name to bring in the customers, while Pan would dearly have preferred an opportunity to take in an unknown who simply danced well.

Inferior film or not, Fred worked for *Second Chorus* as though he really was Nijinsky reincarnated and was about to give a command performance before the Czar and the entire Imperial Family.

The numbers, for once, were not all improvised in the studio and then developed there in front of mirrors. He did much of his planning for *Second Chorus* at the South Carolina home of Phyllis's aunt and uncle, Mr and Mrs Henry Worthington Bull. The estate at Aiken had wide open spaces that were far away from Hollywood. No risk there of being interrupted by anxious studio executives or secretaries passing on messages about rehearsal facilities.

On the manicured Aiken lawns he marked out the charted course of each routine – using white paper squares secured to the ground by stones. Each step – and each leap, too – was painted on the grass once he had touched down.

From Aiken, he maintained his correspondence with Adele and their mother – adding a few details of his *Second Chorus* routines to the family chat and his expressions of concern about the war. When they managed to get the occasional telephone call to each other, not easy in war time, he was still 'Sap' or 'Babe' and she was 'Funny Face', just as in the old days.

He could tell her, too, that Fred Junior was, at the age of five, showing the makings of a dancer himself. 'Whenever he hears music', said Fred at the time, 'he rattles around a bit.'

Not even in *Second Chorus* could anyone describe Fred's dancing as 'rattling around a bit'. But there was not much that was kind that could, in fact, be said about this story of a college boy band leader. When you realise that the college boy in question was forty-one-year-old Fred Astaire, you get some idea of the lengths to which the imaginations of audiences were expected to stretch. The story line that Fred constantly failed his exams to stay an undergraduate was not really a valid excuse.

High spots of the film were the scenes featuring the Artie Shaw orchestra – with Fred conducting the players in the midst of an elaborate dancing routine. Dressed in white tie and tails of course.

Like most of the films, it represented something like six to seven months work. It could have taken much longer, and not simply because of the problem of making Miss Goddard into a dancer. Paramount executives were reported at the time to wake up in the middle of the night in cold sweats—not knowing whether the writers of the piece would ever finish the story. When it was all finally and safely locked in the can, you could almost hear the sighs of relief around Hollywood.

Before anyone had seen the film, the studio grapevine had immodestly and inaccurately spread the word that the picture was going to be a sensation. Columnist Sidney Skolsky decided to take their word for it and said that Fred seemed 'more excited about *Second Chorus* than any picture since *Top Hat*'.

And he quoted Fred as saying: 'I picked this one myself. It's not an important story, but I think it's interesting and gives me a chance to be back entertaining. That's all I ask.'

The *New York Times* were most impressed with an interesting phrase that cropped up as the title of Fred's leading number in the picture, 'Dig It'. It was just about the first time that it had been heard outside of a Greenwich Village jive joint.

'Until Astaire adopted the expression, "dig it" was a swing term without precise meaning. He took the words literally, pressed his toe forward and down as though digging, rocked back on his heel and came up with a brand new dance step.'

The *World Telegram* concentrated on the picture itself, and was dissatisfied:

Fred Astaire's new picture at the Paramount is called *Second Chorus* but it doesn't call for any encore.

In it, he has Paulette Goddard for his leading lady and he dances once with her. But attractive and pleasant as she is, she's no Ginger Rogers – either as a dancer or as a comedienne.

Nor has the film itself any of the charm, slickness, or inventiveness which made those early Astaire–Rogers attractions such lively and entertaining fun ...

[The sting was in the tail.] Mr Astaire dances admirably and plays the role of Danny O'Neill with ease and assurance ... Good, too, were Miss Goddard, Burgess Meredith and Charles Butterworth ... but the sum total of their efforts is a lot of good talent wasted on nothing.

No one doubted that Fred and Paulette Goddard had made their first and last picture together. Early in 1941, the name of a new partner was announced. She was only twenty-two but she had a name that evoked memories of Fred's days in vaudeville.

You're Easy To Dance With

Fred Astaire could not possibly have known that the day he signed a contract with Columbia Pictures he was helping to write a chapter in the history of the cinema.

On the surface, going to Columbia was an odd thing to do. True, it was an outfit that occasionally had its moments of glory – the Frank Capra films were an example – but no one considered it any more a prestige studio now than they had when Gable was unceremoniously unloaded there.

Astaire, however, was more concerned with finished products than with the prestige of the people for whom he worked. Had he not been, he would never have stayed so long with RKO, which at one time was even more poverty-stricken than Columbia.

He also had one distinct advantage over other players who crossed the studio threshold. His name.

Harry Cohn, the iron dictator of Columbia whose reputation made him a cross between Hitler and Judas, wouldn't dare drop cigar ash on Astaire the way he did on to almost everyone else. It is even possible he muted his usual vocabulary in Fred's presence. But Astaire didn't go to Columbia because he liked Cohn, or because he was attracted by the story idea they presented to him – although it did for once take note of the fact that other nations were at war and American kids were thinking about putting on uniforms. What interested him far more was a girl he had heard was under contract at Poverty Row.

She hadn't made much of an impact, even at Columbia. She had been making a Blondie picture or two and had also had odd parts in other B pictures. But he hadn't seen them. Nor had he met her. But it was her name that fascinated him – Margarita Cansino.

By the time Fred had signed his contract, the girl had been given a new name by Cohn. The mogul thought that Cansino had no magic about it – even for an old vaudeville musician and song plugger like himself. Besides, it looked 'too foreign' for the theatre marquees and he wanted her to be the all-American girl, if not Miss America herself. (He was reportedly considering that, too.)

The name he chose for her, he thought, was much more suitable, much more American. And it was only partly made-up, because he used her mother's maiden name. She became Rita Hayworth.

Fred's interest was in her original name. He knew that she had to be the daughter of Eduardo Cansino, the man whose act with his sister Elisa had topped so many of the bills in which he and Adele were only supporting players. According to his daughter, Eduardo was second only to Nijinsky – a name that Astaire himself had heard a time or two.

Fred had watched her work and liked what he saw. Now, Harry Cohn told her that she was to get her first starring role – and her new name would be perfect for it.

He called her to his office and, as usual when it came to choosing a new Astaire partner, Fred was there, too. He had told Cohn that he believed any child of the Cansinos must be exceptional, because she would have had the best training in the world.

Rita admits today that she was more terrified about meeting Astaire than about almost anything else in her screen career. When they were introduced, she couldn't even pronounce his name properly. The sentence that tumbled out of Fred's mouth at that moment seems, on reflection, rather like the cliche that invariably followed an offer of 'I can get you a part in pictures.'

What Fred actually said was: 'Would you like to do a picture with me?'

All Rita could think of to say was 'Yes, I would.'

It was a very excited and very shy Rita Hayworth who took her

158

first tentative steps alongside Fred on the Columbia lot for a picture to be called *You'll Never Get Rich*.

As the days went by, Rita became less shy and more sure of herself. But she says now she never stopped being excited at working with Fred Astaire, a 'real gentleman'. She also experienced the usual penalty of any Astaire co-star – hard work, Astaire style.

It began slowly and with the apparently effortless Astaire limbering up, gradually formulating ideas, as he moved his feet and swung his arms.

'Well, let's try to do these little steps,' he told her. And she tried to follow him – better and faster than he had seen most of his previous partners manage.

'How can you do that so fast?' he asked her – and then provided his own answer. 'Of course, I know why – it's because your training is so excellent from your father.'

'Yes,' Rita replied. 'I've been dancing since I was three or four years old.'

Each dance routine took hours, but his personality put her at ease even if her feet didn't feel that way.

The starring debut of Rita Hayworth is now the only thing for which *You'll Never Get Rich* deserves to be remembered. It was a very slight story about a Broadway dancer who gets drafted. The locale of an Army rookie introduction centre was based on a real military camp, but Fred's uniform – he becomes an officer, of course – looks stagey and no one really imagined you could ask Fred Astaire to peel potatoes while in training.

It should have been much more notable – for Cohn now decided to take another leaf out of RKO's book and hire not just any songwriter to do the picture score, but one of the Greats, Cole Porter.

The tunes – 'The Boogie Barcarolle'; 'Shootin' The Works For Uncle Sam', 'Since I Kissed My Baby Goodbye'; 'So Near And Yet So Far' and 'Wedding Cake Walk' – give some idea of the sort of material he provided for the movie. None was in the least bit memorable; in fact, it was the only time Porter wrote a score that failed to produce a single hit.

One of the problems at the time was that ASCAP – which still proudly boasted Fred Astaire as a fully paid-up member – had called a strike and none of the new tunes were getting radio airings. Rita wasn't happy with the way the music was handled in the film, either. Harry Cohn flatly refused to allow her to sing in the picture. Since the film featured a big band, he wanted a band singer for the tunes, so when Rita mouthed the numbers, someone else's voice came out.

'I was not happy with it, I'll tell you that,' she says now.

Hermes Pan was not available to work on *You'll Never Get Rich*, so Fred himself planned most of the routines, with the help of choreographer Robert Alton. The film's director, Sidney Lanfield said he wanted it that way. 'I'm no dancer,' he declared. 'A routine may look perfect to me, but if Fred feels he was the least bit off, I'm willing to shoot again.'

The newspapers welcomed *You'll Never Get Rich* simply because it had Fred and Rita co-starring with each other.

'Filmdom's master of grace and taps, who has been in somewhat of a decline since the cycle of films with Ginger Rogers, finds a glittering partner in Rita Hayworth,' said the New York *Herald Tribune*.

Time magazine, who gave Rita Hayworth the cover, declared of Fred's new dancing partner: 'There could be no doubt that she was the best partner he ever had.'

No one noticed that Rita was barely three inches shorter than Fred – the height problem was always his big worry – her particularly low heels helped, of course.

When Columbia decided on another Astaire–Hayworth picture to follow fairly soon afterwards, Fred greeted the idea with considerably more enthusiasm than he usually accepted a repeat performance. He was as determined as ever not to be part of a 'team' again, but there was something rather special about the red-headed Miss Hayworth, who in a sweater was now brightening up many a real Army barrackroom.

Before the new Hayworth film was underway, there were two other new productions for Fred to consider. The first starred Bing Crosby; the second Phyllis Astaire. They were on holiday when she told him that she was pregnant.

A Couple Of Song And Dance Men

Ever since Ginger had given way to a host of other leading ladies, people had been asking Fred which one of them he liked best. He always shrugged the famous Astaire shoulders and changed the subject. Now, at last, he had a partner he could hold out as being head and shoulders above all the others – and for once the height just didn't matter.

In *Holiday Inn*, he was teamed with Bing Crosby – and from that moment on he had the pat answer to the inevitable question. His favourite partner was 'Bing'. Though he could have had reason to resent Mr Crosby.

For one thing, this was going to be the first Astaire film in which Fred didn't get the girl. For another, *Holiday Inn* produced the most sensational song hit of all time – 'White Christmas', which as everyone who has ever listened to a radio during the festive season knows, was Bing's hit, not Fred's.

But Fred was greeted so enthusiastically on the set that he was embarrassed.

By all accounts, Fred enjoyed *Holiday Inn* as much as any film he had ever made – and worked just as hard in it, shaping the routines as only a perfectionist could.

It was the story of a hotel owner who wanted to keep his place open just for the holidays. Bing was the owner of the Holiday Inn; Fred – the star dancing attraction who unsuccessfully tries to woo Marjorie Reynolds away from him.

Bing had most of the good songs – and 'White Christmas', which has now sold more than ninety million copies (twenty-five million of them Crosby's), was the best. Irving Berlin says of that one – 'It's quite impressive.' And that from a man who has had more hit songs than any other popular composer.

In fact, it was due to Berlin who was one of Fred's closest friends in all his years' hoofing, that *Holiday Inn* ever got on to the Paramount floor. He had long before dreamed up the idea of staging a musical show based on seasonal numbers. One of his greatest previous successes had been 'Easter Parade', and the number played more than any other on the Fourth of July was 'God Bless America' which at one time was considered likely to replace the 'Star Spangled Banner' as America's National Anthem.

The stage show never came about, but a meeting between Berlin and Mark Sandrich in New York clinched the idea of its forming a reasonable basis for a movie. Berlin wanted Crosby for the principal role and since Sandrich was now a top producer for Paramount, Bing's studio, it was a reasonable suggestion. Sandrich, for his part, thought it would be a superb idea to be able to team Mr Crosby with his old star Fred Astaire – who could, he reasoned, play Bing's ex-vaudeville partner.

It was not an easy plan to put before the bosses of Paramount. Crosby was expensive, but he was under contract, so that was fine. Astaire, on the other hand, was a free agent – and he came very costly. It was also war time and the whole nation was constantly being exhorted to economise. Fred Astaire and Bing Crosby in one picture looked very extravagant indeed.

Finally, a deal was settled – with the understanding that at least the leading lady would not be paid too much. In typical Hollywood fashion, there turned out in the end to be two leading ladies – Marjorie Reynolds whom Fred didn't get, and Virginia Dale whom he did. Neither had a particularly devastating effect on the pockets of the Paramount stockholders.

As a result of making *Holiday Inn*, no one had cause for complaint. Berlin, unloading a calendar full of seasonal melodies ranging from

'Let's Start The New Year Right' to 'White Christmas' – with 'Easter Parade' and tunes for Lincoln's birthday and the Fourth of July thrown in between – had cause to laugh hysterically all the way to the bank.

Fred was his usual impressive self – he worked in the traditional tie-belted slacks and sweat shirt for rehearsals and then, when everyone else looked like something resembling a wet herring on a fishmonger's slab, combed his hair, wiped his face and was as immaculate as always.

His tour-de-force was a dance in which he stepped in and out of lighted firecrackers for the Fourth of July number, 'Let's Say It With Firecrackers'. It took twenty-five takes to get that number right.

There were other tunes, not geared to particular holidays – including 'Lazy', which must rank as one of the prettiest of all the Berlin songs, 'You're Easy To Dance With' and 'Be Careful Its My Heart'. When Bing sang 'I'll Capture Her Heart Singing', Fred was ready with the reply 'I'll Capture Her Heart Dancing'.

As fussy as Fred was with his dance numbers, he relied extensively on the back-room boys for advice on his vocal contributions. 'What key do you want it in?' he'd be asked. 'Oh,' he would reply, 'it all sounds comfortable with my voice.'

Walter Scharf, who was in charge of some of the arrangements and orchestrations, would play over the numbers to him first and then they would try between them to settle on a suitable key.

'Fred,' Scharf told Astaire, 'this picture is likely to play for thirty years and you'll be listening to yourself all that time, so we ought to get it just right for you.' No one at the time knew that *Holiday Inn* would be that sort of film and that Scharf's rash prediction would be incredibly true.

'He was still not convinced that he was a top-notch singer,' recalls Scharf. 'If we did our side of the work properly, it was just like butter – that easy. Bing and Fred could get on with a tiger. They just tranquillised each other.'

Orchestrating for Astaire's dance numbers was not so easy. Scharf describes the task as 'like crocheting. You had to catch everything he did; all the nuances and subtleties.'

A deliberate attempt was made in the picture to capture both the charm and the warmth of Astaire's performance. So the orchestra was kept as simple as possible and with no overloading of one section by another. Astaire made it all look so easy. He was the only star anyone could remember who, without fail, arrived on the Paramount set at precisely seven o'clock every morning.

There was one particular *Holiday Inn* milestone that would not go unrecorded during production. Fred wore out his six hundredth pair of dancing shoes since first going to Hollywood; he was sure of the number because they always came from the same little Los Angeles shop which allowed him to have every hundredth pair free of charge.

Bing said that Fred worked so hard in the picture that 'I could almost spit right through him.' He recorded in his autobiography *Call Me Lucky* that Fred lost fourteen pounds while the film was being made.

As always, the film was toughest on Fred's partner – his female partner that is. Bing has never admitted to really doing any serious dancing in the picture. Marjorie Reynolds remembers being petrified making the movie, until Fred whispered encouragement to her at the start of their big number together.

A couple of months before the film opened, Phyllis completed her own major production. Her third baby – the second with Fred – was a daughter. They called her Ava. There is said to be something very special about the relationships between fathers and daughters and, as the years went by, Fred and Ava were more than to prove the point.

The success of Fred's marriage to Phyllis had always been an open secret. They still avoided parties and big social gatherings, but that only went to show the film colony how happy and self-contained they were. At a time when comedians were making popular sport about Hollywood marriages – one tale was that brides were wished 'Many Happy Returns' on their wedding day – Fred and Phyllis were conconstantly refuting the legend.

The title of Astaire's next picture, his second in 1942, seemed to be a paean to Phyllis: *You Were Never Lovelier*. It also made a strong impact on the cinema.

This was Fred's second, and as it turned out, last, vehicle with Rita Hayworth, who really never was lovelier than in this story of four Argentinian sisters. It was based on a film bought in the Argentine by the producer, Louis F. Edelman. The Latin-American locale was immensely suitable, bearing in mind Rita's own background. But the only thing to show the film was set in Buenos Aires was the orchestra of Xavier Cugat. The music of Jerome Kern and Johnny Mercer, however, was spectacularly Hollywood – and Hollywood at its best.

Fred sang 'Dearly Beloved' and 'You Were Never Lovelier' and Rita Hayworth, still unable to convince Columbia Pictures she should be allowed to do her own thing, mouthed 'I'm Old Fashioned' to the voice of Nan Wynn.

Kern made no bones about writing the sort of music with which he felt comfortable. Fred liked Xavier Cugat's style, but Kern refused to write anything specially for him. 'I don't write Spanish songs', he told Lou Edelman. 'I don't write anything unless I can write it well and I can't write Spanish songs.'

Fred and Edelman had a strange relationship on the picture. If the producer spoke to Fred, the answer would frequently be in the form of a dance step and Edelman admitted he didn't always understand what he was doing.

It was up to Rita, however, to comprehend everything that Fred transmitted with his feet and her triumph was not simply to understand, but also to respond. Even so, there were snags. On one of the first days rehearsing 'You Were Never Lovelier', the soles of Rita's new dancing shoes gave way to the shiny surface of the floor. As her legs spreadeagled beneath her, she fell and hit her head. For a moment she was knocked out. Fred rushed over, helped her into a chair and was with her as she came round. 'My heavens,' he kept saying, 'are you all right?'

Possibly because of this, Fred and Rita did much of their later rehearsing on less slippery floors. Once, when all the sound stages were occupied, they took over a hall on the edge of the Hollywood Cemetery. When funeral cars approached, they simply stopped dancing.

Rita didn't have enough dancing roles after *You Were Never Lovelier*, although the later *Cover Girl* was to be a big milestone in her career. She was going to be groomed now as a serious actress and, as she puts it, 'pushed further ahead to stardom'.

Years later, she said in a *New York Times* interview: 'I guess the only jewels in my life were the pictures I made with Fred Astaire.'

In a minor part in the film was a young man who four years later would become the talk of Hollywood, Larry Parks. He was to score a notable success as the screen Al Jolson.

Time magazine said: '*You Were Never Lovelier* presents fresh evidence that Fred Astaire is still a superb dancer and a deft light comedian and that Rita Hayworth is still the most ambrosial lady he has ever teamed with.'

Follow The Fleet

In 1942, Fred started thinking about a new kind of engagement. He called in to see his local draft board.

In March that year, soon after the birth of Ava, he appeared in a list of possible draftees, in the company of Jack Oakie, Spencer Tracy and Humphrey Bogart, but at the age of forty-two he was very low down in that list; he was, in fact, number 156. Yet he didn't want to either escape the hazards that many less favoured men were facing every day or even to be thought to be avoiding them.

For stars like Astaire, the Government had missions which, in their way, were as important as sitting with a gun in a foxhole – entertaining the troops and helping to raise money for the war effort.

Pearl Harbour had totally changed the outlook of most Americans, and just as the name of the base struck down by the Japanese Air Force in December 1941 had become engraved in history, so the words 'war bonds' had become part of many people's everyday vocabulary. They were sold the way soap and cigarettes had been sold in peacetime.

A Hollywood Bond Victory Cavalcade had been organised, taking stars on bond-selling trips from one end of America to another and Fred was one of the first to join this outfit.

It was like the old Orpheum vaudeville circuit again – going from one tank town to another, singing a song one minute, dancing a number the next, and then a few minutes later holding out his hands and asking the audience to buy a bond for America. Fred and the other Cavalcade members played at Service bases, in village halls, at celebrity banquets and in theatres, both big and small. An exhausting experience, but worth every minute spent on it and every dollar saved in war bonds.

Harpo Marx, James Cagney, Judy Garland and Mickey Rooney were among those on the tour.

Mrs Ann Astaire was very proud of her patriotic son, and at Lismore, she unwittingly gave away a military secret – she said that Fred was due over in Britain at any moment to entertain troops there.

Fred had already adopted an RAF squadron and both Mrs Astaire and Adele revealed that he was going to fly the Atlantic to be with them. When he had previously written to the boys at the station asking what they wanted most, they left him in no doubt about the answer. They said they wanted autographed pictures of Rita Hayworth.

After an exhausting bond-selling tour of Ohio, Fred said he had to reluctantly deny the rumours of a transatlantic trip. He said that he had been approached to fly to Britain, but had made no definite undertaking to do so.

His bond-selling tour had, however, been a reality in every way. A total of $18 million had been raised and that included the results of the auction of a pair of his dancing shoes which went for $11,600.

At a rally in New York's Madison Square Garden, an Astaire performance helped take the city's bond sales past the goal of five billion dollars. A war bond was the only admission price to the rally, and there were 18,500 seats up for the asking – for upwards of $25 each. Half of the Garden seats were for buyers willing to spend a minimum of $100. Altogether, the boxes cost a staggering $2 million each to hire. That night alone brought in $86,000,000.

Adele heard about this and sent Fred a letter of congratulations. As she waited for him to decide finally to cross the Atlantic, she continued her own war effort. Acres of ground round Lismore Castle were converted into a farm. From County Waterford she sent Fred another telegram, this time, saying that she thought *Holiday Inn* was the best Astaire film ever. With a little pressing, she confided that she did that after every picture he made.

For Fred, making the bond drives was even harder than rehearsing for a Broadway show or a Hollywood film. In between Victory Cavalcade assignments, he was pressed by the studios to think of his conventional work. RKO still clung to the fond belief that they could persuade Fred to link with Ginger once more and said that they even had a new film prepared by David Hempstead ready to shoot. But it didn't happen quite like that.

Hempstead did entice Fred back to RKO. But the partner was not going to be Ginger. Instead, they had lined up an eighteen-year-old girl who had just had a taste of Hollywood stardom side by side with James Cagney in the picture *Yankee Doodle Dandy* Joan Leslie.

The film was to be called *The Sky's The Limit* with music by Harold Arlen – four years earlier, he had had his triumph with 'Over The Rainbow' for Judy Garland – and lyrics by Johnny Mercer.

Before filming got under way, Irving Berlin returned to Hollywood from his New York home with an offer to star Fred in his forth-coming *Music Box Revue*. The Revue had been Berlin's answer in the twenties to the Ziegfeld Follies. But Fred was not ready to return to Broadway and Berlin was soon planning other things – notably the most successful military show of all time, *This Is The Army*.

Fred was by now letting his mind stray to retirement again. But first, he had to complete *The Sky's The Limit* and then do some more entertaining for the war effort. If he could also go overseas, so much the better.

The big hit tune of the new film was the one that has since become the national anthem of alcoholics the world over – 'One For My Baby'. Fred is reputed to have actually tanked himself up with at least one glass of something strong before filming of the number began – to get into the right, should we say, spirit. But it is safe to add that no one imagined it would have quite the impact on drinkers that it did.

In this number, Fred danced on to the top of a bar surrounded by piles of glasses. As he did so, he caused a flurry of anxiety from all who saw him. Two nurses stood by waiting for what they were afraid would inevitably happen, and even Phyllis made one of her rare appearances on a film set to satisfy herself that he would be all right.

'I'm worried about him,' she confided as he began the routine. He jumped on to a bar stool and from that on to the highly polished surface – demonstrating how much an athlete a dancer of Fred's calibre had to be. From a smooth dance on the bar counter he turned it all into a mad escapade – kicking glasses to the floor as he did so. Finally, out of breath, he jumped down and gave up.

'Hurt?' asked Phyllis anxiously. 'No, of course not,' he replied.

It took the props crew half an hour to replace the mirror and put up a stack of new glasses. Fred tried the number again – while Phyllis and the nurses once more looked on anxiously.

'I won't need them,' said Fred, pointing to the nurses. 'Suppose you slip?' asked the director, Edward H. Griffith. 'You never know. All that glass . . .' But he did not slip and the nurses were sent home.

One of the ironies of those early war years was that the studio had to use real glass – instead of the sugar substitutes they would have adopted for the purpose in peacetime. A massive collection of factory rejects was brought in with full account being taken of the number of takes Fred was likely to insist on. And insist he did.

One extra at the studio was lucky as a result of Fred's search for perfection. He managed to stop him throwing away a pair of dancing shoes. 'I want them for my boy in the Army,' he explained. For this good cause, Fred abandoned his normal reluctance to help souvenir hunters.

Fred played a member of the Flying Tigers squadron in the picture and Joan Leslie, a magazine photographer. In the true spirit of the times, when Fred wasn't in uniform he wore a dinner jacket, not white tie and tails.

He also improvised a number on the spot. In one scene, Robert Ryan and Richard Davies were supposed to entice Joan away from Fred, but couldn't find a way to do it effectively.

'You've got to do something to him – something cruel,' Hempstead told them.

In the end, Fred dreamed up the idea of a snake dance to, supposedly, frighten away the opposition. He climbed up on a table and performed the dance, but instead of frightening anyone, Joan said it all reminded her of Dorothy Lamour.

Meanwhile, the idea of Fred playing a Flying Tiger who spent much of his time out of uniform provoked a few comments in the press. One critic wanted to know how a soldier could go around on leave in civilian dress. Other critics wanted to know what Fred Astaire was doing in a film like *The Sky's The Limit*. The *New York Times's* Bosley Crowther was extremely disappointed with it all: 'Mr Astaire does one solo which is good, but a bit woe-begone, and the rest of the time he acts foolish – and rather looks it – in his quick-fitting clothes.'

The only time Fred really felt foolish was at the race track. He was convinced that when he had a horse of his own racing, the best thing to do was to stay away, because it seemed he could never see one of his own stable getting past the winning post first.

Fred was equally unsure about his next professional assignment – but there was nothing new about that attitude. He always was unsure. He joined MGM for a part in the studio's revue spectacular *Ziegfeld Follies*, which also included stars like Fannie Brice, Esther Williams, Lucille Ball, Kathryn Grayson, Lena Horne and Red Skelton. William Powell played the part of a now dead Ziegfeld recalling the great days of the Follies from his heavenly perch. Astaire was the man he said he would choose to lead a contemporary Follies.

Fred himself had suggested one of his big numbers 'Limehouse Blues' to producer Arthur Freed. He did this spectacular with Lucille Bremer. The film also featured a revival of the nonsense number he had sung with Adele in *Funny Face* – the Gershwins' 'Babbit and the Bromide'. This time, he performed it with Gene Kelly.

Film revues don't usually succeed – but *Ziegfeld Follies* did. And one of the reasons it did was, without doubt, Fred Astaire.

As soon as his commitment to MGM was over, Fred put on a uniform – and for the first time, it was for real. He had enlisted in the USO, the organisation which liked to call itself Soldiers in Greasepaint. The bigger the star, the further away the USO were happy to send him – and as the tentacles of the advancing allied armies spread over enemy-occupied territory, so the field of operations of these entertainers extended. They wore officer's uniforms, but no badges of rank.

Fred stopped in New York on his way to Europe. And, perhaps because it was war time, threw convention, Astaire style, to the winds. He marched into his hotel without his usual toupeé and with his trousers turned up well above the ankles. It was not at all most people's idea of Fred Astaire, the best-dressed man about town. 'My trousers are too long, so I turn my cuffs up once again,' he explained to an incredulous Earl Wilson in the *New York Post*.

No one noticed the avant-garde fashion style when he marched out of the hotel and walked along Madison Avenue. It was probable that the bald pate, combined with trousers at half-mast, had made him virtually unrecognisable.

Fred was told he was going to London – which, as far as he was concerned, was just about the one place he wanted to be more than any other. It meant not only a reunion with the city that had been a second home, but also with Adele – who was barely over yet another tragedy in her life.

Early in March 1944, her husband, Lord Charles Cavendish had died. It was a lonely death. He had been ill for some time, and all that time, Adele was hundreds of miles away working in London for the American Red Cross. Her mother had been nursing him at Lismore during his last days because Adele couldn't get a permit to cross the Irish Sea. It was just before D-Day.

Charlie Cavendish was only thirty-nine. He was buried in his racing colours.

By the time Fred was ready to fly the Atlantic, Adele had got over the initial shock of Charlie's death and was back at work at Rainbow Corner – the social centre in London's Shaftesbury Avenue for the hordes of American Servicemen thronging the capital just before they sailed for Europe. For security reasons, Adele had no idea when Fred would be joining her – and he almost didn't. Three days before he was due to fly out, he was asked if, like so many other show business people, he was superstitious. He told the Army officer making his departure arrangements that he was not. Well, he was told – if he wasn't superstitious, he would be flying in a planeload of thirteen. If he minded that, he could go on another flight.

But no. He took the aircraft with the thirteen and clambered into the rickety structure. The shaky journey in a plane more suited for cattle on their way to slaughter took ten hours after the initial refuelling stop at Ganda. Fred spent much of the trip playing poker.

When he arrived at Prestwick, Scotland, he discovered why he had been sensible not to be superstitious. The plane arriving immediately before his had crashed into the airport's mass of radio aerials and everyone on board had been killed. And that was the one he would have had to take had he considered thirteen to be unlucky.

He was quite shaken. But not too disturbed to appreciate the beauty of a family reunion – if only by phone. As soon as he arrived in Britain he rushed to a telephone and called Adele at the Ritz Hotel in Piccadilly where she had a suite.

The switchboard operator said he couldn't disturb Lady Charles – it was only nine o'clock in the morning. Fred insisted that she be woken up.

A sleepy Adele came to the phone. 'This is Fred,' he shouted down the mouthpiece.

'Fred, who?' Adele asked.

'Fred Astaire – your brother, you sap,' he answered, trying to sound annoyed.

Adele was so excited at the news that came down her end of the phone that all she could offer by way of reply was a fit of crying. It was too much for Fred – he rang off. But they met a few hours later at the Ritz. The Ritz in 1944 wasn't quite the Ritz of 1934, but it was comfort and luxury unlimited compared with the plane across the Atlantic and what would be his subsequent 'digs'.

They had never been apart from each other for so long before and their embrace on meeting spoke very clearly their feelings on being together again.

The next night, they relived that reunion – for the world's press. Adele was at her usual spot at Rainbow Corner, at a table next to the men's lavatory, writing letters. While cameras clicked and flashbulbs popped in the heavily blacked-out club, Fred went over to the table and gave her a big kiss.

Mrs Ann Astaire didn't yet know of her son's arrival in London. 'I'm going to send her a telegram, but whether I'll get over to see her is in the lap of the gods,' he said. On this trip he didn't manage to persuade the gods to help.

One of the first things people wanted to know in London was how much longer he thought he could continue dancing. 'These old bones are beginning to rattle a bit,' he confided. 'I'm still under contract to make a few more pictures but when I have finished them I shall retire and produce films.'

Adele ran Rainbow Corner, and although some of the British worthies who popped in from time to time liked to call her 'Lady Charles', she was quick to correct them. 'My name's Adele,' she would insist. And if a close friend like Col David Niven popped in, there was nothing she liked better than to be called Delly.

In the day time, she did some shopping for the boys – who either didn't have the time to do it themselves or were too shy to buy frilly underwear for their wives and girlfriends at the Service 'PX' stores. In the evening, she wrote letter after letter for the young soldiers and sailors – there was still no separate American Air Force. She wrote them 'not because they can't write, but just because their folks like to hear from somebody else how they're getting along,' she explained at the time.

For Staff Sgt Philip Scheyer, she wrote a letter home to his brother at Staten Island in New York. She didn't go into a long rigmarole about her aristocratic lineage or her Astaire pedigree. She simply said: 'I am the girl who writes for boys on leave – see?' And she concluded the note: 'War is hell – no ice cream here.'

Often, she would take down the letters in a shorthand notebook – like the secretary she in fact now was. At one time, she was writing 130 letters a week and doing her own censoring as she went along. 'I knew what could be said,' she explained as she took the letters to the post office.

Everyone at Rainbow Corner knew her and loved her for the down-to-earth way she spoke their language. 'Where you been the last couple of days?' asked one youngster as he pushed his head through a vast bowl of flowers on her table. 'You're going to get hay fever, Tootsie,' she replied.

She gave the same services to officers as to shy enlisted men. Soon after Capt Frank McDermott had had a letter written to 'Dear Mom' in the Bronx, she handed the pen to him, so that he could add his name in her autograph book, which by now had thousands of GI signatures.

On the table was a photograph of Fred. In the drawers underneath, hundreds of letters of appreciation from 'the folks back home'.

She was still an aristocrat to a lot of the Rainbow Corner youngsters, however – and to even more of them she was undoubtedly English. 'English?' she asked one of them. 'I'm Adele Astaire, Fred's sister.'

'Yeh,' said her doubting friend. 'And I'm Victor Mature's brother.'

'Well, I don't like *him*, either,' she replied, sensing disapproval as well as disbelief, 'I think his acting is terrible.' But Adele's own bit of acting wasn't much good either. The kid really was Victor Mature's brother, and he left muttering a few unkind words about Fred.

When she wasn't writing letters or shopping for the boys, she was dancing with them. She didn't exactly approve of some of their dancing styles – the jitterbug and the jive, in particular.

'When I left the States in '32,' she told one soldier, 'nobody danced like that outside of Harlem.'

'Hey, how about our dance?' one private called to her – and together they did a nifty foxtrot, repeating the performance first for another private and then for a sergeant. Not all of them appreciated the significance of dancing with Adele Astaire. The surname meant something to everyone in 1944, but few of the young Servicemen she was dancing with knew much about *her* days of stardom.

Fred saw what little of London that he could. In Hyde Park he was recognised by a bunch of American Servicemen and together they posed for pictures.

He couldn't avoid the inevitable press conference – though he tried. Before this particular mission started, he hid himself in a corridor, feeling rather embarrassed. Eventually, he was persuaded to go into the room, accompanied by a personal 'bodyguard' comprising several bemedalled officers. It was all carried out with traditional military efficiency. One of the officers spoke first – to introduce the officer who was going to introduce Fred. When the time came for the final introductions, that officer made a speech too.

Fred made his own speech sitting on one of the hotel's gilt tables. 'I shall be giving shows all over the theatre,' he said – and the joke was not missed.

'Mr Astaire is referring to the European Theatre of operations,' said one of the officers.

Fred said he planned to dance but not to sing. 'I think not – I guess I won't inflict my apology of a voice on anybody.'

What about Fred Junior? someone asked. Now Fred had to be more honest than previously, 'He's never going to make a hoofer,' he said. 'He's just not interested in dancing.'

As for himself, he was prepared to do whatever was expected of him. 'They'll plan just what they want me to do and whatever they plan will satisfy me,' he said. He certainly had no intention of doing any filming in Britain.

But he hoped he would have a chance to dance for British troops and, after all this time, dance again with Adele. And they did – at Rainbow Corner.

If people had previously had doubts about Adele's identity, the night that Fred joined her at the Corner, they were put aside. Fred was instantly recognisable and the people there reacted accordingly. With him was his own personal accordionist, Mike Olivieri who had just been half way round the world as a one-man orchestra, and there were a few members of Glenn Miller's celebrated outfit at the club, too. Miller himself had only just embarked on the fog-bound cross-Channel flight from which he never returned.

Entertaining the troops had become an honoured tradition in the United States. It was show business's effort for the country, and those who volunteered for work with the USO were simply doing their own kind of soldiering. Glenn Miller was not the only casualty 'Over There' – to quote the George M. Cohan tune that was virtually the USO's theme song.

When, after kissing Delly goodbye again, Fred boarded an aircraft at London's Northolt Airfield, he knew he could be the next to disappear. But he was consoled by the company he kept. With him on the cross-channel flight, the first leg of the trip to the front line, was Bing Crosby. Bing was as disturbed as he was at having a pilot for the journey who looked no more than seventeen, but they all got over to France in one piece.

Fred and Bing enjoyed being with each other – but if anyone had thoughts of their reliving the experience of *Holiday Inn*, with Bing calling all the shots, there was no cause. For days, the Groaner bemoaned the fact that he was virtually unrecognised by the girls in the small French town where they awaited their next orders. On the other hand, there were swarms of nubile young ladies around Fred – after one of them found an ancient fan magazine which had printed his portrait. Everybody loved Fred Astaire – although he wasn't quite prepared for the welcome from one small boy who told him how pleased he was to meet Mr Ginger Rogers.

As impressed as the young troops were with Fred Astaire, he was more moved himself by what he saw in the places where he and Mike the accordianist entertained.

'They've unbelievable guts,' was all he could say after seeing one group of men return from action. 'They go back in there time and time again to hit the Germans. It's something impossible to forget.'

He danced wherever the authorities would let him go – and

176

generally it was close enough to hear the guns bursting; frequently so close that he had to be advised to move back. Everywhere he went he carried a six by twelve foot mat, so that he could dance as near as possible in the style to which he had become accustomed. Often, he performed wearing heavy Army boots.

For days, he went without a bath, which for the immaculate Astaire was more worrying than the gunfire. He admitted he occasionally felt 'pretty scared'.

The boys, like soldiers anywhere had a one-track mind once they could forget the horror of the fighting. As much as they liked his dancing – and they were as impressed as anyone could be at having a live performance by Fred Astaire – the questions revealed what they were really thinking. In almost every place he and Mike stopped he was asked the same question: 'Say, what's it like to have a pretty girl like Rita Hayworth in your arms?'

Fred was nonchalant with his answer: 'Just fine,' he told them. 'She's a beautiful dancer.'

The head of the USO camp shows in Europe, Bill Dover, was suitably impressed with the Astaire performances. Word got back to him of Fred and the Chicago comedian Willie Shore being caught up in a German counter-attack near the front line in Belgium. It was just before the massive offensive that has become known in history as the Battle of the Bulge – the last, dangerous but finally futile attempt of the Germans to regain the initiative in the war.

Fred and the comedian were moving up towards their next show when the Luftwaffe decided to put on a show of its own spraying bullets and bombs around them like the firecrackers in the Fourth of July number from *Holiday Inn*. All Fred is prepared to admit today is that he landed up in a ditch for a little while. The stories circulating about the incident at the time said that he and Shore were pinned to the muddy ground, and under fire all the time, for twelve hours.

Dover, a Hollywood executive in peacetime, had himself just experienced the thrill of having a German bullet whizz past his nose. But it was the bravery of Fred Astaire he kept talking about.

'Funny thing about Astaire,' he said later. 'He was rather nervous about going under fire for a number of reasons – including his wife and the kids. But he was tremendous after that twelve-hour introduction to fire and it all went without a hitch.'

Fred followed the retreating Germans and watched prisoners being rounded up; probably the only troops in the entire tour who didn't give a second nod to Astaire.

Like other men in the front line, Fred collected souvenirs from his travels. The ones he liked best were a motley assortment of false teeth, which he picked up at a deserted dental laboratory. 'The Germans were running away so fast they left everything behind, including their teeth.' It made good reading in 1944.

The young soldiers were often so thrilled at meeting Astaire that they piled him with presents, including a collection of German Army insignia.

He entertained wherever there were people to listen to him. Sometimes he played to two hundred, sometimes, two thousand.

Fred made no distinction as to rank on this tour. When General Eisenhower asked to see him, Fred performed for the Allied Commander in Chief just as though he had been a buck private.

He did between three and four shows a day; sometimes to 'footloggers' waiting for the next order to advance; sometimes to airmen about to 'scramble' on a raid over enemy territory. If he were lucky, the camp entertainments officers made makeshift platforms for him but frequently he had to use the back of trucks for his dancing. If the mat had to serve as his entire stage, he'd make do with whatever he had around him. In Army hospitals he leapt from one empty bed to another. In barracks rooms he jumped on and off tables – using every gadget in the sparse room as a prop.

The soldiers tried to help out whenever they could. He was almost blinded from the torches shone like spotlights by eager youngsters in the midst of a blackout. They were determined that nothing would spoil the show. He was worried most about those Army boots. 'They stilted me a little,' he confessed. 'But the G.I.s liked it. They love to see you get into trouble.'

Fred and his companions had to put up with many of the deprivations of the troops; when they didn't have a bed laid on for the night, the party slept on the stage of a Dutch theatre. For all the inconvenience, Fred was enjoying these live shows. The tour, which really began with his Victory Cavalcade, represented his first stage appearance in more than ten years.

The real triumph in what must be regarded as his finest hour, came at the end – when in September 1944, he gave the first concert since the liberation in the famous Paris music hall, the Olympia. There were two thousand American troops in the audience. It was Fred's first ever appearance on a French stage.

Afterwards, it took all the strength that the Military police could muster to hold back the hundreds of eager French fans beseiging the theatre, waiting for Fred to leave the stage door. 'Vive Monsieur Astaire,' they shouted as they thrust autograph books in his direction.

Then he went back to the front – where on one occasion, he got so exuberant that his taps flew out into the audience. 'It's more dangerous on the front row with me dancing than it is on the front line,' he quipped.

Fred and Bing Crosby met up again for the journey back to the States, travelling in the *Queen Mary*, which had been converted to a troop ship at the start of the war. They gave a number of shows for the boys on board, including some for the wounded in the ship's hospital.

When he finally reached America, he spoke again of the Allied troops – 'Unbelievable guts'. The boys, he declared, 'left an indelible impression.'

Phyllis met him in New York. Before they left together for California, Fred spent days on the telephone – calling not just his own family, but making several hundred calls to wives, mothers and sweethearts of the Servicemen he had met overseas. Not all of the boys were coming back; but the messages Fred delivered were from young men who had had an experience they were not going to forget – and part of that unforgettable experience was meeting Fred Astaire.

Mr And Mrs Hoofer At Home

Back home on Summit Drive, Fred was much more a happy husband and father than a returning hero. Peter and Fred Junior were given the captured Iron Crosses and other German insignia he brought with him, and if the younger Fred Astaire – now eight years old – had made it clear he wasn't going to be a hoofer like his dad, that was quite all right. Fred was just pleased to be back and Phyllis was glad to have him home.

All Fred wanted to do now was to relax and think very seriously about retirement. *Ziegfeld Follies* had not been shown yet and until it was, Astaire was his usual worrying self. But not even a hit would let him stray from the idea of resting.

He agreed to make one more picture at MGM and then the dancing shoes were going to be hung up for good. Doctors had told him that nobody approaching forty-six should consider taxing his heart the way Fred did every time he danced on a stage or film set.

'I'll just look around and perhaps I'll go for production,' he repeated. 'Maybe, I'll do dramas. After all, several of my former dancing partners went dramatic – Ginger Rogers and Joan Fontaine. Some of them won Academy Awards.' Incredible as it may seem, no one had yet given Fred the coveted Oscar.

He didn't mention his own heart. But of his partners he said:

'Strenuous camera dancing is tough on the ladies. I don't blame any of them for turning to dramatic roles.'

No one who saw Fred's next picture, *Yolanda And The Thief* would have blamed him for turning to dramatic roles either. It was a fantasy played for much of the time against a backcloth that would have suited Snow White. It didn't really suit Fred Astaire or the box office. But it teamed Fred once more with Miss Lucille Bremer, who after her two parts with Astaire in *Ziegfeld Follies* and *Yolanda* decided to settle for marriage. She was a discovery of Arthur Freed, who by now had become the symbol of MGM's musical department – the one man who was giving the famous initials an entirely new meaning, Makers of Good Musicals. Miss Bremer had been one of the ladies of the chorus at the famous Roxy Theatre in New York. In 1939, the Roxy voted her 'The Rockette Most Likely To Succeed'.

All the time that Fred was working on *Yolanda* people were asking the now expected questions: 'What next? Would he really pack it all in after so long?'

For a time it seemed he would not. MGM believed they still had a commitment from him for more pictures and they already had a new title they wanted him to make – an updated version of *Belle of New York*, a Broadway show stopper at the turn of the century.

As Fred rehearsed his numbers for *Yolanda*, songwriters Harry Warren and Johnny Mercer tried to interrupt him to show their wares for *Belle of New York*. Fred, wearing curling 'Arabian Nights' dancing shoes for his latest picture, agreed to lend an ear. As the score was played over, and Fred chewed gum while he thought, he remained noncommital. Finally, a little while later, it was announced that if Fred did do another film for MGM, it would be *Belle of New York* and he would then fulfil the remainder of his contract. Otherwise, everybody was resigned to the fact that he was on the threshold of retirement.

All this only tended to increase Fred's reputation as the champion worrier of Hollywood. If he didn't have new dance steps to concern him, he was going to have to worry about the future.

For the moment, however, he was devoting his worries to *Yolanda And The Thief*. It was a story about a mythical South American country called Patria – 'a cemetery with a train running through it', as Fred describes it in his role as the thief who thinks he can trick the country's richest woman (Lucille Bremer) out of her possessions. The best part of the film was Fred's dancing with Miss Bremer in a ballet sequence, and the comedy of Frank Morgan, ideally cast as another con-man.

One reviewer said the film looked as though it had dance routines designed by Salvador Dali. All in all, not an Astaire film to remember with particular affection.

Even so, there was still an enthusiasm for whatever Fred Astaire did – and one which even now was reflected by the critics. The *New York Times* commented: 'It is a long-established principle that Fred Astaire's name on a picture is a guarantee of fine dancing, and if Mr Astaire retires as he is threatening to do, it will remove one of the truly great American dancers of the age.'

As for *Yolanda* the paper called it 'an excellent and thorough job.'

Meanwhile, there were other things happening to the Astaire family. For one, and with retirement very much in mind, Fred and Phyllis had bought a new ranch – a place where they were determined no one would have the effrontery to mention films or dancing. For another, a colt called Triplicate looked as if it might show more potential than had at first been displayed. But there was one other success that pleased him even more than owning a promising horse.

In June 1945, an excited Fred sent off a telegram to Adele at Lismore Castle: HAVE DONE IT AT LAST STOP HOLED IN ONE YESTERDAY.

To a golfer there could be no finer achievement. And Fred did it with a number-four wood on the thirteenth hole at the Bel Air Country Club in a match with Randolph Scott and two friends. While Fred scored one, Scott had two, another partner three and the last member of the party, four. And it was achieved with the meticulous ease of a dance routine. Fred moved the ball into the hole with the precision he reserved for the studio floor and wielded the club with the sort of grace he used in the golf number in *Carefree*. After that result, who could doubt he was right to take so much trouble?

For Adele, it was another excuse to be homesick. But finally, with the war now over and with no reason to put off a trip any further, she announced she was going to look enviously towards the Atlantic no more. She was going home. After spending the war years commuting between Rainbow Corner and Lismore's 160-acre 'victory garden', she was now going to Hollywood.

There was the usual speculation that this might really mean that

Fred was not only *not* going to retire, but that Adele was coming out of retirement to dance with him. She soon put an end to the chatter. She was simply going home; with Charles Cavendish dead, there was little reason to stay at Lismore simply for the sake of doing so – although she had been told she could use it whenever she wanted to.

The shocking Lady Charles was true to her old reputation. As dowagers on both sides of the Atlantic contemplated the departure of the lady who had entertained royalty, Adele saw no reason to deny that the States had certain attractions for her. She said she was going to spend a great deal of time and money on new underwear – 'particularly little panties. It's been so long since we could get any in England I'd almost forgotten about them.'

New York, when she finally arrived there for her first visit since before the war, was as exciting as she knew it would be – and unlike London, was virtually unchanged from 1939.

A few days later, together with Paulette Goddard, Anita Louise and Ed Sullivan, she welcomed the *Queen Mary* as it steamed into New York Harbour with 11,475 veterans of the European campaign aboard. She knew exactly how they felt.

When she looked out of her window at the Waldorf Astoria, she did so with wide-eyed excitement. But a *Life* photographer who watched her was at the receiving end of her salty tongue: 'I'm not sure I want to say anything at all in view of that lousy picture you ran of me last year,' she told him. 'It almost finished my glamour life, you stinker.' Back in the States, she settled down to catching up on old friendships and before very long would find a new love, too.

As for Fred, his own 'glamour life' was taking new shape through an accident of fate – even though he was still protesting that he was hanging up those dancing shoes, come rain or shine.

Yolanda And The Thief might well have been the film he retired on had there not come a frenzied call from Paramount Studios, where Bing Crosby was struggling through a new film – based, yet again, around the music of Irving Berlin. The trouble was that Bing wasn't getting on at all well with Paul Draper, the leading male dancer in the picture, *Blue Skies*. Draper was meant to be dancing with the attractive female lead, Joan Caulfield and to share a great deal of the banter with Crosby. But it wasn't working out that way. He had a slight stammer, which didn't seem to matter on Broadway, where he had appeared in a number of shows and had always managed to control its worst effects. But nothing seemed to go right on the *Blue Skies* set.

To make things even more difficult, tragedy struck the unit soon after the film got under way. Mark Sandrich, the man who was as responsible as anyone for smoothing the path for Fred Astaire in Hollywood, was appointed producer and director – but quite suddenly, at the age of forty-five, died of a heart attack soon after work on the picture started. The day after his death, Fred was among the first to call upon his widow and their two small sons so acknowledging a debt he undoubtedly owed. On the set of *Blue Skies* the loss of Sandrich was felt in a different way. Draper was even less confident with the new director, Stuart Heisler– and with Sol C. Siegel who took over as producer – than he had been under Sandrich.

Every time he and Crosby were in a scene together, Bing's temper became more and more frayed. Finally, at about three thirty on a Friday afternoon, he walked off the set and said he was taking his boys swimming. What he, in fact, did was to go to the Paramount front office and have an urgent talk with Siegel and studio executives. The following Monday morning, Paul Draper was no longer on the set, but Fred Astaire was.

The effect on the rest of the cast was rather like a bolt of electricity in a storm. Instead of being galvanised into action they were fixed in their tracks, entirely stunned by the august Astaire presence.

Miss Caulfield, who could be a dab dancer in her own way, was so scared at the prospect of having to dance with Fred Astaire that she persuaded the director to give her number to the Spanish dancer Olga San Juan.

She has regretted it ever since. 'But I couldn't dance with Fred Astaire – I was so petrified.'

Choosing Fred Astaire to succeed Paul Draper was an inspired move and Fred had no compunction about taking over from another actor. In this case, he wasn't second choice in the conventional sense of the term.

No one else, in fact, could have made a Berlin duet with Crosby seem so perfectly made-to-measure for themselves. 'A Couple of Song And Dance Men' would undoubtedly have become their signature tune had Bing and Fred decided to form a permanent duet. The fact that they didn't can only be the public's loss.

Until *Blue Skies*, another Berlin tune had been principally associated with Harry Richman. After the film, it was as much Fred Astaire as 'Top Hat' had been. 'Puttin' On The Ritz', in fact, was Fred in the old style – almost as if by donning top hat, white tie and tails to sing this number he was signalling the end of war and austerity and saying that he was back in business. Instead, he was still saying that it was his swan song. Hermes Pan had been on war service and Fred brought him back to directing the dance routines in the picture. Between them they devised a backdrop for 'Puttin' On The Ritz' that would have done credit to the most lavish scenes in the Astaire-Rogers series. By a clever special effects, Fred appeared to dance in front of seven other Fred Astaires, all dancing separately.

As for the story, it was no more important than Fred Astaire film plots had ever been. But when there was Crosby to tease and Berlin numbers to which they could sing and dance it mattered even less than usual. For the record, it was about a pair of vaudeville artists who split up; one to continue dancing, the other to run a succession of night clubs. It covered the period 1919 to 1946 – or from 'I've Got My Captain Working For Me Now' to 'White Christmas' and beyond.

The film was a tremendous success – and Mark Sandrich would have approved his successor's change of cast. Surely now, everyone seemed to be asking, Fred would relent and forget about retiring? But Fred said No, he would not forget.

Soon after the film was released in September 1946, the public – aided no doubt by an astute publicity department at Paramount – made it quite clear they didn't like the idea of losing Fred Astaire from their screens. A mammoth petition was launched – collecting signatures day after day in theatre after theatre. After two weeks, the management at New York's Paramount Theatre announced they had 10,000 names written on two rolls of paper, both 50 ft long and 18 inches wide.

'It will be sent to Mr Astaire,' said the manager, 'as the biggest petition of this kind ever presented to anyone.'

If that was something of a publicity stunt, and the public reaction couldn't be completely put down to that, there was not much doubt about the attitude of the city council at Omaha, Nebraska. The leading citizens of Fred's old home town launched their own petition to beg Astaire to reconsider his decision to pack it all in.

He was even more speechless than usual when faced with a mass of praise from ordinary people. 'I am a little surprised and gratified,' he said. 'I had no idea this was going to happen.'

'I thought the public's reaction would be – "Oh well, we don't have to worry with him any more." '

But it wasn't. The clamour for more Astaire snowballed. Even the equally shy Irving Berlin joined in. 'If Fred can be persuaded to make another picture, I'll be glad to write the songs for it,' he declared.

Fred said he took that, too, as a 'terrific compliment'. But he was still retiring. 'I've had a pretty full career in show business – I worked hard in every picture and I was beginning to think the public was becoming a little indifferent.'

The *New York Times* decided that was totally untrue and traced Fred to Aiken, where the family now spent most winters. The paper told him 'that the beating of timbrels being heard in the land is none other than a public clamour for the return of Fred Astaire to the screen'.

When people still couldn't understand why such a drastic and seemingly final step should be taken, he said, 'It's been a long grind. Year after year, dancing eight to ten hours a day. Planning, rehearsing, performing. I'm tired.'

So would he now dance just for pleasure? Pleasure? The thought made him shudder. Dancing could only be hard work, and nothing else. 'You might almost call me a wallflower,' he said at the time. 'At parties, I never dance unless I have to.' He had been saying as much for years. But it now made better reading than ever before.

In December 1946, he seemed to weaken. 'Maybe, yes,' he would go back to films, he said, 'Maybe no.' The odds, someone decided, were on 'Yes' – but Fred was still publicly denying it.

In England, *Picturegoer* magazine featured a piece entitled 'What You Owe To Fred Astaire And What You Will Miss.'

Said the magazine's Gerald A. Pratley:

We cannot help feeling a sense of sorrow after hearing that Fred Astaire will retire. Until we force our minds to think and believe it, the full significance of this fact is not realised.

Then comes the shock, followed by an empty feeling, when we visualise the screen without that dancing genius. . . .

Fred Astaire gave us happiness at times when we most needed it. And strength to persevere in the struggle for existence.

What was really worrying Fred – and he never needed any encouragement to worry – was how long he could maintain the standard that had engendered such comments. It wasn't simply that he was tired of hoofing and all it entailed.

'I've tried to fashion something new for each picture,' he told the *Los Angeles Times*, 'But after all, there is a limit. I've never found it easy to perform routines thought up by others. Lately, the feeling has been that people might be saying: "Jeepers – there's old Astaire again, keeps creeping in." '

But that wasn't the reaction of the audiences – anywhere. When Fred lost his $1200 gold and jewelled cigarette case after being besieged by a crowd of admirers at the *Blue Skies* preview, there was a rush to find it and then hand it back to him.

So what was Fred going to do? Direct? Perhaps. But first he had a little business venture to get under way.

That there were commercial possibilities with the name Fred Astaire no one could deny. Just by lending his name to a dress hire firm, he could have made a fortune – but he never would. And, as we have seen already, when a firm did try to cash in on the best-dressed man in Hollywood for an advertisement, the legal feathers began to fly as high as those on a dress worn by Ginger Rogers.

But now he was taking a different attitude. He announced he was opening the Fred Astaire Dance Studios, with the first one on New York's smart Park Avenue, the thoroughfare he had sung about so reverently in 'Puttin' On The Ritz'. Later, he said, there would be more and this was going to mark the emergence of the new Fred Astaire, Astaire the businessman.

There would be eighty-five instructors – men and women with an average age of only twenty-five.

The large ballroom in the 487, Park Avenue premises was called the Adele Room. Within months, the studios were proudly announcing they had a thousand students. Fred emphasised he was going to keep a personal watch on the premises – although he couldn't promise to teach all the people who enrolled for courses. He contented himself with giving the first lessons to the instructors. 'Let's relax,' he said when he turned up for the first session – and as Joan Caulfield, Eleanor Powell, Rita Hayworth and a number of other dancers could testify, that was an almost impossible command to obey.

The ballrooms had all that was considered necessary for establishments of their kind. Music was by touch control. Even the very dance floor 'floated' so that no one dancing would feel the slightest bit fatigued.

To set the whole thing off, Fred devised a new dance to be taught exclusively at the studios – called, of course, the Astaire.

The studios' press department said of it: 'With the Astaire, North America will finally have a distinctive native dance with an infectious and pleasing rhythm that up to now has been expressed largely in Latin American dances.' Ambitious words indeed – and never to be fully realised. But to show his enthusiasm Fred did what he hated doing most of all – 'opened the ball' at the launching ceremony by dancing the Astaire with a pretty girl wearing a 'new-look' ankle-length skirt and a crisp white blouse.

It wouldn't take long before Fred would get very disenchanted with the dance studio business, but for now, with no film commitments to distract him, he was playing the perfectionist. The launch was going ahead with Astaire-like precision.

There would, he announced, be schools in Kansas, Los Angeles, San Francisco and then London. The whole venture was said to be aiming at beating Arthur Murray on his home ground – and since Mr Murray cashed in to the tune of $20 million a year, that was wishful thinking indeed.

As for Fred, even at the beginning, he found a lot more excitement on the race track. And most of it was called Triplicate.

Let's Call The Whole Thing Off

Few would have guessed that Fred Astaire would be happy in retirement. But it seemed he was. If people had seriously believed that he needed to worry to feel inwardly satisfied, a quick glance at the Astaire household in 1946 would have put them wise.

Mr Twinkletoes – as most writers had dubbed him at least once in the career they had seemingly made out of simply recording his dancing successes – was king of his own little domain: the house at Summit Drive, its 'colony' at Aiken and the Astaire ranch.

Phyllis was quite obviously the consort treated as every inch the queen, a role Fred would have gladly assigned her even had she not figured in the Social Register. As for the children, Peter, Fred Junior and four-year-old Ava – they were the healthy, happy and the devoted subjects of them both.

Now at last, Fred could really spend time at the ranch and enjoy thinking about not having to think – particularly about any more pictures. He could also enjoy the cheques coming his way via the stables where in the world of racehorses, Triplicate was fast becoming a superstar.

The $6,000 Fred had spent on buying this three-year-old colt was paying the sort of dividends that would gladden a bank manager's heart. In 1946, he won the Hollywood Gold Cup – a $100,000 race, of which $81,000 went to Fred, together with $6,000 picked up as the result of his betting on the winner. How could he do anything else?

In the same year, he won the $75,000 Golden Gate Handicap in San Francisco and the prestigious San Juan Capistrano at Santa Anita. That was worth $50,000.

His jockey wore a dark blue blouse with a yellow sash and a red cap – the colours of Phyllis's uncle Henry Bull, who had done some steeplechase racing himself as a 'gentleman'.

Fred loyally backed Triplicate to win – and was rightly glad that his loyalty had paid off so handsomely. But he wasn't a big punter and even now says his stakes at the track are modest – for a rich man, that is. He bets $50 to $100, but rarely more.

Every time he went to the races where Triplicate was running, he was driven there by his chauffeur Dan. His relationship with Dan was one of those ideal pairings that novelists like to write books about. There was nothing 'Upstairs and Downstairs' about the way they spoke to each other and Fred would respect Dan's opinions as much as Dan valued those of his distinguished boss, especially the fact that the chauffeur would always place a bet on Triplicate. But one day at the track, however, Dan exasperated Astaire. After a day of betting, Fred noticed that the driver had not exactly been rushing to the window to put up his own stake – or allowing Fred, as he often would wish, to bet for him. For once, Fred lost his cool: 'I really can't understand why you bother to come here at all if you don't bet,' he told the chauffeur. Presumably Dan wondered how Fred expected to get home that day.

Triplicate's success was to last for two years, but finally the horse suffered severe ankle trouble and went off to be a stud in Kentucky. Meanwhile, Fred was beginning to feel as though he were put out to graze himself. It was pleasant enough having nothing to do, but in the house he would still put on his record player and find himself dancing steps he usually liked getting paid for doing.

The fact that an offer came to do just that again was due mainly to Gene Kelly deciding to play a game of volley ball.

Kelly was a different sort of dancer to Astaire; much happier in a pair of jeans and a sweater than in top hat, white tie and tails – and his style went with the dress. If Fred was the suave, urbane gentleman, Gene was the tough stevedore. And, remember it was Astaire who said that dancing was as tough as stevedoring.

190

But they both were athletes and they both achieved stardom. While Fred confined his athletic prowess to the studio floor or the golfcourse, and indoor sporting activities around his pool table, Kelly loved fast ball games. On this one occasion, playing in the grounds of his own house, he raced a little too hard for the ball, fell down and a couple of players stepped on top of him. Kelly couldn't get up again. His ankle was broken.

To a dancer, breaking an ankle can be as dangerous and foreboding as it is for a racehorse. Gene's injury this time wasn't as serious as it might have been. But it did have repercussions – not just for him, but also for MGM. And for Fred Astaire.

Kelly had been signed to make another film based on the songs of Irving Berlin to be called *Easter Parade*. Now what were they to do?

Producer Arthur Freed burst into tears when he heard the news. The studio wanted to get on with the making of the picture, but Kelly would be out of action for two months at least – and probably more. In Hollywood two months represents a great deal of capital. Judy Garland was to be the co-star with him – and she could be a difficult lady to work with. In the end, the studio decided that it had to go ahead without Kelly. At Gene's suggestion, a telephone call was made to Fred, who confirmed that he was now out of retirement.

Astaire was offered his regular salary, reportedly nearly $160,000, to take the part. But I suspect he would have done it for a great deal less. The temptation was not the money – a lot of which would have gone to the Internal Revenue department – but a very good excuse to rid himself of his self-imposed retirement.

Easter Parade

Fred protested that he had never really intended to retire completely. He had merely wanted to have a rest from organising dance routines, which always had to be different for every number in every picture. The way he reckoned it, eighty per cent of the effort in creating the routines went into the process of thinking up the steps and only twenty per cent into the job of actually doing them.

But now, with his mental retirement complete, he was having to flex his muscles and see whether he could get to grips with actually moving his feet to the rhythms of Irving Berlin's music.

The man who wrote the story, Sidney Sheldon, wasn't all that delighted at the prospect of having Astaire step into Kelly's dancing shoes – and not simply because it would inevitably mean that a number of Gene's lines and the situations surrounding them would have to be replaced.

It was after Fred had agreed to take on the role that Sheldon was first told. Arthur Freed called the writer to his office and said: 'Guess what's happened? Gene Kelly has broken his ankle.'

'That's very funny, Arthur,' he replied.

'No really,' Freed insisted. What was more, he told him, there were going to be no postponements. 'No. We're starting on Monday. I've sent a script to Fred Astaire.'

When a writer hears that the man he had in his mind's eye all the time that he sat before his typewriter is not going to be the one to say his lines, he is likely to get somewhat disturbed. Sheldon was. He protested that forty-eight-year-old Fred was old enough to be Judy's father. 'Fred's so much older that you could never get an audience rooting for them,' he said.

But Freed was adamant. Sheldon now admits that he was wrong. 'Part of the reason,' he says, 'was that two very talented people were working together and the chemistry was right.'

Gene Kelly's ankle was not the only bone to break in the preliminary stages of *Easter Parade* and so alter the final complexion of the picture. Cyd Charisse had been selected to play Astaire's 'junior' partner in the picture. But she broke a leg, too. At that appropriate moment, Ann Miller – who had been flexing her own long legs at Columbia Pictures for the previous few years and was one of the loveliest dancers in motion pictures, was newly out of hospital after suffering a fall herself. Would she like to test for the role? Miss Miller was jealous of her reputation – as were most performers who had ever had their names above the title in film billings – and refused. That made Fred as worried as usual. He thought she might be too tall for the part. But as far as she was concerned, a pair of flat shoes would solve the perennial problem of girls who had to dance with Fred Astaire – and the studio accepted the suggestion.

In the end, Fred had three dances with Ann Miller, three with Judy, and another two without the benefit of female company.

Fred's arrival for his twenty-first picture was greeted with enthusiasm by almost everyone. They did so, knowing exactly what they were letting themselves in for. While the other members of the cast and the technicians were gradually pacing themselves through the boring pre-production weeks, Fred was his usual demanding self. And if things weren't working out right, he was ready to turn into Moaning Minnie at the drop of a top hat.

During rehearsals, he put in a seven-hour day, starting on the dot of ten o'clock in the morning, breaking for sandwiches from one to two o'clock – using half that time to take a nap – and then finishing the moment the studio clock struck six.

No one connected with the picture thought it was going to be a walk-over. After twenty films, the man's reputation for perfection had preceded him, and while it was a thrill for most people to be in the same room as Fred Astaire, it was a daunting prospect, too. It extended even to his co-star.

For Judy Garland, *Easter Parade* represented a severe test. Only weeks before arriving on the MGM lot, she had smashed a bathroom mirror and made an attempt at cutting her wrists with the broken glass. She had been under psychiatric care for some time. If that in itself wasn't a big enough problem to wrestle with, there was the additional pressure of seeing her husband replaced as the picture's director – for very personal reasons. Judy's psychiatrist had told MGM that the effect of having Vincente Minnelli directing her in *Easter Parade* could be catastrophic. To her, he wouldn't simply be a husband, but would represent the power of the studio, and little frightened her more than the stern parent figure of MGM. Charles 'Chuck' Walters was brought in in his place.

Judy had worked with Fred before – in the Victory Cavalcade, but now was petrified at the prospect of dancing with him in front of the cameras.

On the first day of any film, there was an atmosphere of excitement and expectancy. There was a tradition at the time that everybody involved in making the picture should see the first take completed and safely locked away in the can. On *Easter Parade*, the atmosphere was electric. It would be Judy's first picture since her much publicised illness and would mark Irving Berlin's forty years of songwriting. But most important of all, it was Fred Astaire's comeback picture.

With bustling studio carpenters dashing around in every direction and extras and assistant directors following them like lemmings rushing off the end of a cliff, Judy just sat behind the camera chatting to Sidney Sheldon. She was called in the midst of an inconsequential joke which Sheldon decided to break off. 'No,' she ordered, 'carry on'. It was strange behaviour from any star when on a film set the director's command was regarded as law; he wanted to start work and needed Judy in front of the camera.

Sheldon was reluctant to interfere with the director's plans. The lights were burning and even at the end of 1947 that represented a lot of money.

'Chuck' Walters might have been forgiven had he thought that Judy's reluctance to go before the cameras was directed at him for daring to replace Minnelli. But Sheldon suspected something else.

'Don't you want to do the scene, Judy?' he asked her. She pulled no punches. 'No,' she said. 'Because in this scene I have to kiss Fred Astaire, and I've never met him.' The two had certainly not met socially when they worked on Victory Cavalcade, and now her mental condition was still, to use the medical phrase, giving cause for concern.

So it was Sheldon who played 'marriage broker' at this moment. Gently, he took Judy by the hand and led her over to Fred – who put her completely at ease, as he had so many leading ladies before. When the cameras were switched off, he did a mock impression of Rhett Butler – while Judy, never reluctant to join in a good joke, parried with her own interpretation of Scarlett O'Hara.

The plot was in many ways little more than an excuse for Berlin's music and Astaire's dancing. But it was still stronger than most of the ones in which Fred had been involved. He and Ann Miller were a show biz partnership, broken up when Ann decides she wants to go it alone.

In pique, Fred looks for someone else. He finds her in the chorus of a small night club and offers to do for her what Henry Higgins achieved for Eliza Doolittle. Judy – or Hannah Brown as she is called in this picture – has as many fraught problems as the cockney flower girl in *Pygmalion* but, like her, finally comes to appreciate her 'creator'.

The story and the dance scenes seemed to fuse perfectly together. Sidney Sheldon had written the tale around the music numbers and left it to Fred to decide what he wanted to dance and how. But there were complications in some of the scenes involving Fred Astaire, the actor. Early on in the production, Sheldon had an urgent call to meet Astaire on the set. Fred said he couldn't possibly do a scene the way the writer had planned it. He wanted it rewritten.

Fred was supposed to tell Ann Miller just how angry he was at being deserted. Earlier in the story, he had turned down the chance of going to Broadway without her, and now she was accepting a solo part that would leave him out in the cold.

'I can't do it,' Fred explained, 'because in this scene I'm supposed to be rude to her.'

Fred Astaire, the gallant gentleman, was worried not so much about his image as about the very idea of being rude to a lady.

'Fred,' Sheldon tried to soothe, '*you're* not rude to her. The character you're playing is rude to her. She has just done something terrible to you.'

Fred replied: 'I know, Sidney. But I still can't do it.' So Sheldon had to 'soften' the effect.

Relations between the two were slightly fraught and not simply because of this particular misunderstanding. Sheldon was fascinated by the perfection of Astaire's dance routines.

On one occasion, Fred was so preoccupied rehearsing a dance routine that he didn't notice the writer was even in the same room. Astaire was puffing and blowing from sheer exhaustion, and sweat was beading on his brow. The only people he thought were around him were the ones he could see – the rehearsal pianist and Robert Alton, the dance director who fitted the over-all dancing effects to Fred's own choreography.

At the end of one very obviously vital spin, Sheldon tapped the still sweating Astaire on the shoulder and told him, joking: 'No, Fred, like this. . . .'

Astaire, as Sheldon recalls it, 'got absolutely hysterical'. And hardly any wonder.

All in all, *Easter Parade* worked splendidly, relations between star and writer apart. The film was set in the heart of the pre-1917 ragtime era, with mentions of Ziegfeld and Dillingham to evoke memories of Fred's own days on the boards. The tunes ranged from 'I Want To Go Back to Michigan' to 'The Girl on the Magazine Cover' – with 'Easter Parade' itself and an additional batch of sufficient new songs as were considered necessary to keep the whole piece alive and fresh – which is exactly what it turned out to be.

Fred sang and danced: 'It Only Happens When I Dance With You' and Judy Garland heard Peter Lawford tell her he was simply 'A Fella With An Umbrella'. But the real show stopper was a number that owes itself more to Irving Berlin than anyone else. The production was already well in hand when Berlin turned to Arthur Freed and suggested simply 'Let's have a tramps' number'. When Freed said 'Yes,' Berlin produced one of those songs that becomes a milestone in so many different people's lives – as well as a classic piece of cinema. 'A Couple of Swells' actually had the suave Mr Astaire with a tooth blacked out, wearing a filthy frayed collar, a patched tail coat, dirty shoes, a two-day growth of beard and – believe it, you must – a top hat that had probably not been in one piece for a generation. Everybody loved it – especially Judy who was dressed almost identically.

It came in a part of the film that was a show within a show, but is now remembered vividly by people who have long forgotten not only the context of the number but the title of the film itself.

Fred did not just dance, sing, act and strum a ragtime violin in *Easter Parade*, he also indulged again in one of his long-felt passions. He played the drums in a way that would have delighted Gene Kruper and excited the audience by dancing between taps on the skins, to the tune, 'Drum Crazy'.

When the film was sneak-previewed in London, Reg Whitley in the *Evening Standard* said all that ever needed to be said of Astaire:

> Partnered by snub-nosed Judy Garland, he sings and dances with the vigour of a teenager through a film which sets a new high standard for musical comedy on stage or screen. . . . The brilliance of Fred Astaire inspires Judy Garland, who gives her finest performance to date.
>
> Here is a really magnificent film which, from a production angle, begins where the fast-moving stage shows *Oklahoma*! and *Annie Get Your Gun* leave off. I predict with confidence that it will become the talk of every town in the country. And of every country with towns big enough to show it.

What Reg Whitley hinted at was an absolute fact. *Easter Parade* had a lot in common with both *Oklahoma*! and *Annie Get Your Gun*. For while *Annie Get Your Gun* which was also by Berlin, consolidated the revolution in stage musicals begun by *Oklahoma*!, *Easter Parade* set a pattern that would be followed by film musicals for more than a decade. It was a new kind of movie with a new kind of flavour. Certainly, not even Fred Astaire had ever made anything like it.

The *New York Times* had just one wish: 'Let's hope that he'll never again talk of retiring.'

To put the paper's mind at rest – and those of a few million fans, too – MGM quickly announced that Fred Astaire would make another big MGM musical and that Judy would again be the co-star. She and Fred were not dancing partners, much more two individual stars who happened to be working in the same picture together, and, as Sheldon said, the chemistry was right.

The new film was to be called *The Barkleys of Broadway* and everyone was certain that Astaire and Garland would make a brilliant job of it. The story was written by Betty Comden and Adolph Green, who always seemed to have a very nice double-act together – reading the script to the assembled company at the beginning of a film.

Judy commented to Fred after the first of these: 'If we can only do as well as they did, we're OK.' Unfortunately, Judy wasn't OK. She started putting on weight and she was constantly ill. The old mental depression that had taken her to a nursing home before *Easter Parade* was back.

Plans had not advanced very far before the studio made the momentous announcement that Judy Garland was going to be replaced. And followed it with a still more momentous statement: the replacement would be Ginger Rogers.

Can't Stop Talking

It seemed an incredible, if inspired, choice. A telegram had gone off to Ginger's ranch at Oregon and she had accepted not just a part in a film called *The Barkleys Of Broadway*, but the role of once more being Fred Astaire's partner.

Of course, the news set the gossip columnists into their favourite state of apoplexy. There was going to be one more glorious episode in the Hollywood story labelled 'Astaire–Rogers' and everyone knew how much the two loved the idea of working together again.

That was certainly the popular impression. The old, frequently quoted stories of disagreement between Fred and Ginger were completely forgotten and nobody tried to dig them up from the morgue. In short, the old team were back in harness again – even if neither of them now liked the term any more than they had a decade earlier.

It was also good for the studio – if it only meant that Fred forgot about that retirement talk. Now, he said, he would stay in business for 'as long as audiences want to see my pictures and so long as I can keep on my feet.'

MGM naturally thought that anything RKO could manage in the thirties, they would be able to achieve at the very end of the forties – and if it worked, well, who knew what could be made to happen in the fifties? They certainly knew the value of the Astaire–Rogers combination. Even in pre-war box office terms, when people paid just pennies to see films, RKO's take from the series was an estimated eighteen million dollars.

Certainly, no one was more excited about the prospect of what looked like being an historic moment than Charles Walters, whom producer Arthur Freed had selected to direct the comeback picture. He looked forward to it with all the enthusiasm of a small boy about to be taken to the zoo.

Getting Ginger had not been quite as easy as people had thought it would be and Chuck Walters had his time cut out just persuading her. In fact, there had to be a great deal of negotiating before final agreement was reached. Above all, she wanted to see the script which Betty Comden and Adolph Green had prepared for Judy. When it arrived, she agreed there was no great difficulty in adapting the words and actions Miss Garland had been expected to perform to her own needs.

The importance of her first meeting with Fred on the set was not lost on the crew. Mr Walters received them in due ceremony – with tears running down his cheek. He just couldn't believe his good fortune. As things turned out, he now remembers, Fred and Ginger weren't quite as overjoyed at being together as he was at the prospect of directing them.

Fred himself has always protested that he and Ginger got on splendidly. They did their work together without rancour and with a professional approach. They respected each other's search for perfection. Ginger has persistently denied that they were anything but the best of friends.

But there is not much doubt either that Fred was slightly less enthusiastic about this pairing than he was willing to admit. The RKO pictures were things that had already happened and he was now developing his acute dislike of dwelling on the past. Almost fifty years old, Fred was determined to think only of the future – with all the bright prospects that improved colour and the other talked-of changes in filming techniques offered. Was making a tenth film with Ginger – after all that time away from the 'team' – a step backwards? That could possibly explain the reserve which Charles Walters says he detected on the set.

Another explanation could be the way Fred was looking at Ginger. She had seemed to change during the ten years they had been apart

200

professionally. Her manner was the same. Her smile was as sweet as it had always been. Her appearance was as immaculate. But there was a difference. It struck Fred as quickly as it occurred to Chuck Walters and the crew. Ginger was looking uncomfortably tall. She finally admitted that her heels were rather higher than they had been in the old days – and agreed to scale them down. Even so, nothing about the *Barkleys* set was quite like the old days in the thirties.

But the serious problems came in the wake of Judy Garland's dismissal from the project. One day, Judy turned up at the studio while Ginger was working and somehow managed to break through the security cordon and get on to *the Barkleys* set. She stood behind the camera muttering until ordered to leave by Walters. When she refused to go, he forcibly removed her – as she shouted not particularly nice things at Miss Rogers.

None of the difficulties, however, prevented *The Barkleys of Broadway* from being both a successful and an entertaining film. It is open to speculation whether it would have been better or worse had Judy Garland been Fred's partner.

Certainly with her, there would have been a minstrel number. It is also unlikely that Fred would have appeared in top hat, white tie and tails without Ginger looking elegant and pretty in a long ball gown, which Judy would have found difficult to emulate. Time had still not made Fred's 'penguin look' old fashioned, but it was plainly the one concession to the old Astaire–Rogers image he was willing to make – as though he were allowing the film to establish its identity and so qualify in the collection.

It should not be forgotten that there was a great deal going for the *Barkleys*, even without the seemingly magical combination of Astaire and Rogers. Harry Warren wrote a delightful score for the picture and Ira Gershwin provided a set of lyrics that were as good as any he had produced in his entire career. For the big dance number, Ira suggested resurrecting a piece he had written with his brother George – 'They Can't Take That Away From Me'. No one wanted to take that away from the film.

The story was much less flimsy than the others had been – although the trend for this had already been set with the last film, *The Castles*. Newspaper reports said the new picture was based on the life of the celebrated actress Gaby Deslys. Certainly, one incongruous part of the picture comes when Ginger takes it into her head to do a Sarah Bernhardt – and recites the Marseillaise to a stunned but appreciative *Academie Francaise*.

Charles Walters has misty eyes when he insists that Fred and Ginger seemed to love each other in front of the cameras – and a misty memory. Basically, the Barkleys were almost always at war with each other. They were a married dance team who were constantly quarrelling. He wanted her to continue dancing; she wanted a dramatic career – the irony of that situation didn't strike many people at the time, but it was just the sort of thing being reported at the time newsmen were speculating in the thirties, about the Astaire–Rogers partnership's future.

Oscar Levant was on hand to lend his own peculiar species of dry wit to the picture and his contribution worked as well as anything else did in the *Barkleys*. But the dances worked best of all, none more delightfully than 'My One And Only Highland Fling' which presented the cinema with yet another Astaire characterisation, Fred in a kilt.

This was one number for which it was not difficult to imagine Judy Garland stepping into Ginger's dancing shoes. Indeed, it would have been a splendid follow-up to the 'Couple of Swells' number they did in *Easter Parade* – and doubtless it was meant to be just that.

Fred's best solo number came when he was surrounded by a dozen or more pairs of dancing shoes with no feet in them – for 'Shoes With Wings On'. Fred and the seemingly ownerless shoes were fighting each other for attention – and leading what could accurately be called a merry dance all around.

This was Hermes Pan's sole contribution to the *Barkleys* and was one of the most splendid examples of trick photography ever devised, as difficult to choreograph successfully as Gene Kelly's dance with cartoon characters in *An American In Paris* and Julie Andrews's adventures in *Mary Poppins*. But this was much more inventive, for the shoes had to dance as though they were really being worn while the people inside had to be entirely invisible.

If this was trick photography, the tricks deserved an Oscar. In the end it was all brought off by a combination of black velvet screens – so that only the shoes and not the feet inside them would be seen – and a great deal of back projection. The number ended with Fred attempting to destroy the ownerless dancing shoes with a broom, not quite as elegant an instrument as the one used in *Top Hat* and not quite as successful in terms of the action because the shoes refused to die until he used a pistol. But it was beautiful choreography.

The press liked the film – even if only because a new generation of critics were for the first time able to write about Astaire and Rogers together. *Time* magazine seemed to forget what it had said about Rita Hayworth and commented: 'Ginger is still the best movie dancing partner that Astaire ever had.'

The London *Daily Express* termed it: 'One of the gayest, most enjoyable musicals in years. The plot. . . . Ira Gershwin's lilting lyrics, Harry Warren's catchy music and brilliant dresses all add up to a hit.

At forty-nine, Astaire has lost none of his skill afoot, vocally or as a comedian.'

Ginger was spotted at a preview of the picture and proved that she hadn't lost any of her old nerves. She sat entirely still throughout the whole film without muttering a word to her companion, although she occasionally seemed to be mopping her brow. Once, however, she did allow her composure to slip – to give Astaire's 'Shoes' number a hearty round of applause.

Just as in the old days, everybody wanted to know what the next Astaire–Rogers film would be. There was indeed talk of more, but it dwindled away. No plans were actually announced, and there was to be no eleventh Astaire–Rogers film. The two had done what the fans had been begging for, and once done, it was enough.

The Band Wagon

So what now? It was the question asked every time any one had ever mentioned the ending of the partnership with Ginger previously, and it was again the question in 1949. Now it seemed less important, because the film industry had changed and the film musical had altered with it. As for Fred Astaire, at the turn of his half-century, he seemed very happy indeed with the way things were.

There was a polish to the screen that it had lacked before, and the dancing and singing were both sophisticated and more real, both of which pleased Mr Astaire very greatly.

The question of partners continued to crop up, but there was devastating news about his next film. He was going to stop dancing before the picture was halfway through. His new partner in the picture would be Red Skelton. The film turned out to be *Three Little Words* which was to prove the first of a glorious series in an even more glorious Astaire decade.

It was different from anything Fred had done before. There would be more comedy than previously and because he stops dancing so early on in the scenario, more acting opportunities for him, too. It once again had Fred in a biographical role – playing songwriter Bert Kalmar to Skelton's Harry Ruby. Such dancing as Fred did do was opposite a little charmer who was to make a fair impact on

Hollywood in the fifties, Vera-Ellen (the hyphen was always used in her billing).

Much of the glamour in the picture revolved around the beauty – she was, in fact, a beauty consultant as well as an actress – Arlene Dahl, although her big number threatened to turn into a reprise of what was not exactly Fred Astaire's happiest memory of the films with Ginger Rogers.

She stood at the top of a large staircase with a pink fan, frightened above all else of falling off and crashing to the ground. She was also frightened of sneezing, for with every step she took, more feathers from the fan flew in all directions. One or two of them lingered around her nose for so long that she was certain a calamity was imminent.

When she finally did reach the ground, with Astaire ready to sweep her firmly off her feet, there were a few whispered words of comfort from him too which was calculated to put any leading lady at ease.

Fred's dancing exploits in the picture end when Bert Kalmer is supposed to have a serious fall and takes to songwriting with his baseball addict partner Harry Ruby. In between, there are the usual jokes, the usual girls – one of them a delightful young lady called Debbie Reynolds – and the usual love story. The tunes, all by Ruby and Kalmar, were standards like 'I Wanna Be Loved By You', 'Nevertheless', 'Who's Sorry Now', 'You Are My Lucky Star' and the title tune. There was also the added benefit of the occasional period piece like 'So long – Oolong'.

Fred certainly liked making *Three Little Words* and the box office take proved he had chosen a pretty good vehicle for himself. The critics apparently thought so, too. The New York *Herald Tribune* said that both Astaire and Vera-Ellen were 'at the top of their form'. It was a sentiment echoed by most American writers.

In London, however, the whole species of which *Three Little Words* formed part, was examined more thoroughly and with far less respect. The *Evening Standard* said:

Forget that in *On The Town* recently at this same cinema, American screen musicals suddenly and excitingly grew up. Here we are back again with another biography of a team of Broadway songwriters. . . .

It would all be as dated and conventional as the Kalmar-Ruby numbers themselves – were it not for the stars. But Fred Astaire is so very engaging as the lyricist who really wants to be a magician; Red Skelton so likeably gauche as the baseball-mad composer; and Vera-Ellen so infectiously happy as a new partner for Fred Astaire that criticism is charmed and laughed away. [It was at that point that the *Standard's* critic put into writing what every Astaire partner wished to read more than anything else.] Vera-Ellen is certainly the best leading lady Astaire has had since Ginger Rogers – with the same grace and much the same sense of humour. A pity she and Fred have comparatively little dancing to do. As an actor, he has improved out of all knowledge, but this is the kind of story which should be danced and sung, but not acted.

Every now and again, Fred worried as much as the critics about the rash of so-called screen biographies – *Three Little Words* contained the occasional germ of truth but hardly worried itself about mere facts. In an age when true stories of people who could be given some kind of musical peg were being rushed to the studios as quickly as they could be dashed off the typewriter, approaches were made to Fred, too – to agree to have someone play *him* in a film. It was basically an academic question for the future, since Astaire was still working and his face was known to every small boy on both sides of the Atlantic. But studios liked to buy options – if only to prevent their competitors making a picture first.

Fred said 'No' – just as everybody expected him to do. When five years before, Warner Brothers had made the George Gershwin story *Rhapsody In Blue*, the young dancer friend of the composer was given an entirely meaningless name, although most people suspected it was meant to be Astaire. Soon after *Three Little Words* was released, Fred inserted a clause in his will. He directed that no one should ever attempt to make a film biography of him.

About this time, he said of his own film appearances: 'When I see myself on the screen, I'm immediately sorry about the whole business. I want to get up and walk out. And sometimes I do.'

Now he wanted to protect future generations from the same sort of 'suffering'.

Most of all he wanted to protect his private life. By now he and Phyllis had achieved what everybody told them would be impossible. They had kept the public away from their front door. By avoiding the razzamataz and steering clear of the big public occasions, Fred could live two distinct lives.

When he and Phyllis did entertain or go out for dinner the evenings were as private as those anyone outside Hollywood enjoyed in their own homes. Frequently, the David Nivens and the Astaires dined with each other. Often, it was the Astaires and the Cole Porters. The importance of the guests didn't make Phyllis treat Fred any differently from the way many another wife would relate to her husband. It was at the ranch one night that Phyllis suggested that Fred and Hermes Pan might benefit from washing the dishes. They got as far as the kitchen – and then decided that it was all rather a waste of talent. So instead of washing the dishes, they smashed them on to the floor. It saved a great deal of work.

That story would have thrilled the fan magazines – but they didn't get hold of it. They contented themselves with 'revealing' – it certainly wasn't the sort of thing either Phyllis or Fred would have published – that the Astaires slept in single beds and that Mr Astaire always wore silk pyjamas. He didn't waste his time confirming or denying the stories, but they probably irritated him to distraction. The fact that Fred sometimes attended police line-ups was a little more difficult to deny. He had got to know the men at the local precinct and it seemed a lot more lively than simply reading detective stories.

Fred also kept up his interest in the dance schools although he spent much less time on them than previously. He had about forty of these now, the largest was the one in New York and there were plans to continue expanding.

Lessons were in mirror-lined cubicles and each school used to send back messages indicating the most popular dances they taught. For years, the rhumba was at the top of many of the branch lists. 'We are going to ask Fred to think up a new dance' said an executive of the company.

Pupils paid $8 a lesson – a lot of money for those days, but the instructors were hand-picked. The Astaire managers decided to look for the college boy and girl type, but none of them had to be particularly good-looking. 'The person who is too good-looking is too self-centred to be a good teacher,' one manager explained.

Fred and Phyllis still spent as much time as they could with Adele. Now, however, the Lady Charles Cavendish had a more mundane name. She had married Kingman Douglas, a former senior Army officer who was also well-connected in American society, and by doing so she had lost her title. Now she was a mere 'Mrs'. It didn't seem to worry her and, as for Fred, he was delighted that she was happy again. She was now the mistress of a Southern plantation at Middleburg, Virginia.

Although the Irish seat of her late husband was back in the possession of the Cavendish family, Adele was greatly loved by them and still considered to be one of their own. She was told she could continue to use Lismore Castle whenever she wanted to. It was still a wonderful place for her summer holidays.

Fred knew he was welcome with Phyllis and the children at Lismore, too, although they didn't use the privilege often. Fred, in fact, seemed to be welcome wherever he went. The New York Racquet and Tennis Club were proud that he had decided to join, and hoped he would do for them what he had achieved for the golf clubs of Beverly Hills, but it was clear there was to be no real contest between them. A man who could get round the course in the middle 70s took some pulling away, no matter how keen the competition or the flattery. One writer commented at the time: 'He appreciates flattery, but he isn't fooled by it.'

Even in golf, he protested he knew his limitations. When someone asked him about the magical legs that people still remembered had been insured for a million dollars, he said: 'The only time I remember my legs is on the golf course – when I find I can't get them in the right position. I get very annoyed with my legs sometimes.'

What did annoy him immensely was 'the constant chewing over my age'.

He explained:

They're always referring to actors or ball players or fighters as ageing or balding. There's no deadline on activity. The important thing is what a fellow does and how well he does it. I think I look peculiar lots of times. It's very confusing to look at yourself and be objective. I always figure I could do better.

If Fred ever felt that he could be dancing faster or playing better – or even just that he wished he had never made a picture at all – the emotions were all applicable to his next movie, *Let's Dance*. Even Hermes

208

Pan has allowed himself to suggest that Fred should have saved his effort and done something else. Betty Hutton was teamed with him in this and as Pan and everyone else agrees, it was miscasting of the classic sort. Fred insists he and Betty Hutton got along fine but others sensed some tension.

Fred needed to dance with a graceful lady, but Betty Hutton was used to exercising her lungs like a female Tarzan.

There were, however, occasional moments of delight even in *Let's Dance*, the best of them featuring Astaire the piano player as much as Astaire the dancer; in one scene he showed just what an adept dab hand at the keyboard he could be. He didn't merely play the piano, he danced around it, to the accompaniment of a cat's chorus. It was Hermes Pan's idea to stuff ten cats inside the piano and release them only when the number was completed!

That was precisely what happened – and why the Society For The Prevention Of Cruelty To Animals didn't immediately protest must be one of the biggest mysteries of all time. Had the number been filmed in England, Fred Astaire would have become an immediate outcast and consigned to the nearest unemployment line.

As it was, the cats scrambled all over the set and up into the flies. Fred had little more to do than explain just how ecstatic he was about cats. He is, in fact, something of a cat fancier – not quite in the way he is of horse flesh, but simply as an addict to feline charms. Except for those inside the piano, all cats seem to love him and he loves them.

The number apart, *Let's Dance* was a disaster and looking back today from afar, it was the only hiatus in those glorious Fifties. *Royal Wedding* which opened in February 1951 was more in the usual romantic Astaire niche. The story of a Broadway brother and sister dance team who come to London in time for the marriage of the then Princess Elizabeth and Prince Philip was right up Fred's street.

Of course, there was a distinct similarity to the story of Fred and Adele, the film brother and sister take a show to the elegant British capital and the girl falls in love with a peer of the realm. And as in the film version of the one show Fred didn't do with Adele, there were title problems with *Royal Wedding*. As *Gay Divorce* became *Gay Divorcee* in America, so *Royal Wedding* became *Wedding Bells* in Britain – the British were thought to be rather sensitive about the use of the word 'royal'.

As in countless other Astaire pictures there were also casting problems. Selected to play Fred's sister was June Allyson, the nearest Hollywood had come to a 'Sweetheart' since Mary Pickford. And by all accounts she revelled in the idea. Matters were complicated, however, when she became pregnant.

As a result of this inconvenience, MGM tried to show that, despite all that had happened in the past, it had a heart. The studio boldly announced that Judy Garland would play with Fred Astaire again – and so give everyone the opportunity of enjoying once more the duo who had made such an impact in *Easter Parade*. But that, too, was more easily said than done. Chuck Walters was relieved of the task of directing the picture because he said he couldn't face the agony of another Astaire–Garland project. He knew what he was doing.

Judy started turning up late for rehearsals and then began missing them out altogether. Before long, she was summarily dismissed just as she had been from *The Barkleys*.

Judy's dismissal came by telegram – a long, meandering legal document sent to every one of half a dozen addresses where she was considered likely to be staying. It was the end of any notion that she and Fred would make a good investment for MGM and more good entertainment for the public.

Films like shows, however, have to go on. The choice for Fred's partner finally settled on Jane Powell who sang and danced beautifully, and because she was about eight inches shorter than Fred, presented not the slightest problem of being seen in close-up with him.

Alan Jay Lerner, who wrote the screenplay and the lyrics, was not as overawed by what he had created as were a number of people who sat in canvas-backed chairs on film sets. He said he was frightened that the picture was going to charm itself to death.

One of the numbers in the film that prevented that happening was a comedy tour-de-force that deserves to be re-run whenever anyone has the bright idea of showing a history of the movie musical. It is all summed up by the title 'How Could You Believe Me When I Said I Loved You When You Know I've Been A Liar All My Life'. Astaire and Jane Powell sing it in one of the film's stage interludes and time after time it set audiences clapping – which is normally a pretty unrewarding thing to do in a cinema. But the fact that the screen can neither hear nor react didn't stop it happening. Burton Lane and Lerner created the number in the course of a short car journey. Lerner mentioned the title in one breath of inspiration and Lane just happened to hum the tune.

Peter Lawford was also in the picture and Sir Winston Churchill's actress daughter, Sarah, was too.

Fred danced in this film in nightclubs, on a stage and in a gymnasium – where he did one of his most famous routines with the least temperamental partner of his whole career, a hat stand. But the dance that made people positively hold on to their seats was one in a small room. Fred seemed to dance like a fly on the ceiling and, without support, on the windows and walls too. 'How on earth is that done?' people were supposed to ask – and for the most part they did. The secret has since been revealed – although never satisfactorily copied. Fred danced in a room that formed part of a revolving drum. Since the camera went round with the rest of the drum, the audiences were left with the illusion that Fred was actually dancing upside down and sideways. Clever stuff, indeed.

If Fred could defy gravity in the picture, he didn't completely succeed in defying the critics. One British writer said:

There are only a limited number of things that can be done with one's feet and Mr Fred Astaire has about exhausted them all. . . . Despite Mr Astaire's ingenuity and the familiar newsreel shots of the royal wedding, *Wedding Bells* remains a second-rate musical that leaves Anglo-American relations just about where they are now.

Perhaps it ought to be explained that Britain was not altogether happy with America's stand in world affairs – the Korean conflict was not going very well and martial aid was causing a number of domestic tiffs. Most people, however, seemed to think that Fred Astaire would always be an insurance policy against any serious rupture between the two countries and it was even suggested he would make an ideal Ambassador to The Court of St James's, but it never happened.

However he was given a token of appreciation for his contribution to motion pictures and from the people who knew best of all how important that contribution had been – the film industry, itself. They presented him with a special Oscar, marking his outstanding part in the Hollywood story. Appropriately, the award was accepted by

Ginger Rogers, as Fred was out of town when the presentation ceremony took place.

The citation for the Oscar stated that it was given for 'the artistry that has brought a unique delight to picture audiences and has raised the standards of all musical pictures'.

If Vera-Ellen, as the critic had said, was the natural successor to Miss Rogers, the ticket-buyers were invited to show their approval or disapproval of the fact in Fred's next film.

Together they made *The Belle of New York* the movie Astaire was due to film just before he announced his temporary retirement in 1946. It was the film he had promised Arthur Freed he would do should he ever come out of that retirement. The five pictures that preceded it seemed to indicate that he constantly tried to put it off. Fred never liked *Belle* and, after it was made, neither did many of the critics. But like *Royal Wedding* it looks very much better today than it did at the time – and the songs by Henry Warren and Johnny Mercer were both tuneful and good. It was very loosely based on the old Broadway show and the story was set in that same turn-of-the-century era, but there were a number of 'fifties hallmarks about it and altogether the film deserves a better fate than it has ever enjoyed. The principal weaknesses are in the crude attempts at trick photography and a few hints from *The Barkleys of Broadway* in that direction would not have gone amiss.

Vera-Ellen, like all the Astaire leading ladies at one time or another, was somewhat in awe of Fred. And like all the others, she was amazed at just how worried Fred could be over whether or not a number was working out. But she was tickled by another Astaire characteristic, producing pictures of his horses from his wallet in much the same way other men showed photographs of their children. He had quite an extensive stable by now, although none of them looked like being another Triplicate. There were high hopes particularly for Triplicate's younger daughter Stripteaser – hopes that never were to be completely realised. Until Stripteaser could come to the fore, his ambitions were directed at Witch Wookey and Blue Border. They didn't materialise, but Fred put it all down to experience.

He was trying to slot *Belle of New York* into the same category, but its failure concerned him just the same. He has said in his autobiography that the only thing *Belle of New York* gave him was a fortune.

Charles Walters did direct this picture and has been even more uncharitable about it than Fred. He said he hated everything about it – and mainly because he didn't think there was any real chemistry between Astaire and Vera-Ellen. I must say the finished result didn't give that impression, and there certainly had been a great deal of that mysterious reaction known as chemistry between them in *Three Little Words*.

The real problem was that no one really knew what the other person was supposed to be doing. With a thoroughly organised and well-prepared star like Astaire that was supreme carelessness.

Fred, it seems, didn't like the orchestrations, most of which, he has said, were much too slow for his tastes.

'Everything was gaiety and charm and I'd say "Cut" and you could see his face drop,' Walters recalls now.

To make matters worse, the proceedings were just about three-quarters completed without there being a third act – and although there were rarely intervals in those days to divide pictures into natural sections, film scenarios were conceived as if there were. So, while Fred and Vera played their parts before the cameras hoping no one would notice that they had no idea about their next move, the writers Robert O'Brien and Irving Elinson were sitting in another corner of the sound stage scribbling.

Eventually, they got out a completed story. It had several similarities to the original Broadway production which had been the very first American show to come to London's West End – and was about a playboy who falls for a girl Salvationist. But the music was new and so was the dancing in thin air that both Fred and Vera-Ellen did to show they were in love. It was as corny as that – but sometimes corn can be enjoyable and *Belle of New York* is so today.

It also gave Fred the odd interlude of fun. It provided an opportunity for taking Fred Junior to San Francisco for a ride on the cable car – the nearest thing around to the nineteenth century New York tram used in the film. 'He got a bang out of them,' said Fred Senior at the time. 'And I got a bang idea for a dance routine.' If he did it wasn't noticed by the other people working on the set of *Belle*. One writer said that while making the film, he was 'morose and hardly fit to be spoken to'. He said of himself round about this time: 'I'm not easy going. I've got a bad temper. When I get mad, I throw chairs around.'

On the ranch, where the family was now growing oranges and

grapefruit as well as raising the horses, Fred was an entirely different man. Stripteaser was fussed over like a baby. If she didn't actually feel like one of the family it was not the fault of any of the Astaires.

The ranch was a superb escape valve, a place where Fred could be the country gentleman who loved to play jazz records or work out on his own set of drums. It was also the place where he could consider all the offers that constantly came in. There was talk soon after the completion of *Belle of New York* of launching him in a new Betty Comden and Adolph Green story called *The Strategy of Love*. The title's pedigree didn't seem the kind of thing Fred Astaire would attempt – it was based on a fourteenth century guide to romance, but was updated as the story of a television writer who attempts to woo a modern young miss.

Ever since the remainder of Fred's hair first began going grey, he had worried about the implications of his dancing with much younger girls. That could be the principal reason he rejected *Strategy Of Love* – despite the entreaties of Arthur Freed and the rest of the MGM hierarchy.

Much more readily, he accepted another Freed production, *The Band Wagon*. That, of course, had been the title of one of his happiest Broadway experiences, the last show he and Adele did together.

There were a few similarities between the stage *Band Wagon* and the film, but not enough to notice. The main one, of course, was the presence of Fred Astaire. The other similarity was in the music. The scores of both were provided by Arthur Schwartz and Howard Dietz. Four of the tunes had, in fact, been in the earlier show – 'High and Low'; 'Dancing In The Dark'; 'New Sun In The Sky' and the merry-go-round German spoof that made such an impact on Broadway in 1931, 'I Love Louisa'. That being said, everything about the new *Band Wagon* was different – and new, in every way.

It was new because the film had a definite plot – about a screen star of the recent past who decides to make a comeback via a Broadway show – while the stage version had been a revue without any pretence of a story. It was importantly new because it linked Astaire with probably his most competent dancing partner to date, and certainly one of the most beautiful, Cyd Charisse. And it was new because it also featured a young lady whose memories of Mr Astaire are neither as pleasant nor as adulatory as those of most of her predecessors.

Nanette Fabray had the second female lead in the picture, she played the young girl writer who, with Oscar Levant, had just completed the very show that would give the star played by Astaire his new break. She sang and danced – and did both charmingly. She acted as though the situations were actually happening instead of merely learning a collection of lines written for her by Betty Comden and Adolph Green. But she and Fred Astaire did not get on – and that is putting it mildly.

Today, she says she found him 'very stand-offish, aloof and kind of private.' Well, Fred Astaire has always been very private. But it went deeper than that.

She and Fred were shooting the scene that introduces the 'I Love Louisa' number. The first take was in its stride when, she says, Fred interrupted everything and called a halt. At first, Miss Fabray thought it was the number of extras hovering around that caused Fred momentarily to lose his cool. If it was, he put the blame elsewhere.

'Stop,' she recalls him saying. 'This will never do. I'm not going to stand for that.' But stand for what? Nanette insists to this day that she doesn't know. All that Fred would say was to repeat 'I'm not going to stand for that,' and to add 'I went through that with Betty Hutton and I'm not going through it with you.'

Betty Hutton's partnership with Fred was a nightmare in every way, but the young actress couldn't feel responsible for that. She asked Fred again what she had done wrong and again he wouldn't tell her.

The scene was in an hotel room where the young kids of the show's chorus had intended to celebrate their pre-Broadway opening. Instead, they were holding a wake – but an enjoyable one and taking out of it every ounce of fun that they could. It was into that room that a thoroughly dejected Fred Astaire walks and, somehow from the boys and girls there, takes on the same spirit of jollity. With Nanette, he sings 'I Love Louisa', but because of the problems between them, problems that to this day the lady says she finds incredible, nothing got into an acceptable state for a very long time.

She asked the director, Vincent Minnelli what the matter was and all he would say was 'Whatever it was you were doing, just don't do it.' It was then that the puzzled Miss Fabray decided to approach Astaire yet again. 'Please,' she recalls telling him, 'please tell me what I did. I'll do anything you say, but I don't know what I did.' To which she says Fred replied: 'Oh, yes you do.'

This was a situation without an end in sight. All that poor Nanette Fabray could do, she insists, was to say; 'I *don't* know, but I'm willing to try again.'

Fred's version of the story is slightly different. He does recall it in his autobiography, but he gallantly doesn't tie it in any way to Nanette. He says that at that moment, he simply lost his powers of concentration and walked off, to everyone's astonishment.

It was indeed an un-Astaire-like gesture. But why? Nanette says she thinks it was because Phyllis was ill at the time but by all other accounts she was in her normal good health. It remains one of the mysteries of Hollywood.

None of the traumas recalled by Nanette Fabray – and she is certainly not the only actress to have been brought to tears by Fred's insistence on his brand of perfection being copied by everyone else – seem to have affected the outcome of the picture. It must now rank as one of the best of all the Astaire films. But she says that it didn't seem to be a happy picture for anybody. You wouldn't get any idea of discord from watching the comedy number in which Fabray, Buchanan and Astaire mysteriously turn into three babies – complete with bonnets and matinée jackets. Together, they sang 'Triplets', a number that is one of the funniest things ever seen on film.

It was producer Arthur Freed's idea to team Fred in a picture with the man who for years had been known as his British equivalent, Jack Buchanan. In *The Band Wagon*, he played the director of the show – a man with illusions of grandeur who thought that he could turn Faust into a musical. Eventually, when it becomes obvious that the only kind of show that can succeed is a song-and-dance musical (nobody has ever claimed that the *plot* of *Band Wagon* was particularly impressive) he and Fred dance together – and inevitably in top hat, white tie and tails. Strangely, it is in this teaming of the 'two Astaires', British and American, that Fred's superiority is seen to the full. Even the top hat didn't look as well on Buchanan as it did on Astaire.

And his top hat was not alone in being a bad fit. His teeth weren't right either. He had just been through a series of dental treatments and was working throughout the picture in a constant state of pain. Again, it didn't show.

It was also, contrary to legend, Jack Buchanan and not Astaire who led the singing in a number which, only now after more than twenty years, threatens to usurp 'There's No Business Like Showbusiness' as the anthem of the theatre. It was called 'That's Entertainment', one of the few pieces written by Dietz and Schwartz for this version of *The Band Wagon*.

By becoming the theme song for that collection of MGM musical clips called, inevitably, *That's Entertainment* and for the sequel *That's Entertainment Part Two*, it entered the comparatively small company of songs that tend to symbolise an era – and in so doing, become part of history themselves.

The writers, Comden and Green, have complained that all they were expected to do for *The Band Wagon* was come up with a story that could be neatly fitted around the songwriters' catalogue.

Another new number was 'The Girl Hunt Ballet', which featured Astaire and Cyd Charisse in the kind of spectacle that now makes buffs of the dance positively drool. It was based on the Mickey Spillane stories which in the pre-Bond era seemed to take as far as possible a combination of a little sadism and a great deal of sex and crime. Fred was the gangster; Cyd, his moll, firstly as a blonde, then her more usual brunette. As they dance, Fred, off-screen, reads the Spillane-like words written for the film by Alan Jay Lerner: 'She had more curves than a scenic railway. . . . She was scared, scared as a turkey in November.'

The two did a more conventional routine, too. In an unlit Central Park, and in a scene vaguely reminiscent of the one with Ginger in *Top Hat*, they sweep along the pathways to the tune of 'Dancing In The Dark'.

The dance director for *Band Wagon* was a little man who at the time was described as symbolising the new young crop of Hollywood geniuses, Michael Kidd. Kidd went on to star in a picture himself, to choreograph and then also to direct a vast number of successful Broadway shows.

It was the uncanny combination of Astaire and Charisse that impressed itself most on Kidd. Uncanny because they really did work together beautifully.

Fred and Cyd had met each other very briefly when they both had taken part in *Ziegfeld Follies* – so briefly that they were on screen for only seconds and Fred had really no reason to remember her at all. It was while she was working on another MGM film that Astaire appeared on the set, without warning and proceeded to walk round and round her like a fox sizing up a new prey. In a way that was precisely what Fred was doing. When Arthur Freed offered her the co-starring part in *The Band Wagon* she realised what the circling had all been about. Astaire had simply been trying to work out how tall she was. When the shapely and amazingly beautiful Miss Charisse was established as shorter than he was, the green light was given to the idea of her becoming the latest Astaire dancing partner.

When the two of them appeared for rehearsals for the first time, the incredible effect of the presence of Astaire was summarised in one small incident. If she had nothing else – and the comparison of her curves with a scenic railway was not totally a figment of Mr Lerner's imagination – Cyd Charisse had a remarkable pair of legs, legs that looked at their very best in rehearsal tights. As she moved on to the floor, no one needed high-powered lenses to spot the saliva on the lips of most men present. When she and Fred started dancing together, all eyes were still on her. But as the number gained momentum, a very strange thing happened. As Kidd now recalls: 'Fred was older than Cyd, lantern jaws, eyes kind of sad, drooping and balding and not one's conception of a beautiful star.' But, totally unexpectedly and suddenly, the eyes moved from Miss Charisse to Astaire.

'There was something startling about this man as he began to dance,' Kidd says. 'You could not take your eyes off him. It was a unique phenomenon. His looks belied his ability. His age belied his abilities. He was virtually ageless.'

As it turned out, people made an occupation of watching Astaire on the set of *The Band Wagon* and not simply watching his dance routines. They were fascinated just by the way he walked. Crowds would gather just to watch him stepping from the rehearsal hall to the set. Other people walk. Fred Astaire moves. On *The Band Wagon* he even seemed to be chewing gum in step with himself.

Nanette Fabray was not wrong in suggesting that Astaire was a loner, even though her word for it, 'aloof' may be putting things too strongly. When all the others involved in the film ate at the studio commissary, Fred sat at his usual corner of the soundstage with a box of sandwiches that had been packed under Phyllis's supervision by the family cook. At the end of a day's work, he would simply disappear.

And he could be difficult – although not always in the way Miss

Fabray has said. Michael Kidd, for instance, had his problems with Astaire. Fred wanted to rehearse new routines and Kidd wanted to pace out his own ideas, too, but he didn't necessarily want to do them at the same time. So when Fred left at five o'clock, Kidd moved into the rehearsal hall himself and stayed there till after six. When Fred learned of this, he stayed on until after six, too. It was then that Kidd said goodbye and sneaked back to the hall – where he stayed until seven or eight. When Astaire got wind of this, he stayed late with him. So a new move was called for. The dance director decided to come in to work extra early – first at eight and then at seven. Every time, Fred beat him to it. In the end, they compromised and decided to work together – to everyone's apparent satisfaction.

Fred had a unique way of working out the steps he wanted and the rhythms he intended to accompany them. Instead of merely pacing them on the floor, he played them on a set of drums borrowed from the studio orchestra. He was becoming very adept at his drumming, incidentally. Today, Ava insists that she remembers her father being so immersed in his playing that he had to settle for a fairly unconventional place to store his kit – in the bath. That way, he could get to them very quickly. Fred denies the story completely – but with a chuckle.

On *The Band Wagon*, he could spend hours with Kidd, so that a single beat would be precisely right to fit the steps they had initiated together. Kidd would say: 'I visualise it like this – dum-de-dum-di-dum.' And Astaire would say 'No. It should be dum-di-dum-di-dum.' It was a war of professionals.

There was one splendid number set in a honky-tonk amusement arcade on New York's 42nd Street which was based on the old Schwartz-Dietz tune, 'A Shine On Your Shoes'. As is not difficult to appreciate, this was a dance to a shoe shine accompaniment. But, like all Astaire routines, it developed into something more. It was a syncopated smash. Other outstanding numbers in *The Band Wagon* included Fred's solo 'By Myself' and the duet with Buchanan 'I Guess I'll Have To Change My Plan'.

All in all, this last of the current batch of MGM films – his contract begun before *Blue Skies* was now completed – looked in the end as though it had been one long romp – which is precisely what a successful movie should do.

The work on the picture wound up just before Christmas 1952. On the very last day, Nanette Fabray says she went into the studio heavily laden with presents for everyone. But nobody was around to accept them. The way she sees it, the cast and crew just couldn't get shot of it all quickly enough.

Fred was happy enough himself with *The Band Wagon*, in fact he has said it was one of his favourites. As for there being problems with my work, 'I don't have problems in my work. Just solutions!' With his mother and Ava, he and Phyllis celebrated their twentieth wedding anniversary by attending the film's world premiere. It was to be a brief moment of happiness.

Fred's only criticism with *The Band Wagon* was that it began ten to fifteen minutes too early. He disliked the opening scene where an auctioneer tries in vain to drum up a sale for the most famous top hat and cane of all time – Fred's, or rather the one belonging to the character he played. Perhaps he was frightened of its being the writing on the wall. 'Otherwise,' he told the *New York Times*, 'the film was a dandy. Cyd Charisse is such a beautiful girl.'

When the writer of that article mentioned that Fred should not forget he had given a lot of people a great deal of pleasure himself, Astaire answered: 'Thanks. I hope so. I've been around a good long time.'

And Fred was slaying them not just on the screen but from the turntable, too. His songs had always been extremely popular, particularly with the men who wrote them, although he never had a million seller record or even a silver disc that showed he had sold half a million.

Usually, these were songs he had sung in his films. The discs, with him singing to lush orchestral accompaniments were recorded after a picture's completion.

Early in 1953, however, he made a series of records for Norman Granz, who had achieved world fame in jazz circles for his series of 'Jazz at the Philharmonic' discs.

Fred didn't expect any major success. Indeed, the Granz records were for a limited audience and the number manufactured was strictly limited too. All in all, he recorded thirty-four songs under the broad title of 'The Fred Astaire Story'. It was a four-LP set – with only the backing of a jazz sextet. Not at all the old Astaire sound, although you could actually hear Fred dance.

The *New Yorker* magazine commented that the set

raises a number of questions: Why devote so much space to the singing of a man who is celebrated primarily for his dancing? As everyone knows Astaire has a slight, appealing voice. Astaire, who has never had the ability to sustain a note for very long, is hard put to fill the pauses that crop up in the vocal line.

Now and then, he is heard resorting to a muttered 'yeh', which he probably felt was appropriate to the noodling work of the musicians behind him.

It was probably the toughest review Fred Astaire ever had. But it didn't worry Fred very greatly. Soon enough, there would be something far more serious to concern him.

Dancing In The Dark

If you were outside the film colony, chances are you didn't even know that Mrs Phyllis Astaire existed. A straw poll of film fans would probably have produced a majority vote in favour of Ginger Rogers as the true identity of Mrs Fred Astaire.

But things were to change, and before very long an announcement would go round the world that would shock everyone who heard it.

The first indication that all was not well should have been noticed the day at California's Santa Anita race track when Phyllis asked to be taken home early because of a sudden headache. But she recovered quickly and there didn't seem much point in pursuing the matter.

Then, just before the following Easter and at another race meeting, she felt ill again. A little later on, she was bad enough to call off going to a dinner party given by Cole Porter.

It was after that night that Phyllis went to see her doctor. He ordered X-rays to be taken. On Good Friday 1954, Phyllis had an operation, followed five hours later by a second one. This revealed what Fred had never dared to allow himself to suspect – a brain tumour. But it was never removed, the surgeons decided it was inaccessible. After these traumas, it seemed perhaps that all would be well. Fred Junior was in the Air Force at Texas and after coming home on special leave was told there was no reason not to go back to his base. The Astaires went back to their ranch.

Phyllis had made such good progress that the X-ray treatments she had been prescribed were now curtailed and the nurse who was employed to look after her was sent home.

Then in August 1954, Phyllis was back at the hospital where her first two operations had been carried out. She had had a serious relapse and a new operation was ordered. After surgery, she stayed in a coma for weeks. Finally, on September 14, she died. She was forty-six.

For Fred Astaire, dancer, film actor, singer, best-dressed man in Hollywood, life was blacker than it had ever been before. Up to then, he had seemingly been spared the tragedies of life that befall a lot of people, just as he had been granted far more blessings than most would ever dream possible. Now the blessings were in the past and the future seemed not just bleak, but meaningless.

He realised just how much he had really depended on Phyllis and how much he would miss her. No more would he hear 'r's' turn into 'w's' or the judgment on another actor or a film summed up in the word 'dweadful'.

There was, however, one saving grace: Twentieth Century Fox had signed Fred to make a film and everyone said he should do it.

It wasn't easy to comtemplate smiling in public – let alone laughing as he played the drums to a hot beat. And he would have to do all that in the picture which was to be yet another version of the classic *Daddy Long Legs*. But his friends told him to do it, and he accepted the advice. Having done that, the perfectionist in Fred Astaire wouldn't allow himself to do anything but behave as he would on any other project. It was just what his friends knew would happen. He worked himself until it seemed there could be no more energy left in his body. Cast opposite him was twenty-two-year-old Leslie Caron – she, with the gamin look that became her trade mark, played the young orphan Fred adopts and who knows his identity only by the long shadow of his legs.

Fred was more than just depressed by Phyllis's passing – he was distraught – but the work did help him forget his misery while on the set. If he had been called Moaning Minnie for years, never had he more reason to be in that guise than now. But work, as always, came first.

It turned out to be one of the best Astaire films ever – and certainly the best version of the story by Jean Webster. It had first seen the light of day, as a very successful play at the Gaiety Theatre, London. Seven years later it was a silent film with Mary Pickford. In 1952, it had its first musical treatment, again in London, but under the title *Love from Judy*.

The Astaire–Caron version, under its original name, had a completely original score by Johnny Mercer, one of the few occasions on which he was able to show his amazing talent for writing both the words and music; the ballet music was by Alec North. The title of one of these tunes became a classic explanation of the effects of the interminable problem of an older man falling for a younger girl, 'Something's Got To Give'. Mercer adopted a very wise scientific rule to form the first line of the song 'When an irresistable force such as you meets an old immovable object like me'. He also produced the number that Fred regards as his favourite above all other songs – 'Dream'.

In addition, there was also a dance that was better known for its music than for its steps, 'The Sluefoot'.

Leslie Caron liked *Daddy Long Legs*. 'For once,' she said, 'I play someone for whom everything smiles.' She had just played a poor waif in the film *Lili*.

When the film opened in London, the *Evening Standard* commented: 'The sizzling "Sluefoot" number danced by Fred Astaire in the new wide-screen film *Daddy Long Legs* will swamp the current rock 'n roll craze right out, some people think.' That was wishful thinking on both the writer's part and a lot of other people's too. The paper's critic added: 'Astaire will be 56 next Tuesday but he dances like a teenager.' In another piece, the *Evening Standard* said about Fred: 'Astaire, now more than ever like a weather-beaten Stan Laurel, seems to have gained in grace and fluency of movement.' But the critic added: 'Only in one or two numbers by Roland Petit does the screen dissolve into the magical enchanted world of the screen musical, the last resort in the cinema today of the surrealist imagination of early film impressionists.'

Alas, that wasn't going to last, either. But Fred was doing his best to keep it going.

Princess Margaret attended the London premiere – which most people saw as much a tribute to Fred Astaire as anything else.

Leonard Mosely in the *Daily Express* – perhaps trying to atone for earlier less charitable views – commented, 'Worth every penny. But, as Princess Margaret will see, Leslie Caron will never again be able to pose as an innocent urchin.' He hadn't yet seen her in *Gigi*, of course.

The New York *Sunday News* simply said: 'Astaire is still tops as a song-and-dance man.'

As for Fred himself, he was putting on a brave front. But his misery at the loss of Phyllis was taking on a strange form. Other men might have sat at home and moped. Fred did a peculiar thing. He went on an escapade sizing up the local mail boxes – for an illegal purpose. As everywhere else in the United States, the letter boxes near his Beverly Hills home are red and blue. He suddenly had an idea – if he painted the middle of the boxes yellow, they would be in his exact racing colours.

Fred didn't go as far as actually painting the boxes, but he did stick yellow Scotch tape around their midriffs; driving from one box to the next and looking to see who was watching him as he did it.

As it turned out, nobody did see him perform this dreadfully illegal deed. If they had, as he has said, goodness knows what they might have done to him. The fact remains that the boxes stayed red, yellow and blue for at least a week.

As far as Fred himself was concerned, he tried not to remain blue, but it was difficult. Because he was not a garrulous man, he couldn't even begin to look for solace in crowds. Even if he had been the kind to enjoy parties, he was now clearly too eaten up to contemplate the idea of drowning his sorrows in a Hollywood atmosphere.

There are Astaire friends who wondered how he ever took the plunge with Phyllis in the first place as he had always seemed such a loner. And none of them imagined he would now go looking for a replacement. Phyllis was irreplaceable and he knew that their own special brand of marriage was, too. Besides which, there was always the inbred reluctance to admit that the perfect love affair was over. Even now, twenty-two years later, there are days when he secretly thinks she is going to walk through the door as though nothing had happened.

When *Daddy Long Legs* was over, there was talk of Fred even shutting himself away from the one place where he had proved he could best forget his troubles – the film studio. He made his television debut in 1955 on the Ed Sullivan Show, but that was basically to plug the film and he didn't get paid for the experience.

The rumours of an Astaire retirement were heightened when a big new film for Twentieth Century Fox called *Dry Martini* was mentioned in connection with Fred, but it just never came off.

Then Paramount said they were going to star him in a film to be directed by Jean Negulesco, and written by Henry and Pheobe Ephron, the same trio who were responsible for *Daddy Long Legs*. Like *Daddy*, it would be a musical with Sammy Cahn writing the lyrics to Jimmy Van Heusen's music.

This was to be called *Papa's Delicate Condition* – the delicate condition referred to being the gentleman's appreciation of the delights of the bottle. The film would be based on the life of a man called Jack Griffith, which had been written by his daughter, Corinne Griffith, a silent movie star. As Sammy Cahn told me, it represented a career-long ambition for him – to write for Fred Astaire. He even agreed to audition for the master. When it came to the day they were to demonstrate one of the tunes, Cahn says he was rather more enthusiastic than Van Heusen who regarded the idea of an audition as being beneath his dignity.

But demonstrate it they did. The song was 'Call Me Irresponsible' and it was planned for the moment in the film that the man with the delicate condition was trying to explain to his wife why he had spent so much money on buying a circus – just so that his little girl would be happy.

The pair got halfway through the song, Cahn says in his masterly book *I Should Care*, when Astaire ordered them to stop. Commands from Astaire could never be ignored and when they came, the people involved usually got more than a little worried. This time, the song-writers need not have been too put out – Fred told them it was one of the finest songs he had ever heard. He also revealed why Van Heusen and Cahn had been invited to supply the score, it was because Johnny Mercer was not available.

But neither 'Call Me Irresponsible' nor any of the four or five other songs they wrote for the picture were ever sung by Astaire. In fact *Papa's Delicate Condition* was made without Fred; Jackie Gleason took the role intended for Astaire. The reason given was that Fred had an obligation to MGM to fulfil first. But that took time, too.

For the moment, Fred was still trying to reconcile himself to what was irreconcilable – life without Phyllis. He would wake up at three o'clock in the morning, just about the time when he used to get some of his brightest inspirations, and the depression would hit him deeper than ever before. He would say to himself 'What's the use?' About this time, he told the *New York Times*, 'I have my family – my stepson, my daughter, another son – my work, but not the incentive. You hear of these things happening, then it actually happens to you – and you're lost. My wife was a remarkable woman. Never around the studios. Always at home when I needed her.'

Fred was talking while publicising *Daddy Long Legs*. The *Times* said he 'looked tense and tired; he thrust his hands in his pockets.' And he told the paper: 'I always needed her judgment, too. I especially wanted her opinion of this new picture.'

So what was he going to do? Finally, he came out with it. His dancing days were at an end, he was sure. But he didn't want to give up work. Instead, he would settle for the director's chair.

'I can't go on dancing for ever,' he declared. 'The public would only accept me in dancing roles. I could never become just an actor.' It wouldn't be long before he would be eating these words, but he went on, paraphrasing as he did that first screen test report: 'I haven't one feature that even remotely resembles that of a movie star.'

The trouble with Fred was that he was in limbo, unable to accept the fact that he was now alone, yet not really sure he could work in the same old way, either. The old haunts that he and Phyllis enjoyed so much were too painful for him to retain them exclusively for himself. From the time that she died, for instance, he couldn't return to the ranch. When years later he happened to go past the place, the experience was almost unbearable.

Without Phyllis, he was depending on his mother and on Ava for feminine company. In July 1955, the three of them went to Europe on holiday. Ava was thirteen, and he started escorting her to the odd film première – as much a treat for a young girl on the threshold of her teens as company for a star.

Now, in England, they dropped in to look at the horses at Newmarket. Fred bought a yearling filly called Rainbow Tie for 1,500 guineas and put her under the care of his old friend Jack Leach – who had long since given up riding and had followed his brother Felix as a trainer.

Fred had been buying horses in England under Leach's guidance, keeping them in Britain to race in the country for a year or so and then taking them over to the States. He promised to return to see Rainbow Tie do her stuff the following year.

Leach was still a great friend of Fred's. It was he, of course, who had introduced him to the 'Racing Swine'. He used to swear that Astaire told him he only kept on working so that he could afford to race.

But Fred tried to keep his racing as secret as possible, sometimes registering his ownership in either a stable's name or that of a ranch, some were registered in the name of Blue Valley Ranch or Blue Valley Stable.

'It got too embarrassing,' he explained. 'People would come up and ask me if my horse was going to win. I said I didn't know and if the horse won they would accuse me of holding out on them. If I said he's got a chance, and the horse lost, they complained that I gave them a bum steer. You can't win either way. How do I know what a horse is going to do in a race?'

In between, Fred had weakened and agreed that perhaps his dancing days were not, after all, over. He consented to make a film for MGM called *Wedding Day* and admitted that the most enticing part of the deal was that he was going to co-star with Audrey Hepburn. Before long, it was decided to change the title to *Funny Face*, like *Band Wagon* an evocative name straight out of the two Astaires' Broadway careers. And also like the film *Band Wagon*, it had very little to do with the original show.

All there was, in fact, to connect the two was the title and the fact that the Gershwins supplied the music. Four of the numbers were taken from the original stage production – 'Funny Face' itself, 'S' Wonderful', 'Let's Kiss And Make Up' and 'He Loves And She Loves'.

Leonard Gershe and Ronald Edens supplied the other tunes which they had originally planned for a Broadway show that never came off. The story was also the one they had planned to put on Broadway under the name 'Wedding Day'.

The path to true success in films, rather like the one to true love, rarely runs smooth. And so it was with what became *Funny Face*. There were impossible contract difficulties getting the picture under way at MGM. Eventually, the whole deal was sold to Paramount, who had had Audrey Hepburn under contract in the first place. Audrey insisted Fred did the picture with her.

It was the story of a fashion photographer who finds what was shortly to become known as a beatnik in Greenwich Village. He takes her to Paris where, of course, all good movies must be photographed. What neither the story nor Paramount took into consideration was the fact that it sometimes rains in Paris. It certainly did when *Funny Face* was being shot. Numbers suddenly had to be given a rainy background where originally no one gave rain a passing thought. And the sun came out only when it was not wanted. It would have been much easier if it kept raining throughout the same scene, but artificial rain had to be created by hose pipes when, obstinately, there was none of the genuine variety.

By far the hardest problem caused by the weather was the effect it had on the dance numbers. On one celebrated occasion an entire area had to be resurfaced with new earth and grass, because everything underneath was waterlogged.

Another problem was controlling the Paris crowds. This was partly solved by dressing some of the extras as gendarmes. One of the people they had to control turned out to be Hermes Pan who was on holiday in Paris and investigating what looked like a familiar scene – without realising who was involved in it. Fred immediately changed Pan's hotel booking so that they could be near each other. It was a great reunion for them.

His big solo in the picture was a complicated bull fight mime – in which he used his raincoat as a cape. But one of the most endearing parts of *Funny Face* was the moment Fred played with his hat. He simply tipped it off his head with a cane. It looked the simplest routine in the world, the sort of thing with which fathers amuse their children at parties. But fastidious Fred Astaire rehearsed it with all his usual dedication.

Fred did his own choreography including a pas-de-deux with Audrey Hepburn. For her, it was the most important professional dancing she had yet done. Fred danced too, with Kay Thompson, who in a charming character study played the magazine editor.

There was an important historic feature about *Funny Face* – historic, that is, as far as show business is concerned. For the first time, songs from the soundtrack of a film were put on an LP record instead of them being re-recorded later on in another studio.

The critics liked *Funny Face* well enough. The *New York Times*'s Bosley Crowther commended its 'appropriate décor and visual style' the New York *Herald Tribune* said that the picture was 'that rare thing on the screen – a polished musical'.

The *New Yorker*, in a review that must have sincerely gratified Fred after the slating for his record album, commented: 'Put *Funny Face* down as an amiable bit of seasonal fluff and rejoice that Mr Astaire's middle-aged bones can still rattle with an infectious beat.'

In Britain, the enthusiasm was more muted. *The Times* said: 'This is the American "musical" at its worst: not even the presence of Mr Fred Astaire, who was in the original stage production, nor that of Miss Audrey Hepburn can save the day. It may be extravagant to discuss a "musical" ' (the inverted commas indicate that this was written in the days of *The Times's* much more serious 'Top People's' era) 'in the terms proper to a serious creative work, yet there is that in the film's attitude towards the "intellectual", whether in Greenwich Village or Paris, which offends. It is not amiable parody and it is not telling satire.'

The *Evening Standard* was a lot kinder. 'With six tunes and a title salvaged from a thirty-year-old George Gershwin show' (the arithmetic as far as the tunes were concerned was somewhat amiss), '*Funny Face* is a musical that really sings. Directed by Stanley Donan, it has a wit, a zip and a charm rarely touched since "On The Town". *Funny Face* is as smart as next season's styles, and as intimate as a dinner for two.'

The *Daily Mail* said: 'Mr Astaire shrugs his way through this smart strident film with his usual effortless air of claiming no responsibility for his feet and his new leading lady dances right into our hearts as well.'

Fred obviously liked it all very much indeed. If he hadn't, he might not have been quite so willing to take Ava to Paris the following summer to see where the picture had been filmed. They stopped off in Britain on the way and booked into a modern black and white painted hotel at Aldwick Bay, near the resort of Bognor Regis.

The idea of society figure Fred Astaire booking into a small fifteen-room hotel that normally contented itself with families carrying suitcases and buckets and spades, made the mind boggle. But Fred and Ava had no intention of going down to the beach – at least publicly. He paid the same three guineas a day as everyone else. The mock Tudor, Bay Court Hotel was simply a convenient and out-of-the-way-place for the Astaires to stay while they were attending the nearby Good-wood race meeting. For there, Rainbow Tie would finally be showing what she was made of.

Rainbow Tie in fact started fourth favourite at six-to-one. But it ran up a lane and turned out to be too far back in the field. Fred didn't lose too heavily. As one writer put it, 'He didn't put his pink shirt on him.'

Seeing Rainbow Tie run – and lose – was not the most notable part of that visit to Goodwood. Fred and Ava were there for the entire meeting. The day before Rainbow Tie's 'performance', Fred was invited to visit another racing enthusiast. He was approached by Lord Porchester, equerry to the Queen, and asked if he and Ava would like to come to Her Majesty's box the following day. That entire evening Ava practised her curtsey, while Fred rehearsed the exit he would make after the formalities of the meeting.

When they did meet in the box of the Duke of Richmond and Gor-don, the conversation was almost entirely restricted to horses – although Fred allowed himself, as he recalls in his autobiography, to mention for the Queen's benefit that he had danced with her mother. To which she replied: 'You mean *she* danced with *you*.'

The big problem was trying to work out when the Astaires should leave. The Queen solved the difficulty for them by suggesting that they probably wanted to go and see what Rainbow Tie was doing.

After Goodwood, Fred took Ava to Paris – and now she felt really grown up. A tour of the dress salons was laid on specially for her.

What sort of girl was the fourteen-year-old Miss Astaire? That seem-ed to be the sort of question every journalist wanted to know. Fred thought it was his duty to be frank. He told reporters:

'She isn't stage-struck, film-struck or anything struck. She's just a sweet, simple girl who likes ice cream sodas and isn't too fond of school. She is interested in my work, but that's all.

'Ava doesn't take after me as far as dancing goes. Naturally she goes to the occasional dance.'

In Paris, they sat at pavement cafes with soft drinks in front of them, attended street auctions and visited all the famous haunts visited by sightseers for centuries.

Naturally, people asked Fred what he did with his time when he wasn't actually filming. He told them that he now had 120 dance schools to look after, including the first one to open in Los Angeles. He hadn't wanted to have one there before, because he thought it was too close to home and he might be bothered too often.

People wanted to know when Fred would take what they regarded as the obvious next step in his career, namely television. There was still a reluctance among the Hollywood studios to allow their big contract stars to appear on the small screen – because they feared it would harm the take at the box office – but Fred had never had that sort of contract.

He simply protested that he wasn't interested.

'I don't see any reason to do television when you've got an active movie career,' he said at the time. 'My type of work is awfully difficult and, as long as I don't have to, I would just as soon stay out of television.'

It was the sort of reaction Sammy Cahn got when he suggested that Fred join him in a TV project. Cahn was anxious to capture what he had so narrowly missed just a short while before: the chance to write for Fred Astaire. As he told me: 'It was the dream of my life.'

Cahn and Van Heusen had only recently had a great success writing 'Love And Marriage' and other tunes for a musical TV version of Thornton Wilder's classic *Our Town*. Frank Sinatra had sung it in the live show and, as a result, the writers were awarded an Emmy – the first ever given for a song.

They wanted to revive the *Our Town* musical idea and Cahn thought that Astaire would be ideal casting. 'After all, we had had an actor to do it, then a great singer, so why not a dancer?' he reasoned.

The people in the TV company were ecstatic about the notion and Cahn was deputed to see Astaire.

As Sammy recalls now, it was the beginning of an unhappy story. 'I say this on oath,' he insists. 'Fred Astaire told me: "I can't go out and do a show for an hour and a half. In a film, we do a three-minute sequence. We cut, we rest, we change..."'

Cahn adds: 'I realised he was making proper sense and I dismissed it.'

The matter was allowed to rest there, but it did come up again a few years later. For the moment, as Cahn said, it seemed to make sense that Fred didn't want to do television.

But Fred did branch out into one field from which he had previously always held himself aloof – advertising. In April 1957, an advertisement appeared in the *New York Times* for American Airlines. It showed a picture of Fred and added the legend: 'Fred Astaire's favourite step – aboard America's famous DC-7 Mercury for luxury.'

At least, it did not trade on Fred's reputation as one of the world's best-dressed men, and Fred's reputation as the world's greatest dancer was still completely intact. In 1956, production began on what we now know was the last glamorous film musical of the entire Astaire career, *Silk Stockings*, the film adaptation of a Broadway show which itself was a version of a movie classic. Back in the 1930s Greta Garbo had carved a niche in cinema history by starring in *Ninotchka*, the story of a Russian woman diplomat who is led astray in decadent Paris. Cole Porter had written the score and it all seemed to bode very well indeed when Fred and Cyd Charisse were again dancing together on a film set at the MGM lot.

Cyd was excited at being with Fred once more and it seems that he was, too. As a gesture of his appreciation, on the day they began work he presented Cyd with a cage-full of red-billed finches – the red intended to represent the Russian she was playing in the film.

The offer to make *Silk Stockings* came to Cyd Charisse at a moment when fixing her time schedule resembled a juggling act. Her MGM contract was such that she went from one film to the next and had to think about a third before the second was completed.

Producer Arthur Freed did, however, give her a say in the matter. She could, he said, either do *Les Girls* with Gene Kelly or *Silk Stockings* with Fred Astaire. She said there was no contest and chose Astaire. It wasn't just that she was working with Fred again – although that was a very important consideration – but also that she recognised Ninotchka as the best role in her career. She could also see a lot of a man she greatly admired, Cole Porter. Porter told her he would rather have Astaire be the first to sing his songs than anyone else – because only he showed them the care that a songwriter appreciated.

It was obviously a happy combination for Astaire and Charisse. Cyd knew that Fred had the right to approve his partner, and after *The Band Wagon* he knew what he was getting. Even so, Arthur Freed had had his time cut out trying to persuade Fred to take the role in the first place. He just had the feeling that people wouldn't accept him as the romantic lead to a girl so much his junior.

Eventually, at the suggestion of the director, Rouben Mamoulian, Freed arranged a lunch for the three of them. After being wined and lunched, Fred took his pen and signed the contract. The film was going to be made.

Again Miss Charisse's long legs and her beautiful figure made it difficult for eyes to switch to Astaire, yet once more, his dancing persuaded audiences and crew alike that there was still something special in him, too.

Leonard Gershe, who with Leonard Spigelgass, wrote the screenplay, was not altogether sure that casting Fred was totally successful. He said that the conniving film producer who Fred played needed something that he never had – 'commonness'.

The film must go down in history, if only because it was the very last picture in which Fred wore top hat, white tie and tails. Since Astaire always wanted to live in the present, Hermes Pan, now back at work with his old pal, had to persuade him to adopt the costume for a number called 'The Ritz Roll 'N' Rock'. Fred thought the whole outfit was rather passé, but to the people watching it all, it just looked like Fred Astaire – and no one asked for more.

The film also had comedy with the help of Peter Lorre in one of his last and least sinister roles, and Janis Paige as the film star who, incidentally, comes to Paris to make yet another version of *War And Peace*.

It was up to Mamoulian, having solved his casting problems, to decide just what sort of film he wanted it to be. The picture was to be in Cinemascope, which since it was first introduced as the answer to TV had been voted by directors the most difficult medium in which to work. It was an ungainly size, the proportions were all wrong and before long it would be replaced by Panavision and similar systems.

Mamoulian felt that the emphasis had to be on dancing, above all else. And since never again was Fred to be seen on film doing the sort of routines he did with Cyd Charisse in *Silk Stockings* it was a wise choice.

Fred, as usual, worked his taps to a shine – but had enough energy left over to take part in a fake scene which he laid on as a sort of practical farewell present for the director at the end of the filming.

Mamoulian loved working with Astaire. It was, after all, a meeting of two perfectionists. 'You'd think,' he said after *Silk Stockings*, 'that his entire life and future depended on the outcome of each dance. He keeps at the top because he does the impossible. He improves on perfection.'

234

For once, Fred himself revealed a secret of his craft. 'It's always murder to get that easy effect,' he said. 'I don't try to make things look easy. I'd like them to look hard so that people would know what work went into them.'

It certainly impressed Arthur Freed: 'The man is absolutely ageless,' he told reporters when the film was safely in the can, 'Why, I'm only a couple of years older than he is and I look like his grandfather! After only three hours, I'm ready to drop. I've been so exhausted that they thought they'd have to give me oxygen. Fred just looks at me and tells me to rest and keeps on dancing for six hours more.'

The reaction of the critics for this very important film in the Fred Astaire story was mixed.

It might have been less so had not the title provided such a good excuse for puns. The New York *Mirror*, for instance, took advantage of all they were offered: 'Putting it bluntly,' said their critic, '*Silk Stockings* seems to have a number of runs.'

The New York *Journal* was kinder: 'The Melvyn Douglas part, portrayed behind footlights by Don Ameche, is stepped superbly by Fred Astaire. This is not to write that Fred and Cyd didn't act. They did, and very pleasantly, too. The fact remains, however, that the ageless, agile Astaire is primarily America's greatest male dancer.'

And the *Daily News* seemed to have thoroughly liked it, too. Their critic wrote: 'MGM's screen version is infinitely better than the Broadway show, for the simple reason that it has far greater talent participating in the acting, singing and dancing ... Astaire is Astaire and need I say more?'

And, of course, to Ava, Fred was always simply Daddy – Daddy with all his quirks, as well as his talents. Fred didn't like being seen dancing when he was not on the stage or film set, because it embarrassed him. When Ava 'came out' – she was included in the debutantes' list because her mother had been 'in society' – Fred and Ava danced together for the fathers' and daughters' waltz. They were the only ones out of step.

But now, at the end of the 1950s, Astaire's public wouldn't believe that he could be out of step with their tastes, and they were still wanting more. Over the past seven years, in fact, he had been showing a newer, more up-to-date image, and when you talked to him, you knew there was still a lot more he wanted to do.

No Strings

It was a new world. The war was now fading as a memory and a whole new generation of people made up the audiences for entertainers like Astaire; people who were just children when he was dancing for the troops, who were not born when he and Ginger were the most popular stars on the screen. They were now the ones who seemed to have this changing world at their feet.

They had money, they spent fortunes on records, on going to the movies and on buying the first colour television sets. For Fred Astaire, feeding those sets became a notion he found difficult to resist.

His plans were still topics for conversation. Would he retire again? And, more important still, would he marry again? The answers were slightly more evasive to the first question than those to the second. He had no doubts at all about his personal life. 'I had one of the happiest marriages a man could want,' he said. 'For twenty-two years, it ran and when it closed, when I lost her, I couldn't work up an interest in anyone else.'

But what about television? Now, he did appear to be weakening in that direction. He followed up his appearance with Ed Sullivan with stints on the Arlene Francis and Art Linklater shows. On the Person-to-Person programme, he once more showed his talent with the drums. But Marie Torre in the New York *Herald Tribune* reluctantly prophesied that this was merely a passing fad, not something Fred was likely to take as a spur for the future.

'The recent Fred Astaire appearances on television,' she wrote, 'have sprung hope in the hearts of video pursuers who have been falling over antennae trying to shake loose from the movie lots. Sad to relate, however, any TV man with Astaire in his eyes is merely having a pipe dream.' And Fred certainly did seem to be saying as much himself. Ask him why he did make his excursions on to the small screen and he would reply disarmingly: 'I like to visit my friends.'

Then, in August 1957, came the news that both Fred and Charles Laughton had been hooked by CBS. They would each star in a General Electric Theatre film. Fred's would be a comedy fantasy by Jameson Brewer called *Imp On A Cobweb Leash*.

It was aired in December that year and was well received. In fact, so well received that Fred decided that for the first time he was going to think very seriously indeed about yet another new career – in television – possibly even doing his own thing on the medium, dancing.

Matters came to a head when Astaire and the Chrysler Corporation reached an agreement that opened up entirely new vistas for a man who began entertaining in the first decade of the century. Chrysler agreed to package a television programme that would go out live and in colour. As for Fred, he would not only star in it, but produce the show, too – under the banner of his newly-formed company Ava Productions.

It was at that point that history looked as if it were about to repeat itself. Who, everyone wanted to know, would be ... yes ... Fred's partner? When he told them, the headline writers inevitably described her as the new Ginger Rogers. Fred could have told them they would do that but restrained himself.

But in many ways, for once, they were right. Fred had selected a young girl whom he always agrees was one of his most accomplished partners. She was also one of the youngest and one of the most beautiful. Her name – Barrie Chase.

Fred had first noticed Barrie when she had had a small supporting role in *Silk Stockings*. Blonde, very slim and short enough to make Fred look tall, she was enchanting and also very hard working. The daughter of writer Borden Chase, she was twenty-two when she signed for the show. She had first made a name for herself on skates – at the age of three when she was offered a job with Sonja Henie's troupe.

She was a fan of Fred's long before working on *Silk Stockings*. She had seen *Top Hat* and several of the other Astaire–Rogers films two or three times. When they first met, she was working on another lot nearby. Fred found his way to the set and watched her as she danced. 'It made me shake all over,' she recalled.

Fred paid her the usual compliments and drove her wild with his search for what might have seemed unreachable perfection. He would cuss, shout and make her run out of the room crying, but when she came back after two hours alone soothing her wounded pride, he would pretend that she had never been away.

He was not, she points out, a Santa Claus with frosting. The show was called *An Evening With Fred Astaire* – but like any other Fred Astaire production, the evening was really the result of several months of hard work.

David Rose, one of the most talented of Hollywood's music makers, conducted the orchestra and provided musical arrangements of numbers that ranged from 'Change Partners' and 'Baubles, Bangles and Beads' to 'A Foggy Day' and 'Top Hat, White Tie and Tails'.

He was amazed at the detail that went into preparing the dance routines. As he recalls: 'I walked into a rehearsal and there was dead silence for five minutes, with Fred and Hermes Pan just staring at each other. Then Hermes said to Fred that he had the answer to their problem. He should step off on the left foot instead of the right. They had been debating for fifteen minutes which foot to step out on. Every step he took just had to be accounted for.'

It was easy to see that the show lightly called a Fred Astaire 'Special' was special in many ways – and not just simply because it starred Fred Astaire. Previously, no one had even considered having more than a quintet or perhaps a sextet for a TV show. Astaire brought in David Rose to head a forty-piece orchestra.

As always it wasn't easy for anyone to get to know him. While Barrie Chase resorted to tears, Rose and Bud Yorkin the producer wondered why Fred kept himself so aloof. He didn't mix very much with the others on the set, simply concerned himself with getting out a perfect programme. Not that it lessened their respect for him. As Rose says: 'I was no different from anyone else in Hollywood. It was an honour to be with him.' He was not demanding at all. He just watched and said: 'Here, you know what to do.' The orchestra knew just what beats they would have to mark so that Fred could come on with the sort of precision he demanded.

The show was full of innovations. Fred did the unheard of thing and sang a medley of ten songs. The big risk, and the thing that worried Fred most, was that it was all live. The company had a once-only try at getting it right. As it turned out, they got it very right indeed. The show won nine Emmy awards.

The Emmy that Fred himself won for the best actor of 1958 – the show was aired on 17 October 1958 and repeated on 26 January 1959 – caused a row in the industry. Some critics said that it should have gone to a dramatic actor, not a dancer. When he heard that, Fred said he would give the Emmy back – but was persuaded to keep it.

That was not the only problem. *Variety* had reported: 'Fred Astaire's reluctance to do another spec this season (it's natural that NBC would overture him pronto in view of his last week's click) reportedly stems from the fact that the hour show according to "inside sources" resulted in a loss of $75,000 to the packagers. This includes the many weeks of painstaking rehearsals etc. Astaire and producer-director Bud Yorkin had a cut of the MCA package.'

He wrote an angry letter to the show biz bible's editor:

Kindly retract erroneous article in last week's *Variety*. Here are the facts: The entire package is mine, via Ava Productions Corp. MCA merely acted as my agent with the sponsor. Nobody had any cut. All expenses were paid by me and the show definitely turned in a sizeable profit. Though I was not interested in that phase, I would like to make it clear that I'm not completely nuts. I particularly directed that no expense be spared in carrying out my plans, ideas and designs for the show which I had been working on for some time. Thanks, love and kisses and I will do another when I get the time,
Fred Astaire.

Although the show was live, it had been taped for the second showing It was at that point that Sammy Cahn came into the picture once more. He again considered starring Astaire in yet another version of *Our Town* – and was sent off, so he says, with a rather large flea in his ear. Purely by chance, Cahn ran into Fred outside a book store in

Beverly Hills. 'I said, "Gee I'm so glad to see you," ' he recalls. 'Remember the time that I came to see you about our show and you said you couldn't do it because you didn't get the chance to rest . . .'

As Cahn tells it, the situation became explosive. 'I didn't finish the "st" in rest,' he says. 'It was as if you had pulled out the pin from a grenade. The most gentle human being developed a hide. He said, "How dare you suggest that I need a rest?" '

Says Cahn: 'It was as though he were going to hit me. And I said, "Forgive me." I knew of no way that I could salvage the idea.' And now Cahn says he takes this opportunity 'to apologise to a man who has pleasured me so much.'

Certainly, Fred's Special had set new standards. The original production had a rating of 18.9 – phenomenally high. The repeat registered a rating of 26.2. It was an encouraging sign that tapings of programmes, of which this was one of the very first, would be the big thing for the future.

The *New York Times* said: 'Mr Astaire's show enjoyed such individual distinction that it is probably not wise to draw too many conclusions from its success. In any case, the experience with Mr Astaire's show does invite interesting speculation.'

There was also some very interesting speculation about his relationship with Barrie Chase. Fred was constantly worried – among other things to be worried about – concerning suggestions that there was something immoral in his partnering a girl who was not only so attractive, but also so young. When critics commented that the pair represented a combination of June and December, he would light-heardedly ask: 'Couldn't they have said, June and October?' But he did worry about it, and so did Barrie.

However, for a time after the Special had been aired, they would go out for quiet dinners together.

Occasionally, he could be brought out to comment on the 'affair'. 'Barrie is a sweet girl of twenty-three,' he said. 'But I'm sure she's not interested in me. She is talented and we have much in common.'

People were still talking about their TV show together – and the effect it was likely to have on the industry. The taping of the show and its second performance had 'swept all before it', network executives reported excitedly – and asked for an immediate guarantee that there would be another Astaire–Chase outing on the box.

Fred was as enthusiastic about the idea as anyone else, but he had also been tickled by another proposition: Stanley Kramer wanted Fred to make a film for United Artists. It would be in black and white and his wouldn't even be the top name above the title. But it was too exciting a prospect to resist – he wouldn't have to dance a step or sing a note in it.

Look To The Rainbow

In 1959, Fred Astaire produced his autobiography *Steps In Time*, with every word written by himself – because, he said, a ghost writer couldn't express his thoughts the way he felt them. The book would be, he believed, a chance to put those thoughts on record. Certainly, he had no intention of making a fortune out of what was never intended as a literary exercise.

One of the thoughts he expressed in that book was that he did not like challenges. Yet *On the Beach* was undoubtedly going to be the biggest challenge of his career. In this Stanley Kramer film, Fred played a British scientist involved in the last human journey following a nuclear holocaust. The year was supposed to be 1964, immediately after the entire northern part of the world had been devastated by the Bomb and just before the nuclear fallout was making its deadly way southwards. Gregory Peck was the commander of an American submarine working out in Australia, Anthony Perkins his junior officer and Ava Gardner the loose woman with whom Peck gets involved. Together, they and the scientist decide to make a journey back to the States in order to see what Armageddon had left behind. By the time they return to Australia that continent is as dead as everywhere else.

There seems nothing for any of them to do but patiently await death – so all four decide that if they are to die, they will do it in their own way. Perkins takes his wife aside and with her swallows a suicide pill; Peck takes the submarine back to America; Ava waits for a lonely end in Australia while the scientist extinguishes himself sitting in his racing car as the exhaust fumes sweep around him in the locked garage.

Fred said it took him thirty seconds to make up his mind to play the part of Julian Osborne, the scientist. Kramer had regarded Astaire's decision as proof enough that he did take up challenges.

'I've thought about doing straight roles,' Fred said at the time, 'but always hesitated and finally gave up the idea on the grounds that the public (or that part of the public who wants to see me at all) might not accept an Astaire who neither sang nor danced. I figured that if a director of his standing thought I could do it, that was security enough for me.'

He admitted he had had doubts over being able to do justice to the role – but was satisfied that Kramer didn't throw him out before the film was finished.

He said he had decided now, finally, not to do any more dancing pictures. The sceptic could have remarked that he had said that more than once before. But this time it did seem that he had finally made up his mind and with no reason to bluff, really meant it. 'I've done them all, you see. Over thirty pictures – and that just about exhausts the possibilities. I was determined not to become a dancing freak at sixty.'

It had certainly been something he had frequently thought about. A non-musical role became more a practical possibility, he felt, after the success of *Imp On A Cobweb Leash*.

The only real worry about *On The Beach* was that he had to smoke in the film – and he hadn't done that for four years. It was a justified concern, for once he started, it was impossible to stop again. Impossible, at least, for the next two years. He finally had his last cigarette to date in 1961.

There were other problems with the picture, problems that didn't threaten Fred personally. United Artists wanted to give the picture a 'global' première in some twenty capital cities, including Moscow. The State Department stepped in and refused to allow an export licence to the Soviet Union – because, they reasoned, the story of a nuclear holocaust was hardly a subject calculated to promote good international relations.

Fred enjoyed his time working in Australia. While there, he bought a chestnut colt for 6,100 guineas and tried twelve times to get the Victoria Registrar of Racehorses to agree to a name. Finally, he said: 'Call it anything.' And so it was. The colt – no great winner – became 'Anything'.

Fred arrived back in the States to find that he was as much in demand as ever. Would he make another TV spectacular? Finally, he agreed that he would – but first he was going to do another straight role on television and would sport a beard for the occasion. This was *Man On A Bicycle* and was as enthusiastically received as the earlier play had been.

He followed it on 4 November 1959 with the second Special and again it was with Barrie Chase. 'Another Evening with Fred Astaire' had them doing a series of numbers that were as much tailored for their needs as the old repertoires had been for Fred and Ginger.

The past was still not something he wanted to talk about. 'Reminiscing is for the birds,' he declared more than once. 'Only the future counts.' And that was why he constantly turned down offers for *Steps In Time* as a possible film subject. 'I'm alive, not dead. Why go into the past? However much they offer me – and the offers come in all the time – I shall not sell.'

Again, too, people asked why he still bothered to work. His answer to this was always frank. 'There's no substitute for a wife. Not the kind of wife I had. I work now because I don't know what I'd do otherwise. I still feel very much alone. Somehow, the years slip by and I don't know where they go.

'I'm surprised how many people remember me, let alone want to see me,' he said. 'I'm not a very sociable guy.'

But they did remember and did want him. They also wanted to know his views on modern music, what did he think of rock 'n' roll? 'Anything with a beat is for me,' he declared quite some time after his sixtieth birthday. 'Wasn't it Grandma who thought that the waltz was risqué? And remember what a ruckus the Charleston caused?'

He made frequent visits to England. In 1959, he stayed with America's Ambassador to the Court of St James's, his old pal, Jock Whitney. He went to his Savile Row tailor. It was his first time in the shop in fifteen years and he was served by the same men who had been there on his last visit. He bought a black dinner jacket.

Shortly afterwards, *Tailor and Cutter* magazine proclaimed him to be one of the world's ten best-dressed men. The citation read: 'He is one of the few Americans who can wear a suit of tails without looking like they had to throw it on his back to get it on him. . . . He chooses his clothes with an eye to his lack of inches.'

On the day that the selection was announced, Fred was seen wearing a brown sports jacket, an open-necked shirt and light trousers and chewing gum. When he walked into the smart 'Les Ambassadeurs' club, he was dressed in a pastel coloured soft shirt and a grey tie with Italian suede shoes. His trousers were held up this time by a blue silk handkerchief.

He confessed to the *Daily Express* that most of the things said about his appearance were myths.

I'm convinced that the general idea is that I'm a suave Joe who just dances from here to there and I'm a grinning goof, a kind of sucker for anything. . . .

[And then came the real shock]: I must admit that I don't like top hats, white tie and tails. I'm always arriving at dinner parties not wearing a dinner jacket when I should be, or vice versa. Invariably, too, I don't know how to get there or what time to arrive. Things are always spilling on table cloths in front of me. Not always my fault – but, nevertheless, there it is. Take beet sauce or beet salad. I have had some devastating experiences with beets. The carefree, the debonair – what a myth!

My hats are too small, my coats too short. My walk too loose. I have a sense of humour, but it won't always work for me. I'm always blowing my top at the wrong things. I tell you, I'm a very annoying guy.

For many, it was annoying that he wasn't being seen doing enough dancing. But in September 1960, he made his second spectacular with Barrie Chase in ten months, again with the same sponsor, Chrysler, and again with David Rose leading the music. The show, called now *Astaire Time*, won two Emmys. But Fred told Rose he wasn't sure he wanted to do any more. They were too time-consuming. Other stars who felt that Fred had given them the green light to go into the giant new medium themselves spent perhaps a week, occasionally just a day, planning their routines. Fred took three months at least and plenty of off-set work, too.

Astaire Time, America's entry for the Golden Rose of Montreux award – it didn't win – was the first of the shows to be bought by the BBC for showing in Britain.

Fred's awards were not restricted to his television Emmys. In 1960, he received one of the three annual *Dance* Magazine prizes at a reception at the plush New York Athletic Club. The presentation was made by his first dancing partner – Adele.

In May 1961, Fred starred with Debbie Reynolds in another straight role. This was *The Pleasure Of His Company*, based on a Broadway success. It was about a man meeting his former wife, Lilli Palmer, and his so-grown-up daughter, Debbie Reynolds, with whom he does dance, but only as any other straight actor might have danced if the action called for a ballroom scene.

The course of *The Pleasure Of His Company* did not run entirely smooth. The $3 million production had to grind to a halt when it was only half completed because a Screen Actors Guild strike closed all production. It was impossible to finish the work before Debbie Reynolds and Lilli Palmer were due to start new contractual engagements. So it was put into cold storage for six months.

Producer William Perlberg told Fred: 'You're 61, so please take it easy for the next six months. If you drop dead, we're finished.'

He survived and the film went back into production.

The *Daily Express* in London said that 'Fred . . . steals the film (and the girl, almost) from Tab Hunter, who is not yet twenty-four. He makes Hunter look like a clod. Admittedly, the situation could hardly have been better rigged to give Astaire the opportunity to show off his blithe spirit and hale condition.'

The *Observer's* C. A. Lejeune, recalling her old hero, commented: 'With his creased, old-fashioned charm and two of the most elegant arms in show business, Fred Astaire tries genuinely to make the ridiculous playboy attractive, but he is handicapped most of the time by lines which sound as if they have been lifted out of a travel brochure.'

The *Times* noted that 'even Fred Astaire is robbed of most of his charm.'

It was an age when much of the magic that went with Fred Astaire's image had been transferred to the young occupant of the White House. One gossip columnist was delighted to report that 'Fred Astaire is the brother of Adele Astaire, who married Lord Charles Cavendish, uncle of William John Robert Cavendish, Marquess of Hartington, who married Kathleen Kennedy who was a sister of John F. Kennedy.' Certainly, when the President visited Ireland, he almost called in on Adele who happened to be staying at Lismore Castle. He ordered his helicopter pilot to make a hundred-mile detour – simply so that he could hover over Lismore and wave down to Adele, but without dropping in.

Fred still joined Adele at Lismore when he could. In fact, he kept his contacts very much alive on the other side of the Atlantic. With Anna Neagle, he planned the first Astaire dance studios in Britain – a deal which was before very long to cause him to lose a great deal of money. Fred was now Chairman of the board, but was very much in the background.

If, as Fred had said, he didn't like the 'chewing' over his age he could still joke about it. 'I know I've been in the business a long time,' he said on his sixty-second birthday. 'I used to be expected to kiss the leading lady on the lips. Now all I have to do is buss her on the forehead!'

In 1962, Fred had roles in five television straight plays, all of which fitted into the general heading of Fred Astaire's Premiere Theatre. Actually Fred was on the screen almost every week for two years, hosting the series in much the same way as Dick Powell and Alfred Hitchcock had done, but the five plays, *Mister Easy*, *Moment of Decision*, *Guest In The House*, *Mister Lucifer* and *Blues for a Hanging*, were the only ones in which he acted, too. It was yet another facet of the varied Astaire career. And like the other experiences in show business, he seemed to enjoy it all immensely.

'If you are a host,' he told the *New York Times*, 'your job is to try to hook an audience. Of course, they don't use such language when they discuss these matters in executive television circles!'

In fact, what the ABC executives had told him was that he had to 'integrate' himself into the series which was sponsored by the Aluminium Corporation of America.

He had approval of his part of the script and he tried to handle it in his own way. 'I try to keep away from clichés. I am a sort of story teller. But while I have to be part of the show, I also have to be detached from it. Whenever possible, I try for a tongue-in-cheek style. But I never want to get smart-alecky.'

His success secret – and it *was* a successful endeavour – was to realise that an audience could turn the switch at any moment. So he knew his task was to keep the people gripped. 'My theory is that if an audience stays ten minutes, it will stay to the end.'

His experience as a dancer was also an advantage. 'You move better. You seem relaxed and that, I think, makes the audience feel more relaxed and more inclined to stick with you. At the same time, a dancer learns to hold an audience's attention by the way he moves. This gives the audience a sense of expectancy of growing excitement.'

That was much the same feeling film director Richard Quine had when he ensnared Fred to star in the film he was making for Columbia, *The Notorious Landlady*. Like *The Pleasure of His Company* and most other Astaire films the story line really wasn't important, the important thing was seeing Fred at work again. This time, it was about an American diplomat in London, and the intrigues revolving around his subordinate Jack Lemmon and his 'notorious' lady friend Kim Novak.

Quine wisely took advantage of what some other directors had chosen to ignore – the very thing that had people on the set gaping when Fred made his big musicals of the fifties. His walk. Fred didn't dance in the film, but his walk looked, as usual, as though it had been choreographed. And to exploit that walk, Quine made him march down a very long carpet, so that every movement could be seen by the audience.

He also supplied Fred with a pool table so that he could indulge his passion. It was not entirely a selfless thing to do. There was as much pleasure in watching him play pool as seeing him walk.

Fred and Quine became firm friends. When Fred finally moved out of the Summit Drive home that he and Phyllis had planned together, it was Quine who was one of the first to see his new, smaller house – an elegant bungalow with a Grecian porch. In the den that looked out on to the garden and swimming pool, Fred had installed a pool table.

On that first day in the place, Astaire danced through the house with Quine and Ava in train. He had a bunch of records in his hand and after the first had been placed on the hi-fi and the house was full of music, Fred and the others danced from room to room, switching on the light in each as they passed it.

Astaire helped Quine with his hobby – collecting hats. Since Fred has always been rather reluctant to allow people to take souvenirs of his past glories, the day he turned up at the director's house, carrying the original top hat from *Top Hat* – and there could be nothing more symbolic of Fred at work – was indeed one to remember. Quine was so delighted with this, that he placed it at the top of the special hat rack he had prepared for his collection and had a spotlight focussed on it. Fred was less than impressed. 'For heavens' sake,' he said, 'Put that light out. It looks as if I'm dead!'

The biting pain of losing Phyllis had eased, but he still missed her dreadfully. The worst part of all was not being able to share with her the important things that happened to him. He would still wake up in the middle of the night and find his way to the bedroom piano where he would toy with the idea for a song or two. In 1962 alone, he had three published – 'Girls like You' with Tommy Wolf; 'You Worry Me' for which he supplied his own lyrics; and 'I Love Everybody But You', for which Ava was allowed to share some of the credit. Why, she protests to this day, she does not know. It is possible she hummed a chord and Fred thought it was worth building a song around. It is equally possible that it was just one of those presents which fathers enjoy giving to their daughters.

For two years, Fred Astaire's contact with the public was limited to the few people who managed to spot him in the streets of Beverly Hills, possibly doing a bit of shopping or perhaps driving one of the two Rolls Royces he now owned – one of these was a legacy, together with some shares, from Phyllis's aunt, Mrs Maude Bull. They might also have noticed him if they shared his fascination with the world of crime.

Occasionally, when there was a major crime in Los Angeles, Fred could be seen hovering on the sidelines. He used to love following police 'prowl' cars.

Often, the police gave him a cheery 'Hi, Fred' when he joined them. One night, after a bank hold-up, he arrived just in time to see the thief apprehended. He walked alongside the police as they escorted the man to their car. Just then, the robber handed Fred a piece of paper and asked him: 'Mr Astaire, could I have your autograph?'

Fred scribbled his name on the same paper on which the man had written the plans for his ill-fated expedition.

The hobby did have the occasional unexpected repercussion. Once, a raw police recruit brandished a gun at him; he thought Fred was the wanted man. On another occasion, he had to rush out of the way as a burning wall narrowly missed falling on him. More than once, he had to avoid police gunfire.

If people did come close enough to Fred to pin him down, it seemed they mostly wanted to know his opinion of the current dance and music crazes. What, for instance, did he think of the twist? 'I think it's great,' he said, 'a combination of the shimmy and the snake-hips. I stopped doing it fifteen years ago.'

In 1964, he was closely associated with another dance called the Watusi. It was featured in a play with music in which Fred danced yet again with Barrie Chase – who, had she been with him on the large screen, would by now have more than earned the title of the Second Ginger Rogers. Had she wanted it, that is. Chances are, she was more than happy being Barrie Chase.

Think Pretty was – as the *New York Times* put it – 'a hopelessly intricate and pedestrian story about the recording business. . . .' The paper's critic, Jack Gould, was kinder about Fred: 'For a few tantalising moments of seeing Fred Astaire dance once again, the viewers of last night's presentation of *Think Pretty* had to wait a long hour of ridiculous situation comedy.'

The moments of pleasure, insisted the writer, were all too rare.

'The prospect of seeing the couple in light and lilting movement turned out to be nothing but a come-on for routine silliness from Hollywood. The brief glimpses of Mr Astaire's rhythmic responses to melodies only compounded the feeling of being cheated. The programme's gag writers should have watched his feet for a lesson in the art of communication.'

Yet Fred was still 'the ageless dancer'.

The *Daily News* drew the inevitable comparison with the past.

Memories of Fred Astaire's classy ballroom routines with Ginger Rogers in those vintage movies were erased by the Peter Pan of the dance when he shook his way through the Watusi on television last night.

Astaire belied his age (sixty-five) as he seemingly bounced around with partner Barrie Chase in the dance, a rage of the younger set.

The colour cast was a pleasant piece of fluff which tried to capture the flavour of Astaire's famed flickers. Even the title song, warbled by Astaire, sounded like an imitation Irving Berlin. Yet the way Astaire delivered the lyrics, it all sounded just right.

It seemed that Fred had made the Watusi respectable. 'It isn't so much a dance as it is a way of keeping time to the music,' he explained. Perhaps, as he so often did, Hermes Pan put it all into perspective; 'All you have to be is a good mover and uninhibited.'

Fred had not been begging for the opportunity to appear on the small screen. 'I didn't say, "Please can I dance again?"' he insisted at the time. 'I had to say, "Please, let me alone. I'm not in the mood to do it right now."'

In 1965, Fred surprised everyone by taking a subsidiary role in four episodes of the TV soap opera, 'Dr Kildare'. It was one of the better series, one that was exported, but a soap opera just the same. He followed it in January, March and April 1966 by hosting three variety shows in the Hollywood Palace series. Fred's television career seemed to be confusing Mrs Ann Astaire, who still lived with Fred and who in her late eighties was mostly very much aware of her surroundings. But every time she saw a commercial, she would call over to Fred: 'What are those people doing in your show?'

She liked doing things for herself. If she went out shopping, Fred would have to send his chauffeur out to bring her back.

Meanwhile, Fred was rapidly losing enthusiasm for his excursion into the world of commerce, the Fred Astaire Dance Studios. He disposed of his interest although the chain still retained his name. Afterwards, the organisation came into difficulties with the Federal Trade Commissioner – who charged that the company 'operated in a misleading and coercive manner'. He ordered it to change its ways after finding that the Washington studio 'failed to provide full-time or bona-fide courses to winners of telephone quizzes'. The winners were subjected to a 'rapid succession of unrelenting sales talk'. The company was said to use blank or partially-filled contract forms to create the impression that lessons cost less than they did.

But if the Astaire Dance Studios were no longer his affair, the Fred

Astaire career was – and he reacted to what he considered unwarranted criticism in the tried and true manner: not by sitting down and forgetting it, but by writing back to the critic.

A small magazine called *Films In Review* upset Fred and he pulled no punches in saying so. 'Your publication has been somewhat familiar to me for a number of years,' he wrote to the editor. 'Now one of your reviewers has overstepped his status with a grossly insulting commentary on me. The man's opinion of me as an artist matters little. It is his deliberate attack and effort to describe me as a decrepit old ham trying to hang on by a thread or something, that I resent vehemently. I will not tolerate this presumptuous, patronising attitude.'

He didn't like what he considered to be a snide comment on Fred's hair. The writer commented that Fred wore a 'dyed wig'. Said Astaire: 'I wore just exactly what I have always worn in all my recent TV specials and pictures.'

If people were talking about Fred's appearance – and the short, grey wig that he wore *was* both modern and stylish – it was nothing, compared with the shock experience of seeing the results of his first film in six years, *Finian's Rainbow*. It is now fairly obvious that this was to be his very last musical, the last picture in which Fred Astaire danced solo. But it was a very different Fred Astaire, stepping out very different dances.

It wasn't simply that he didn't wear a top hat, white tie and tails – as we have seen, he had grown fairly tired of that outfit. But the elegant, suave Fred Astaire was actually seen with at least two days' growth of beard, threadbare cuffs on his torn jacket and a naughty glint in his eyes. Nor was he doing a new version of the 'Couple of Swells' tramps number. This was all for real; all very much part of the story. He was a caricature of an Irish immigrant who had stolen a crock of gold from a leprechaun. Since America's wealth appeared to be buried at Fort Knox, here was his big opportunity to plant the stolen wealth nearby and wait to see if it would grow as he believed Fort Know had grown.

Seeing Fred on the set of *Finian's Rainbow*, one writer commented: 'You half expected to find him on a toadstool in a woodland glade handing out three wishes.'

He pranced and danced like a ten-year-old but he was, in fact, beginning to look his age. Even if that were deliberate, the effect was fairly shattering. *Finian's Rainbow* was a twenty-year-old story which had first seen the light of day on Broadway in 1947. It was then a sensation in the States, a flop in London. The best part of the film was undoubtedly Fred, both from the audience's point of view and from those of his co-stars, Tommy Steele as the leprechaun, and Petula Clark who played his daughter. It was a fascinating combination, Astaire and Clark. None of Fred's magic as a potential dancing partner had faded when Petula turned up on the set, petrified for her first try-out steps with Astaire. She had been rehearsing for three weeks with Hermes Pan, yet – to adopt a phrase she used in the BBC Radio Two tribute to her which preceded a mammoth series based on Fred's own life – she still felt like a 'baby elephant on my feet'. Her own fear was eased as her dancing improved – and it did, even though no one chose to call *her* the new Ginger Rogers.

There was more to their partnership than mere dancing, however. They also sang together, after the first recording had been completed and the tape played back, Fred jumped in the air and shouted: 'I sang with her! I sang with her!' It turned out that he had been as worried about matching up with her singing talents, the views of Cole Porter, Irving Berlin and the Gershwins notwithstanding, as she had been about dancing with him.

To Tommy Steele, too, it was a moment to treasure. Like everybody working on Astaire pictures before him, the young Cockney who had started his playing in a coffee-bar skiffle group was most impressed by the man's constant search for perfection – as detailed and intensive a search as for any crock of gold. Fred would work at the task from nine in the morning until six in the evening and carry on at weekends, too.

Steele has described Fred's ankles as seeming to hang from his legs. In rehearsals, Tommy demonstrated a new step. 'Where did you get that from?' Fred asked him. 'Gene Kelly,' Steele replied, to which Fred commented: 'He never could do that one!'

Fred made a number of suggestions to the director, Francis Ford Coppola – who was later to become best known for directing *The Godfather* – most of which were ignored. Fred said nothing while the film was in production, but a few years later allowed himself to say that Coppola wasn't suited to directing a musical.

The critical comments at the time were mixed. Most of the adverse criticism came from Britain. The London *Evening Standard* commented: 'Now we know. There's schmaltz at the end of the rainbow.' The *Evening News* said: 'There's just a drop too much of the Oirish' and the *Daily Telegraph* headed their review: 'Blarney is to blame.'

There was a sub-plot about a black botanist trying to cross mint with tobacco and this caused more problems than the director could have imagined possible. *Time* magazine commented: 'The simplistic notion of the '40s that Negroes are just like whites beneath the skin is more than an embarrassment now.' And in South Africa, the name Fred Astaire was besmirched as never before – for associating himself with what they regarded as an anti-Apartheid campaign. The film was banned in that country. They seemed most upset about the incident in the picture involving a bigoted US Senator who suddenly loses his prejudices. The South African Publications Control Board decided it was all against Government policy. Prime Minister Balthazar J. Vorster's Government was to relent about this a few years later and eventually allowed the film to be seen by South African audiences.

Fred made it absolutely clear that *Finian's Rainbow* was definitely his last dancing picture. And now that he was past sixty-eight years-old, no one bothered to argue.

For once, he was philosophising about the art of being Fred Astaire: 'I've never gone in for physical exercises or any of that stuff,' he told Victor Davis of the *Daily Express*. 'It takes me just a couple of days to get into the sort of trim where I can think about the dance sequences. I'm like a racehorse. I ready myself for the distance, no more, no less. I've never had to work at it constantly like an athlete.' That was an interesting statement. If he has never liked to consider himself a Nijinski, he had frequently referred to himself as an athlete. There was also more than a little thought behind his closing sentiments: 'I've HAD romantic dancing, though. I've done it all and don't want to do it any more. This time, thank goodness, I don't get the girl. Matter of fact, all I end up with in this film is a rainbow.'

Fred's family suspected that he thoroughly enjoyed playing old tramps, although they secretly preferred the old image. Fred was mainly concerned about being thought too old, although he protested that he was not.

He said at the time:

I don't know where the time goes. People immediately mention my age. They mention everybody's age. I'm not too conscious of it. The only thing I do notice is that everything goes by much faster than it seemed to before. You can't explain that to a young person. If they only realised! I'm one of the fortunate ones who's had a long career and don't think I don't appreciate it. There are so many people that don't function around my age. You have to be lucky and try to be reasonable with yourself in order to survive a rough world. I don't have any particular philosophy – why I did that or why I didn't. I don't know why I did.

I want to do something worthy to follow what I've done. I don't take jobs to pick up a buck, you know. I'm lucky enough not to have to do that. I have to like what I do.

If people did think that perhaps the image of Fred in *Finian's Rainbow* confirmed that he was a seedy old man, something had to be done to alter the situation – and quickly. So Fred and Barrie Chase did another TV spectacular together. This was a much more up-to-date Astaire than even the other Specials had shown him to be. He appeared with such established figures of the late sixties musical scene as Simon and Garfunkel and Sergio Mendes.

The *New York Times* loved it: 'The tireless and ageless Fred Astaire bridged the generation gap last night in a precise display of footwork attuned to both popular old favourites and examples of such varied beats as come from the Young-Holt Trio, the Gordian Knot and the delicate compositions of Simon and Garfunkel.'

And the paper's critic Jack Gould loved the all too brief moments when Fred danced. 'The staging alone held the viewer's attention as Mr Astaire and Miss Chase cavorted with beguiling effortlessness in moments of outright horseplay or soothing fluid movement. . . .

'Mr Astaire no doubt could dance to the dial tone of a telephone.'

He certainly could dance with Barrie Chase and make people forget the years that were otherwise very much on their minds. The age difference seemed to gain very much more importance when they were seen together off the dance floor. And they *were* frequently seen together. Despite Fred's age, there were people who still tried to make an affair out of his friendship with Barrie Chase. Would they marry? The embarrassing questions continued and the only answers anyone got were from their close friends who said that they didn't think it likely – since Fred still felt his principal duty was to look after Ava.

In 1968, Ava married Carl Bostleman, Junior, an interior decorator who was a member of a Boston society family. The ceremony conducted by an Episcopalean minister was at Fred's house. The Astaire family – particularly Aunt Delly – were not very enamoured of the match, but Ava appeared to be greatly in love and Fred gave her away in marriage. Now all three Astaire children were married. Would that give Fred the opportunity to marry Barrie? The speculation grew – and amounted to nothing.

The trouble seemed to be that the more Fred Astaire did in films or television, the more people wanted to know about him. To be seen with a pretty young girl was virtually inviting a lynching by self-appointed moralists. They did nothing more than cause embarrassment. One can only imagine how Fred felt when 'an intimate little dinner party' which he attended after a Cole Porter festival at New York's Lincoln Centre turned out to be copy for the *Daily News* gossip writer Suzy. 'After swimming around in champagne for about an hour,' she wrote, 'the coruscant collection repaired to the first-floor dining room for a smart little supper, Adele Astaire . . . was all golden and glistening as she toyed with her salmon mousse.'

That could be one reason why Fred didn't like parties in the 1960s any more than he had thirty years before. He did, however, have that work bug again.

In the summer of 1968, Fred got all dressed up in cut-away coat, wing collar, cravat and a shiny black top hat – and was thrown out of Buckingham Palace. To those who were upset at the idea of a stubble-chinned Astaire the year before, the shame of seeing their idol turned away from the palace – where they thought he should feel so much at home – was beyond imagination.

The scene was for a film called *Midas Run*. But the thumbs-down actually happened to him. The picture in which Fred had third billing after Anne Heywood and Richard Crenna had a very slight story about a British civil servant who engineers the theft of gold bullion from Italy. It is all supposed to be a demonstration of the man's disgust at constantly being thwarted in his hopes of getting a knighthood. When the plot succeeds beyond his wildest dreams, he finally makes the trip to the Palace to be dubbed by the Queen. He was supposed to stand by the gates, smile to the crowds whom everyone knew would be waiting there, and then march smartly across the courtyard.

It was at that moment that a policeman put up his hand and said that not even Fred Astaire could expect to get any further. The trouble was that the producer had not applied for a permit from the Lord Chamberlain's office before setting up the scene.

The news so upset one of Fred's fans, Mr Ferdy Chard of Hampstead, that he wrote to the Queen suggesting that Astaire should be knighted for real. He didn't get very far. Mr Philip Moore, the Queen's Assistant Private Secretary, wrote back in reply: 'Since recommendations for honours are made to the Queen by the Prime Minister, it has been forwarded to No. 10 Downing Street.' Alas for Mr Chard, and a great many other Astaire fans, the penny failed to drop – although there is no doubt whatever that Fred would have been knighted years before, had he been British.

That apart, filming proceeded according to plan. It was also a picture with a family involvement. Fred Junior had a small part as the co-pilot in the airliner transporting the gold. Much of the work was done in Italy and it was the first time Fred had been there. Although he said he loved the country, it made him aware of two difficulties, one resulting from snakes and the other from pasta. He told the Christian Science Monitor: 'Every Italian sucks pasta down from birth and seems to thrive on it – and most foreigners do, too. It's not the pasta itself that is the matter. I like the stuff. Do you know that the company has put on two hundred pounds since it came to Italy?'

The snakes bothered him mostly on the local golf course, which as usual he could not resist visiting. The rough there, however, seemed 'like a primæval jungle'.

He had another worry, too. Everywhere he went, people asked 'Where's Ginger?' And it was nearly twenty years since his last picture with her and thirty years since the end of the series for RKO.

In London, he was annoyed when someone suggested he might make a comeback with Adele in *Lady Be Good*. As he said at the time: 'Have you ever heard anything so stupid? It's ludicrous. Do you know, I can barely remember the thing – beyond the fact that Adele and I enjoyed doing it.'

Midas Run was the nearest an Astaire film ever got to receiving an

'X' rating – since Miss Heywood was seen bare-breasted in a couple of sequences. They were filmed after he had finished work on the picture but they upset some of his most devoted fans. People wrote asking how he could possibly be associated with that sort of thing. Fred took the view that since he wasn't in the scenes himself, it didn't matter a damn to him.

If films were sometimes distasteful to him, racing never was. Back in London, he loved chewing the fat with old friends like Jack Leach. 'Well, how are all the racing swine?' he asked Leach when they met. As Leach reported, the pair of them were just 'two young bald-headed bachelor boys going out on the town, pretending we had not lost any of the dash that we certainly had in the 'twenties.'

Leach wanted to talk about Audrey Hepburn. Fred simply replied that he thought she would win the Oaks in a good year. But he wanted to talk about racing – and they did. Over the years, Fred had accumulated every single English form book dating back to 1923.

His books enabled him to win at least one bet with Leach. He told him that Lord Rosebery had a horse called The Bastard that broke a record at Newmarket. Leach insisted that The Bastard was not good enough. When he returned to Hollywood, Fred sent Leach a cable: THE BASTARD DID BREAK THAT RECORD AND WHAT'S MORE HE STILL HOLDS IT.

It was the record of Fred's age, however, that still niggled. When a writer reported that sixty-nine-year-old Fred was already seventy, his hackles rose to Astaire-like proportions. He sent him an angry note, saying: 'Hey, cut that out.'

Ava toyed with the idea of following Fred into the theatre in some capacity, but her domestic responsibilities took over instead. She introduced her father to some of her friends. Among them was Robert Wagner, the perennially young film actor who in an earlier age would have been listed in the casting directories as a juvenile, whom Fred had in fact known since he was nine years of age. Wagner was at the time starring in a series called 'It Takes A Thief' (or 'To Catch A Thief' as it was called in Britain). He said he would love Fred to play his father in an episode of the story being made at the end of 1969. The one episode became four – four very successful miniature movies which were repeated the following season. To Wagner it was a career milestone – particularly since Fred taught him how to make up as a clown. To Fred, it was yet another opportunity to demonstrate his versatility.

Of the dances of the day, he said: 'The shake; the frug. That's the scene today – but I wish they wouldn't call it dancing!'

As for the future, he sat back now and contemplated: 'There's nothing I want to do that I haven't done. I don't give a damn if I never do another picture or another show. After all, you don't go on doing the same thing forever. If someone asks me to do something worth doing and I want to do it, then I will. But it will have to be awfully enticing to me.'

Yet come the enticements did.

That's Entertainment

No one expected much of Fred Astaire in the 1970s. His appearance was distinctly craggy and if you didn't watch the way he moved across the room – like one of his beloved racehorses ambling through the paddock – you might have been tempted to suggest that Fred's days as a great star were finally over.

He was in good health, but he knew it wouldn't be clever to try to tax his heart by doing the routines that had set him apart from every other hoofer in show business. If he *had* dwelt on the past, he might have decided that retirement was what he now wanted.

But he had other ideas. When Dick Cavett invited Fred to be the sole guest on his television show in November 1970, he took over the evening as though he were a young sprite proving to Broadway he was as good as his reviews said he was. He sat on a chair, talked to Cavett and did a dance or two.

A month later, he took on an appearance not totally different from the one he adopted in *Finian's Rainbow*, this time playing the sheriff to a bunch of equally superannuated Western characters in *The Over The Hill Gang Rides Again* for ABC Television.

Within four weeks of that, the Astaire voice was heard on another ABC show. This was yet another career first for him. His voice, together with those of Mickey Rooney, Keenan Wynn and Paul Frees, was superimposed in an animated TV film called *Santa Claus Is Coming To Town*.

His children were still vitally important to him and if none of them had chosen to follow in his footsteps, that was all right, too. Pete was a sheriff in Santa Barbara, Fred Junior had become a rather shy farmer and Ava had divorced Bostleman and married a tall artist called Richard McKenzie who bears a striking resemblance to Leonard Bernstein – and whom the family adored. The day that Ava and Richard were married, Fred was a judge at the annual Emmy award ceremony, so he could spend less than an hour with the couple. He found time, however, to pose for just one wedding group picture and kidded McKenzie: 'Look after my little girl and see that she looks after you.'

It was the start of a close friendship between Fred and Richard – although the McKenzies would, before long, move to London. Soon after their marriage, Richard borrowed one of Fred's Rolls Royces and broke down on the journey. Drivers passing by were treated to the spectacle of Fred Astaire in one Rolls coming to the rescue of his son-in-law in the other. His affection for Richard was an extension of his deep love for Ava, who could persuade him to do things that no one else would have thought possible. She even managed to get him to part with some of the dress suits and shoes he had been hoarding for years – so that she could offer them for charity at a 'garage sale' held at his home. People who flocked there hoping for souvenir bargains were soon disappointed. Fred took out all the labels before letting anything go.

As far as he was concerned, he didn't look for souvenirs of his career and saw no reason why anyone else should either. But when one of the networks put on a late, late Astaire-Rogers film, it had the biggest mail bag for years in response. The insomniac audiences simply begged for more. Other networks followed suit and a big Astaire–Rogers revival was under way.

Fred tried not to see his films on television. But on one occasion, he did have the set switched on when an Astaire film was playing. 'And I had to stay to the end to see what happened.' He admitted at the time: 'There was a pretty good routine in it. I was pleased with that. In fact, it looked so darn good, I wondered how I ever did it. It would be awful if those routines looked crummy now. It would kinda make your life look pretty foolish, pretty empty.'

261

Anything that made him look old-fashioned was guilty of the biggest sin of all, so he agreed that he had to show the public what he was still capable of. In October 1971, he made a second solo appearance on the Dick Cavett Show and for ninety minutes left no one watching in any doubt that he was still an entertainer to study. He followed that three months later by hosting a tribute to his friend George Gershwin in a show called ''S Wonderful, 'S Marvellous, 'S Gershwin.' He was joined in this, among others, by Jack Lemmon, Ethel Merman and Peter Nero.

Ava agrees that he might not have carried on working had her mother still been alive, but even in the 1970s it still represented that irresistable enticement.

He did another TV show called 'Make Mine Red White and Blue' in September 1972 – when he was already seventy-three. In the following January, he had a cameo walk-through part in the John Lennon and Yoko Ono film *Imagine*, which just proved that he wasn't frightened off by the newer crowd.

Indeed, he charmed them. No one was more affected by the Astaire personality than British skeleton-shaped model Twiggy. She was another of Ava's friends to be introduced to 'Daddy'. She told the *Evening Standard* in London at the time: 'It was my biggest excitement of all time. He invited us for tea at his house and I was so nervous and excited that I didn't know what to say.'

But Fred took to her as she did to him. She and her companion, Justin de Villeneuve, went for dinner with Fred and the McKenzies. After the meal, on the way back to the car park, Fred did a twirl in the middle of the pavement.

No one ever suggested there was any romantic link with Twiggy. But when Fred escorted another young lady on more than one occasion, the gossips had a hey day – richer than any since they were last able to report about a possible romantic link between Astaire and Barrie Chase, who was now married to a Los Angeles doctor.

Fred's newest date was Frank Sinatra's younger daughter Tina. She was twenty-three, the same age Barrie had been when they first went out together. 'I love him,' said Tina – and then, just as the pencils were poised and the microphones connected to the tape machines, added: 'In the same way as I love my father.

'People find it difficult to understand this kind of relationship. How two people can be so close and yet not be romantically involved and planning marriage.' Said Fred: 'I think it is quite romantic that we are being linked together, but romance is beyond my age.'

Fred and Tina had been spotted at a quiet tête-a-tête dinner to celebrate his seventy-third birthday. It was proof that unlike so many great stars who could be passed by without a second glance once their hair had gone grey or had completely disappeared, Fred Astaire was now as magic a name and as recognisable as ever. When the new Uris theatre was opened on Broadway, more eyes were focussed on Fred and his first dancing partner Adele than anyone else. Fred tried not to let too many photographers come near them, but Adele loved every minute of it – and answered the clicking cameramen by taking her own pictures of Fred and every other celebrity around and about.

Adele had now been widowed for a second time and was living quietly either at a suite at the New York Waldorf Astoria or at her home in Phoenix, Arizona which had a golf course for a back garden. She spent her summers at Lismore. Fred would visit her when he could.

At home in Beverly Hills, their mother, fast approaching her century, was very much still in charge of looking after her 'Sonny'. At the age of ninety-five, she fell off a chair on which she had been standing to examine some curtains and broke a hip – but she recovered and agreed to use a wheel chair in future.

At Phoenix, Fred would play gin rummy with Adele's neighbours – or even smile over her language (she is particularly proud of a cushion which she embroidered and which has pride of place on her couch. On one side is some pretty needle-point, on the other, the legend, 'Fuck off'). In Ireland together, they would just occasionally sit and talk about old times – surprising the people with them that the names mentioned so casually just happen to be those of a couple of kings of England. Sometimes, they simply watched television. One day, Fred was watching an imported American quiz show. When he realised the people running the programme had got an answer wrong, he telephoned Hollywood to tell them so. He still hated going to parties – because there was certain to be some matron there who would say for the rest of her life that she had danced with Fred Astaire.

He kept in touch with a lot of his old friends – occasionally, for instance, playing golf with Bing Crosby or talking on the telephone with Irving Berlin. Berlin is an accomplished primitive painter; for

Fred he produced a series of canvasses featuring birds, all fitted with top hats and carrying canes. He told Fred that they brought back memories of the Astaire films and he thought he might like to keep them. One followed on the other. When Fred asked him why the birds never seemed to have any feet or hands, Berlin said that the answer was easy: 'I can't paint feet or hands.'

When Fred met Gene Kelly they would just occasionally talk dancing. 'The bane of our mutual existence,' said Kelly, 'is that the critics tend to compare us. We had two different styles. If I put on a white tie and tails I look like a truck driver going out.'

Every now and again, Fred would still have dinner with his old friends, Hermes Pan and Ann Miller.

But the cinema still remains an important part of his life and he considers it his duty to see all the films being shown in what used to be the movie capital and when it comes to the annual Oscar selections, Fred goes to most of the films so that he can cast his vote knowledgably as a member of the Academy.

A woman box office attendant in a cinema showing X-films on Hollywood's Melrose Avenue tells the story of a man with a hat pulled firmly over his eyes going up to her to buy a ticket. She informed him that the tickets were only available for members of the cinema club and asked if he wanted to join. He said 'No,' and walked away. But he had not got into the street before the woman started screaming: 'Say, did you see who that was? Fred Astaire!'

When Fred doesn't like some of the things written about his or other people's shows, he has been known to send the critics who wrote the offending pieces anonymous letters recounting his displeasure; he makes sure they are posted miles from his home – just in case anyone identifies the source. One of these letters, he was delighted to see, was printed in *Time* magazine.

Early in 1973, Fred had found himself a new task – be it ever so reluctantly. The Film Society of the Lincoln Centre in New York announced they would hold a gala in his honour. It would be a black-tie occasion, one that they hoped would raise something like $85,000 towards the society's funds.

Fred had to be talked into it – it all seemed rather like exposing himself in public and he was reluctant to do that. But he finally agreed and, in particular, consented to select thirty-five clips from his films – no mean task, considering there were something like two hundred numbers in thirty-one pictures to choose from.

'I see the list and wonder how the devil I did so much,' he said after the bulk of the task was completed. But, in case anyone got the wrong idea, he was quick to add: 'We laugh at those old pictures Ginger and I. We're good friends. But I don't want to go on talking about them the rest of my life. I live in the present.'

When the big evening arrived, the entire Philharmonic Hall was packed to overflowing. Finally, after the clips had been shown, Fred stood up in his box, dressed, as the Christian Science *Monitor* reported 'in a black tie and wide smile'. Adele was standing next to him to provide moral support and nearby were an assortment of her successors as leading ladies – Cyd Charisse, Joan Fontaine, Arlene Dahl and, of course, Ginger Rogers. Ginger, stunning in her platinum blonde coiffure, took a bow when Fred referred to her.

'I've got to go easy,' he said in his little speech, fighting to get the words out. 'There's so much emotion here – this is the most exciting thing that's happened to me. It's hard to describe the feelings of affection and appreciation.'

The organisers wondered whether an audience's attention could be sustained for nearly two hours of just seeing clips of old films; beginning with Clark Gable saying to him in *Dancing Lady*: 'Oh, Freddy, will you run through that number now?'

Every clip received an ovation from the 1200 people who had paid between $10 and $100 a ticket. Some 'honorary benefactors' paid $1,000 and even the press were expected to pay to get in – and did so willingly.

Later, a reception was held to Count Basie's music at the nearby New York State Theatre, where dozens of fans lined up to shake Fred's hand, to kiss him or just to collect an autograph. About half an hour after shyly walking in, Fred and Adele retired with the guests cheering them on their way. Some of them were dancing, doubtless imagining that for a moment, they, too, were Fred Astaire and Ginger Rogers.

The *New York Post* reported: 'No top hat, no white gloves, no tails, no cane. That was for the movies. Just a black tuxedo and a black tie. But each time, he took a step, he looked as if he were going to dance.' As for the film clips, 'they proved that Astaire not only danced better than anyone in films, but almost single-handedly invented the form.

It was a journey to another time when a skinny, balding unprepossessing man could just tap his toe and everything was all right.'

Earlier in the day, a reporter had asked him how he felt about being described as personifying the sophisticated and debonair. 'It's right on the nose,' he replied. But he wouldn't dance publicly at the gala – 'because most people expect me to go right off the floor!'

So was this the end of Astaire in show business? Had all the cheers meant that Fred had had his swansong – and swandance? If anyone thought so, they were soon put right.

Early in 1974, Fred and Adele were seen in public again – and this time they did do a step or two. The successors to MGM had put together a massive collection of clips from the time when the letters stood for 'Makers of Good Musicals' and called it *That's Entertainment*. Fred was one of the 'hosts', linking the various segments of film and began with a demonstration of how shabby the train that had been used in *The Band Wagon* had become. What it really demonstrated was how perfect the musical and Astaire had been.

A year later, Fred and Gene Kelly did a similar job with a sequel, *That's Entertainment Part Two*. In between, however, Astaire was nominated for an Oscar, for the best supporting actor of the year. He didn't win the Academy Award, but the picture in which he had been featured was to be remembered principally for the Astaire role – a con man in *Towering Inferno*. Later he received a British award for the role.

He didn't have stubble on his face this time, but there was no pretence at making him anything but a con man who was ageing. And when he danced – as he did, even if only in a ballroom scene with dozens of other people – it for once didn't matter that his partner, Jennifer Jones, looked rather taller than he did.

Fred and Ginger came together again for a brief moment in February 1975, a moment that recalled their past glories. Fred was made a member of the Entertainment Hall of Fame in Hollywood – an honour reserved for 'Twentieth century creators and performers for what they did that will last.' He still liked the idea of making a lasting contribution in the field of songwriting and in 1976 his song 'Life is Beautiful' – with words by his friend Tommy Wolf – was introduced by Tony Bennett and is well on its way to becoming a standard.

People doubted if Fred could still sing. So in the Summer of 1975 he flew to London, where the BBC radio series and a season of the

Astaire–Rogers films had given birth to a big Astaire revival, and cut two new record albums, one with a fellow juvenile called Bing Crosby. They also did a TV show together.

What did matter was that he was doing what he wanted to do and the people buying the tickets and the records wanted it, too.

Let's Face The Music And Dance

Fred Astaire will never dance again in a film and when he next makes a picture he will be unlikely to carry the cane that came to symbolise the debonair Mr Twinkletoes. If he did, people might think he was using it for support.

At seventy-seven Fred needed neither physical nor moral support. He had established not merely a branch of show business that was all his own, but had found an acceptance that bordered on idolatry, as well as a place in the history books. The man who had been dubbed the Entertainer of the Century was something more than that; he was and is a phenomenon of his time.

Ask him why he has succeeded and he will probably put it all into his idea of historical perspective: 'If I were a young dancer trying out for a part in the movies today,' he said in 1974, 'I'd never make it. My one natural talent is dancing and that wouldn't get me much of a part in a modern screen musical. I'd probably end up in the chorus of *Hair* or *Godspell* or something. A lead dancer nowadays needs to be a combination of choreographer, actor and singer.' Which, of course, is exactly what Fred Astaire always has been – although he insists: 'I was never a fan of my own voice and I never really got a chance to act.'

He began in vaudeville, starred on Broadway and made a new career out of television. But it was in the movies that Astaire came into

268

his own. And it is to the movies that he has always looked closest – first to study the market, more recently with something of a paternal air. He says the X-rated film has cheapened Hollywood and he cannot understand why exhibitors are allowed to show pictures that a few years ago would have had you arrested if you tried to screen them in your own front room. But now he says he detects an improvement on the way. 'All the signs make me extremely optimistic.' He thinks it good that producers go out of the studio to make their films, for instance.

Fred remains a very religious man. It was his religious faith which he insists sustained him during Phyllis's illness. Now, he can be seen most weeks at a small Beverly Hills church, taking part in the worship as an ordinary member of the congregation.

He doesn't like the harping on age – although even he admits he has been old for a long time. The past still does not interest him. 'I see the occasional movie. I like dramatics and that's it. That's my life story.'

Ask him whether he is happy about what he has done and he will agree that he is – although he would have liked to have won either the Epsom or the Kentucky Derby and although he has written a hit tune, only wishes he had made a record that topped the charts, too. The ideal day will be the one that a producer comes to him with an offer to star as a trainer in a film about race horses.

Because he does not think of the past, he enjoys the present, although nothing will ever be the same as when he had Phyllis at his side, and every time he has a big success, his one wish is that she were with him to share it. Ask him about today's music and he won't give the sort of answer others of his generation would be expected to deliver. He particularly likes 'the British kind of rhythm' – which is more than he said when he first started coming to London and setting the city on fire. Then, there didn't seem to him to be any British rhythm at all.

Rouben Mamoulian who had directed him in *Silk Stockings* said about him: 'He's a supreme artist. But he is constantly filled with doubts and self anger about his work – and that's what makes him good. He's a perfectionist who is never sure he is attaining perfection.'

One of his friends put it almost as seriously: 'He will probably be playing Hamlet at a hundred and ten.' It remains one of the few things he has not done – so far.

But then he has always known his limitations – or claimed that he has. A few years ago someone predicted that he would still be dancing when he was ninety. 'The hell I will!' he said then. 'I guess the one thing that worries me is knowing when to stop. I don't give a hoot about clinging to a career. I don't want to become the oldest living dancer in captivity, a freak, a sideshow or antiquity.' So we can chalk that up to Fred Astaire, too – he knew when finally to put away those dancing shoes.

As for himself: 'I don't understand what people see in me. I don't look like a movie star and I don't act like a movie star. I'm just an old So and So from Omaha.'

And what about those people who talk about the 'art' of Fred Astaire? Those who belittle his originality and say that he was a second Nijinsky? To them he always has the same answer: 'I don't really know how the dance started and I don't give a damn where it's going. I don't think about art. All I know is that there were musical comedies with people dancing, so that's what I did. I just danced.'

Index

273